WRITING MASCULINITIES

Also by Ben Knights

FROM READER TO READER: Theory, Text and Practice in the
Study Group

THE IDEA OF THE CLERISY IN THE NINETEENTH CENTURY

THE LISTENING READER: Fiction and Poetry for Counsellors and
Psychotherapists

Writing Masculinities

Male Narratives in Twentieth-Century Fiction

Ben Knights

Professor of English and Cultural Studies
University of Teesside

First published in Great Britain 1999 by
MACMILLAN PRESS LTD
Houndmills, Basingstoke, Hampshire RG21 6XS and London
Companies and representatives throughout the world

A catalogue record for this book is available from the British Library.

ISBN 0–333–73356–8

First published in the United States of America 1999 by
ST. MARTIN'S PRESS, INC.,
Scholarly and Reference Division,
175 Fifth Avenue, New York, N.Y. 10010

ISBN 0–312–22245–9

Library of Congress Cataloging-in-Publication Data
Knights, Ben, 1947–
Writing masculinities : male narratives in twentieth-century
fiction / Ben Knights.
    p.   cm.
Includes bibliographical references and index.
ISBN 0–312–22245–9 (cloth)
1. English fiction—Male authors—History and criticism.
2. English fiction—20th century—History and criticism.
3. Masculinity in literature.   4. Narration (Rhetoric)   5. Men in
literature.   I. Title.
PR888.M45K58   1999
823'.9109352041—dc21   98–54313
                                                             CIP

This book is printed on paper suitable for recycling and made from fully managed and sustained forest sources.

10   9   8   7   6   5   4   3   2   1
08   07   06   05   04   03   02   01   00   99

Printed and bound in Great Britain by
Antony Rowe Ltd, Chippenham, Wiltshire

Contents

Preface

One response to another book about masculinity might be a kind of weariness. Is this not a subject which has been sufficiently, indeed abundantly, debated over the last fifteen or twenty years? And in a debate in which the voices of the already audible and privileged can be heard yet again, this time lamenting their audibility and privilege? Yet the subject of how male identities and plots are shaped and charged with legitimacy through story-telling seems to me important enough to risk that response. The political and economic context – the breakdown of traditional employment patterns, the return of atavistic nationalisms and of fundamentalist religion, the dissolution of social democratic institutions under the onslaught of the new free market liberalism – all have the potential to reinforce fortified masculinities, and to delegitimise innovative styles of living. Between them they make more rather than less pressing an inquiry into the means through which male norms are created and sustained.

My own interests and practice as a teacher lead me to an indirect approach. Believing in the cultural productivity of fictions (and of the social and intellectual processes through which they are read and valued), I have chosen to work with literary materials. And not necessarily with the most obvious, the kind of books to which one might initially turn in order to find representations of masculinity. It is often necessary to seek masculinities at the edges rather than the centre of the field of vision.

As a book both about masculinities and reading, this is intended as a contribution both to gender studies and to literary and cultural criticism. Throughout it has been influenced by classroom practice, and many of the discussions here were developed in their earlier stages in dialogue with students. I would like to mention especially those who bravely took part in the first Durham University Continuing Education module 'Words and the Man' and subsequently those in the 'Masculinity in Fiction' modules at Teesside University. I am very grateful to all of them. Masculinity, as Scott McCracken has remarked, 'is not found in a reading unless you go looking for it' (in Roberts (ed.) 1993) p. 17). The object of this book, as of those courses, is to go looking for it.

The process of writing has taken far longer than I originally envisaged when I first proposed to write a book on masculinity and fiction. Along the way I have benefited from the help and support of many people, not all of them personally known to me. Eve Kosovsky Sedgwick's writings, especially *Between Men* have never been far from my desk. Peter Middleton's *The Inward Gaze* has been a source of inspiration. I suspect his book has influenced this one far more than the specific references suggest. The (anonymous) Macmillan reader gave advice and encouragement beyond the call of duty. Closer to home, it is a pleasure to acknowledge dialogues over years: with David Fuller, Diana Collecott, Tim Bond, Bill Williamson, and above all with Pam Knights (who also supplied some of the most valuable suggestions and references). I wish Malcolm Sweeting was still here to thank – for all his support, but in this instance for a conversation on a walk on the Cleveland ridge. Students in the group processes courses in the Durham MA in Adult Education and Learning gave me more than they may have realised. My DUET colleagues have as always been both supportive and challenging, and I think here as well of my fellow staff members of the 1988 DUET on Gender where some of the earlier ideas were tried out: Jane Aaron, Marjan Bhavsar, Nano McCaughan, Andy Medhurst, and Susan Sellers. Tim Middleton generously showed me his unpublished paper 'Re-reading Conrad's "Complete Man": Constructions of Masculine Subjectivity in "Heart of Darkness" and *Lord Jim'*. Su Reid and my Teesside colleagues have been unflaggingly supportive. Jan Hewitt and Robert Burden – pressed as they were with other commitments – generously read and commented on portions in draft. Thank you all.

BEN KNIGHTS

Introduction

In this book I approach the subject of the constitution and maintenance of masculine identities from an oblique angle. I do not intend to review in detail current debates about masculinity.[1] Instead my argument seeks to complement theoretical and historical discussions by focusing on the subject of narrative, grounding that discussion in the analysis of a selection of (mostly) twentieth-century novels. In this Introduction I shall give a brief account of what the book aims to do. I shall start by indicating the presuppositions and beliefs from which it emerges. Then I shall sketch the shape of the book and the course its argument will take.

My working assumption is that masculinities are not given but achieved through a constant struggle with countervailing tendencies. One aspect of this struggle has been a deep suspicion of introspection, conventionally associated with dreaminess, passivity and hence with feminisation. In challenging this norm, it would be disingenuous to remain silent about my own beliefs, and I might add, feelings, though I share with Peter Middleton[2] a suspicion of the prevailing platitude that what men really need is to learn to talk about their feelings; as though emotional literacy were the sole key to undoing the harm patriarchy has inflicted upon us all. It appears to me that the reason why so many 'books about men' are flawed is not due to any failure of intelligence or commitment on the part of their authors, but because of the elusiveness of the subject. This is paradoxical given the cultural dominance of men's voices. Yet there is a sense in which masculinity can be so taken for granted as to be invisible. Which is not to claim for its beneficiaries the status accruing from a hidden history of oppression. Equally worrying is that strand in the 'men's movement' that seeks to colonise the role of victim as well. Nevertheless, anyone who contributes to the critical dialogue is struggling against powerful institutionalised forces to find a register and an appropriate form of discourse. To speak of the Scylla of magisterial impersonality and the Charybdis of self-indulgent effusion would make the problem of speech in this domain evident

1

on more than one level. The available language is already saturated – here with the myth of the hero whose gallant enterprise is threatened with shipwreck by female monsters.

So this book is a contribution to a cultural politics of gender, but one in which the inquiry into what lies behind male masks is carried on indirectly. In this struggle for an appropriate medium I have adopted printed narratives as my subject. But I should not pretend that the personal and subjective element is absent. Reading, writing, and teaching about masculinities cannot be carried on in aseptic isolation from living, and the venture has constantly forced me to confront aspects of my own life and past, of my whole experience of self in relation to others. For example, one male response to feminism has been self-denial and flight from power in embarrassment and shame over belonging to the 'gender of oppression'. This is a reaction I am very conscious of in myself: I am uncomfortably aware of my own implication in much that with another breath I find myself wanting to challenge. That is why I have found helpful the approach adopted by Stephen H. Clark. Examining the response of male critics to feminism, he observes that the point is not that 'there is a healthy libido bubbling under waiting to get out: but that desire itself is experienced in these compromised forms' (Clark, 1994, pp. 33–4). In this spirit he urges 'reading more forthrightly, in a sense more culpably' (p. 219). There is, as Adam Mars-Jones has argued elsewhere, no easy route back to innocence (see Chapter 6).

While any position of cultural critique can generate its own self-righteousness, it is not itself a recipe for purity. As Frank Lentricchia reminds us: 'the radical mind has no privileged mode of persuasion available to it, there is no morally pure, no epistemologically secure, no linguistically uncontaminated route to radical change' (1983, pp. 34–5). Yet the possibility of working for change in the direction of social justice and equality is the hope that sustains this book.

Intended as a contribution at once to a critical cultural politics and to literary criticism, the subject of this book is narrative and specifically narrative exemplified in works of literary fiction. For reasons explained in Chapter 1, the study of narrative texts may feed back into a necessary reflexive consciousness about the narratives in terms of which we all experience and act out our own lives. Another assumption is that writing and the pragmatics of writing are still – even at this moment in the millennium –

important. Literary writing can no longer be regarded as a hierarchically superior technology – but nor is it a superseded form. The idea of the death of writing rests upon a grand narrative of electronic triumph which is itself open to deconstruction. The technology of writing constitutes an invitation to a particular kind of reflective consciousness, to dwell in a social dialogue. Thus in what follows I shall propose the need for a practice of reflexive or estranged masculine reading. At the same time, conscious that such an approach could easily slither into a self-righteous exposure of other people's sexism, I hope to avoid being reductionist or priggish in calling male writers or readers to account. There is no secure position of guaranteed superiority, and the point anyway is that all narratives (however apparently univocal or self-aggrandising) contain within themselves contrary and contradictory strands. At the end of the day I do not intend to advocate a sullen and humourless guerrilla warfare against textual imperialism. The left's traditional suspicion of pleasure may itself have been based upon a hierarchical masculinist dichotomy between the heroic and serious (superior) and the evanescent and pleasurable (inferior).[3]

Texts are not simply mimetic: they are not confined to describing worlds, real or imaginary. They are productive in giving rise to renewed performances of themselves. In those performances readers play a necessary and active part. Another strand of this book derives from my own work in the borderland where the study of text and the study of pedagogy and learning meet. There will be more to say about this in Chapter 1. For the moment the crucial points are that reading is itself an interactive and participative, and thus above all a social process. Dialogue in any case constitutes the ecosystem on which mind and consciousness depend.[4] Specifically, in reading we enter into dialogue with other readers past and present. On this inter-subjective terrain we have traditionally been addressed as gendered beings – but gendered according to a spurious universality attached to the male gender. The object of this book is to enquire – through attention to sample texts – what difference it would make if as readers we start by refusing the gendered subject position so often purveyed to us (both men and women) by texts and by the institutions and conventions of reading. This enquiry is all the more necessary now the canon is once again a tool of state policy. For one more context for this book is the establishment of the National

Curriculum with the concomitant repoliticisation of English Studies and 'the heritage' since the late 1980s.

This book is above all part of a long-drawn out lived response to feminism. It is vital that men should not relax into the assumption that women are doing all the serious work on gender and gender relations. To do so would simply be to reproduce existing structures in a different guise. Men have their own work to do on their relations with women, with children, with themselves, and with the environment.[5] Showalter makes an overlapping suggestion: the 'way into feminism, for the male theorist, must involve a confrontation with what might be implied by reading as a man and with a questioning or surrender of paternal privileges' (Jardine and Smith, 1987, pp. 127–8). One aspect of that work would be to call into question the narratives through which we endow lives with continuity and meaning. To question those narratives would simultaneously be to question our own implication in them, our willing adoption of transferential roles – as heroes bound for triumphant mastery or reciprocally as pitiable failures overwhelmed by circumstances.

To do this through the study of written texts means that we can keep in review the dialectical relations between experience and discourse.[6] There are pitfalls here: 'experience', like 'feeling' has become a touchstone for authenticity, a code for the real, and in turn a form of closure. But any movement whose object is change in the direction of gender equality would do well not to succumb to the temptation to adopt experience as a mysterious and unarguable plenitude. In the field of literary study, critical theory has shelved the problem by ditching 'experience' along with 'the self' and the language of 'emotions', one consequence being that in theory talk the word 'desire', like the word 'subject', has to work extraordinarily hard. While retaining the idea of experience, I shall also want to signal its limitations. Even a phenomenon so apparently personal and undebatable as experience is moulded by cultural and transpersonal formulae. It is as open to manipulation as any other aspect of our identity. Further, over-dependence on 'experience' as our touchstone for reality tends in the direction of passivity, towards the notion of the self as a register for events rather than as an agent powerfully influencing others. It belongs to the vocabulary of immediacy rather than that of transformation. We need to work with an idea of the subject both more dynamic, more flexible and above all more purposeful than is implied in many current uses of the word 'experience'. Towards such an idea discussion of the theatre of identity as it is enacted in a dialogue with novels would be one contribution.

The argument which runs through this book questions the assumption that male identity is naturally characterised by strong boundaries and an active and aggrandising sense of self. On the contrary, the point of studying narrative has been to suggest that rigid boundaries and the self bound for mastery are not natural and unavoidable, but positions whose desirability is propagated through rhetorical and discursive means. They represent an aspiration to be achieved (if at all) through struggle and the vigilant policing of counter-tendencies. As Greenblatt reminds us, 'any achieved identity contains within it the sign of its own subversion or loss' (1980, p. 9). Among a species burdened with the consciousness of biological and historical injury, the narrative enactment of masculinity has encoded a fantasy of rising above and proving superior to the forces of biology and of history. So there may be an instructive analogy between the rhetorical construction of masculinity – what Clark refers to as the 'implicit appeal for a masculine solidarity' (1994, p. 32) – and the rhetorical construction of nationalism.[7] Both are based reassuringly upon a notion of a shared identity rooted in biological affinity, both define themselves in relation to the hostile other, both lead in the direction of purification and the expulsion of impure elements. A proximate community is defined and bonded together against all the forces which need to be expelled. Heterosexual maleness, too, can be described as Anderson describes the nation, as an imaginary community, and like any imaginary community its borders require constant policing, the floodwalls which surround it a scene of unceasing activity to protect it from the encroaching sea.[8]

The horror inspired by those who symbolise creatural existence was long ago explored by Simone de Beauvoir and comparable insights have since been developed psychoanalytically by Dorothy Dinnerstein and in object relations terms by Nancy Chodorow. Put at its simplest, the argument is that given our conventional arrangements for parenting, women become (for both sexes) the focus for human ambivalence towards somatic existence. Fear and loathing of the body and bodily needs may be displaced onto those who through early association can be held to represent the physical domain.

> If there were no longer a special category of person available
> to absorb our split-off feelings of love and anger towards the
> flesh – if man could no longer rely on women to absorb them
> and woman could no longer rely on man to embody for all of
> us a humanness curiously free and clear of the aura of insta-
> bility and contradiction that they carry – these feelings would
> have to be integrated within each individual person.
> (Dinnerstein, 1976, p. 134)

Since it is more difficult for men to take the route of identifying
with the female parent, they thus end up even more deeply
ambivalent towards a being who appears to represent the joys
and the perils of living in the body.

However, the male attempt to cast upon women the guilt and
responsibility for physical existence has implications beyond male–
female relations. Even its effects upon those women who become
victims of physical revenge fail to exhaust the operations of this
malign dynamic. Purification and the maintenance of boundaries
are activities not just addressed to 'the other', but which enforce
conformity upon the other members of the same community. Men
as well as women are the addressees of narratives designed to
purify male identity and to bolster patriarchal power. Classic
masculinity is constructed with an eye to men as much as to
women. Men are themselves victims of patriarchy and the heterosexual presumption.[9] For to collude with a system of power it is
not necessary to be objectively a beneficiary of that system, only
to be persuaded that you are a beneficiary.[10] Such persuasion is
of course the task of ideology. And if you believe unconditioned
existence was once within your grasp, then your revenge when
it escapes you will be all the more terrible.

This book consists of a sequence of interlinked readings of
fictional texts, grouped around a cluster of organising themes.
While trying not to lose sight of cultural and social history, it
does not attempt a historical survey of masculinity or manliness.[11]
In Chapter 1 I first relate this book to contemporary debates in
the social sciences about the 'constructed' nature of reality and
the experiencing subject, then go on to give examples of how a
male subject position may be achieved through narrative. At the
end of the chapter attention turns to some of the institutions –
here primarily 'English' in Higher Education – through which
readings are produced and validated. 'English' it is argued has

from its inception been the stage for a more or less covert struggle over gender and the dominance of patriarchal norms within the subjective domain.

The whole book is influenced by the endeavour to site texts within the communicative interactions of reading. Neither a text's addressitivity, nor the performative activities of audiences, will ever be far from the discussion. It is not that literature helps us understand our lives, but that how we understand literature does. In the readings of which Chapters 2 to 6 are made up, I develop my arguments in more detail, inviting the reader into a process of interpretation and reflection which weaves simultaneously between interpretation of those texts and a critical reflection on the dynamics of the reading process through which meanings are activated. Key themes will, become apparent stage by stage. Nevertheless – without becoming repetitious or, as it were, giving away the plot – I owe the reader some preliminary account of these recurrent concerns.

Earlier on, I pointed to one source of this book in a preoccupation with stories of reading, with reading and experimental meaning-making as a social process. Uniting the 'readings' (in another sense) offered in this book is attention to the sociality of texts, focused through the way in which texts may themselves be read as allegories of reading, but this time specifically interrogated in terms of gender relations. The texts discussed here are seen as embedding prescriptions about the nature of the relations which should obtain between narrators and their audience, as appeals for the solidarity of readers on the grounds of gender, and as invitations to enlist in a group whose own communal identity would be grounded in sharing a privileged relationship both to narrator and to subject matter. Reading is thus seen here as a process of negotiations between readers and between reader and text not only with reference to the contrasting imperatives of pleasure and duty, but also over access to the role of privileged insider, a role fraught with its own dangers. To lay claim to have visited the dangerous place where meaning is made is both a privilege and a stigma. It is a textual performance which offers stability and belonging and yet at the same time threatens to destabilise the superior identity so achieved.

Fictions offer a fantasy space for negotiation. Their force is performative, and relies upon the enlistment of readers to go on re-enacting or subtly varying their scripts. The geographies of subjective space provide a terrain for the articulation of power. This book constitutes an invitation to read the selected texts (and they here stand as representative of countless others) in terms of their address not to a supposed universality of reading experience but specifically to the masculine. In inviting its readers to carry out their own performances on its inner stage fiction both promises the benefits of homosocial solidarity and threatens destabilisation, the perils of ambush by the inner world. Fictionmaking and fiction-enjoying go on in a liminal space which endangers the solidity of the line between public and private along which masculine identity has traditionally been organised. What in a convenient shorthand I shall refer to as 'male fictionmaking' is perpetually engaged on the boundary where the licence it extends to subjectivity and to furtive pleasures is always about to undermine its own stability. We thus have to ask about the nature of the fictional space and the desires vested in the group that assembles there.

The relations prefigured in the text go on echoing and recombining beyond it. In these terms the object of these readings is to make that process visible, and so to enlarge the repertoire of choice available to the reader. Ross Chambers is helpful here. He suggests that

> between the possibility of disturbance in the system and the system's power to recuperate that disturbance there is 'room for maneuver', and that it is in that space of 'play' . . . in the system that oppositionality itself arises and change can occur. (1991, p. xi)

Power, he goes on to argue, must be seen as an allegory 'read as literal' – 'a by-product of that fact being that it is simultaneously vulnerable to oppositional (mis)reading' (Ibid., p. 26).

The brief account of Alain-Fournier's *Le Grand Meaulnes* in Chapter 1 lays a trail to the consideration of the figure of male as artist in Chapter 2. Both in turn become prerequisites for the account of diverse but complementary forms of narrative in Chapters 3 and 4. Recurrent themes will include the refusal of dependency and its consequence, the search for an ideal – unconditioned – but also always already lost domain; the formation and maintenance of homosocial bonds; cultural reproduction and the enlistment of heirs – the management of futurity through symbolic and aesthetic means; the simultaneous investment in and struggle with the power of fathers; the articulation of the boundaries between the public and the private domain; and the relations between centrality and margin together with acts of flight from the centre. The subordination and intimidation of women is one product of this process of homosocial solidarity-building. But so too is the repression – tacit or overt – of homoerotic drives.

In Chapter 5 the theme of masculinity as masquerade will be extended to take in writings by women where the autographical impulse can more obviously be acknowledged to be routed through textual theatre. In invoking the idea of 'writing back' to a dominant norm, this chapter also draws on ideas given currency within postcolonial criticism. Finally, Chapter 6, explores how far all or any of these themes are perpetuated, renegotiated or consigned to obscurity in selected fictions of the 1980s.

This whole book constitutes an invitation to those who are addressed as men to become reflexively aware about that process. In Robert Scholes' formulation: '[W]ith the best will in the world we shall never read as women and perhaps not even like women. For me, born where I was born and living where I have lived, the very best I can do is to be conscious of the ground upon which I stand: to read not as but like a man' (1987, p. 218). Thinking, feeling, and knowing are not confined to the individual but take place in dialogue between persons and between texts. In this book we are concerned with fictional texts insofar as they enact that social process. Maybe insight into that process will in the end turn out to be equipment for change towards another and better kind of society. Throughout, the intention is not to set up images or counter-images of men but to invite dialogue over the way in which texts and our reading of texts summon into being masculine solidarity and masculine norms. Fictions are not, to say it again, simply referential, not just 'about' relationships, feelings, life events. Any narrative is also a blueprint for consciousness, a model of how knowledge may be acquired, organised and above all acted upon. As readers we are not simply passive consumers but active collaborators in meaning. In proposing awareness of and resistance to stereotypical masculinities, I would stress that texts are rarely, if ever, monolithic. Their gaps, inconsistencies and contradictions give us our starting place.

1

Masculinity as Fiction

The 'movement' of my 'inner' life is motivated and structured through and through by my continual crossing of boundaries; by what happens in those zones of uncertainty where 'I' (speaking in one of my 'voices' from a 'position' in a speech genre) am in communication with another 'self' in another position within that genre, where it is at first unclear which position I should be in, that is, which side of the boundary *I* should be on.

(Shotter, 1993, p. 124)

This chapter will fall into three parts. In the first, by way of an introduction to the subsequent study of literary texts, I shall explain why I believe attention to narrative could help us to understand the formation and reproduction of masculine identities. In the second, that theme will be developed in relation to the processes of reading and the relations between texts and readers. In particular I shall argue that men need to become resisting readers of those texts addressed to them as men and as representatives of supposedly universal principles. In the third, I shall briefly locate this study itself within the world of the study of English and of literary texts within Higher Education.

In the Introduction I suggested that this book was not visualised as a contribution to literary criticism alone but also a contribution to a cultural politics of gender. Its object was thus not merely to describe the world of fictions and readings, but in however small a way to change it. It is an attempt to map the junction where several strands of theory meet and cross in an attempt to intervene in an ongoing argument. In terms of critical theory this means drawing on the richly developed domain of the study of reader response, and of the interactions between readers and texts. A number of different but overlapping factors

10

influence the positioning of the reader, and to all these we must give some attention. While none of these influences can work independently of the others, we may to some extent tease them apart for the purposes of analysis. Thus we might broadly speaking see one set of influences as having to do with the assumptions about knowledge, about gender and about maturity available in the culture at large. Fortunately, these assumptions are much more contradictory and heterogeneous than is often appreciated. Another set has to do with the terms of the text itself, above all its power as a discourse, an address that makes proposals about who reads it and according to what ground rules. And another, and overlapping set concern the institutions of education and reading. To each of these we must give some attention. Each will in turn surface at different times and with different emphases in the chapters which follow. Here the object is to establish some general orientations both in terms of subject matter and of the critical apparatus to be employed.

TELLING AND BEING

In linking narrative to the formation of masculine identities I shall be making eclectic use of ways of thinking and modes of analysis from outside the realm of literary study strictly defined. In particular I shall quarry for my own purposes the work of some of those conveniently labelled 'social constructionists'. So in what follows we shall be engaged in an excursion into the borderland where literary study, sociology, social psychology and pedagogy meet.[1]

What follows is difficult to articulate briefly. At the least it will be necessary to spell out a potential connection between reading and living, an embarrassing connection taken for granted in traditional literary criticism, but largely severed by the new formalisms of the 1980s. Let me start not with an intellectual history as such, but with an attempt to explain the relevance to this project of the contemporary intelligentsia's enthusiasm for narrative and discourse. In the Introduction, I sketched the position from which I was writing this book: that while gender awareness and gender studies are often thought of as yet another women's responsibility, men too need to take up a role in the study of gender and the articulation of a cultural politics of gender. A study of literary narrative from a self-consciously masculine perspective would be one contribution to such a cultural politics. To read literary narratives critically and from a gender-aware position may be a route to critical awareness of non-literary narratives as well.

One of the first steps of such a project must be to place in question much that is considered normal, exposing as profoundly ideological the tyranny of so much that passes for natural. One such piece of questionable normality is the commonsense view that emphasises the uniqueness of individual experience and the unique identity of the individual self. A politics of gender – just like a politics of race or class – while it may hope to enhance the individual life, must by definition go beyond such atomism. In doing so it need no longer endorse the sort of mechanistic determinism according to which all individual beliefs or acts are laid at the door of determining and anonymous collective forces. While individualism is commonly (for example in the prevalent neo-liberalism of the Centre for Policy Studies or the Institute of Economic Affairs) articulated in terms of a rhetoric of choice, I shall be arguing that effective choice and real autonomy require a conscious recognition not only of social constraint, but of the mutual production of identities and relationships.[2]

The social and collective structures I have in mind now are those of language and discourse, and in particular of the conventions of narrative. It is here that the work of analysing and arguing with fictions and that of analysing and arguing with structures of thought, feeling and belief, fruitfully converge. In recent years the terrain of narrative, rhetoric and discourse has become an immensely fertile common ground for a number of disciplines, including critical theory, anthropology, sociology, and social psychology.

The matrix for all these studies has been the astonishing success of the post-Saussurean linguistic paradigm: in a whole variety of disciplines, language has leaped from relegation as a dependent variable to being considered the primary pigment of being. Its role has come to be seen as constitutive, not merely reflective.[3] Literary critics, long used to studying style, genre and narrative, have found themselves sharing analytical tools and even to some extent a vocabulary with anthropologists and social scientists. (And are often taken-aback at the impoverished idea of narrative entertained by colleagues from across the corridor.) The sources of this movement include linguistics in the mould of Sapir and

Whorf, Wittgenstein's later writings, the phenomenological sociology of Peter Berger and Thomas Luckman, Foucault's work on discourse at large, Goffman's work on society as theatre, and the work of Pierre Bourdieu (and in Britain Basil Bernstein) on culture and education. In the 1970s a related shift could be seen within Marxism from the economic determinism of the base–superstructure model into a preoccupation with 'signifying practices' under the influence of Althusser, psychoanalysis, and semiotics.

The strands involved are various, and the ensuing work extends along a continuum from 'high' theory to the detailed ethnographic study of conversations and social and professional encounters. From the point of view of this book, the common feature of these approaches is that they accord a central position in the constitution of social and individual reality to language and discourse. They thus have a direct relevance to a study which proposes that being a man or occupying a masculine identity is not an unalterable given – a matter of living out an intrinsic programme – but a matter of social and communicative practice.

Drawing on sources as various as Foucault and speech act theory, social constructionists have studied the way social being and individual identity are produced through cultural performances. Such theorists have taken part in a major rehabilitation of the cultural sphere which in traditional sociology tended to be downgraded to a mere reflection of the 'real' social processes. Symbolism and modes of symbolic exchange have more recently come to be seen as playing a crucial role in how a social order reproduces itself. There has thus been an upsurge of interest in representation, in rhetoric, and in narrative among those social scientists who have become aware that social habits, identities, expectations, even phenomena as apparently personal as subjectivities, are produced through expressive acts. (For examples, see Nash, 1990; Simons, 1989.) Even apparently intransigent material forces, it has been recognised, can only be identified, known or understood through language and culture. Allied to these developments has been the notion of the 'subject', the position from which we experience what we think of as our selfhood, who is addressed and given shape through discourse and the requirement to take up a role in that discourse. Most of the writers alluded to here would assent to Harré's rather structuralist formulation that 'the self is a location, not a substance or an attribute' (1993, p. 4). The notion that culture and identity are inherently unstable, and ceaselessly being produced through communicative acts is centrally important. Such an account of the intersection of social and personal meanings has a very direct bearing on the study of gender (see for example Butler, 1990).

In this book my particular example is the construction of the male reader and of the male as subject and as actor through the discourse of texts. The key point is that, since subjectivity and the particular forms it takes is socially valued and produced, it is also potentially amenable to social and dialogic transformation. In the ensuing chapters of this book we shall study texts with the aim of both identifying and questioning conventional identities and their association with typical actions. In doing so we shall need to be aware that expression (even the apparently personal 'self-expression' we cherish so highly) is not just a neutral way of describing that which 'really' exists somewhere else. Even personal expression or the communication of individual experience depends upon and takes shape within pre-existing formulae and rhetorical strategies. While, on the one hand, language throws only an approximate referential net over reality, on the other, acts of expression and self-expression are in themselves modes of exercising power and influence. Utterance takes place in a social context and generally has a regulatory and normative function. Ordinary storytelling, jokes, and day-to-day conversations can themselves be forms of negotiating power and exerting control. Being a man is as much a matter of style, of intentionally or unintentionally reproducing collective power, as it is one of innocently inhabiting a particular kind of consciousness.

Since this book makes considerable use of social constructionist arguments, it would be as well if – before going on to speak more directly about narrative – I outlined two broad criticisms of the social constructionist movement. In doing so I shall confine myself to those aspects most directly relevant to our purposes: the over-privileging of language and (though this may seem to contradict what I have just said) the obsession with power. Both these facets of the movement are relevant to a discussion concerned with gender. Neither criticism is intended to controvert the importance of the social constructionist project.

Whatever its stated interest in emotions, in social theatre, in the whole gamut of reciprocal social acts, writing in the social constructionist vein tends to privilege verbal language and discourse. (This may partly be because language interactions are easier to record and analyse.) While the semioticians of the 1970s and 1980s professed an interest in all sign systems, and used the term 'language' metaphorically of a vast range of phenomena, Harré and his followers have tended to gravitate back to words and highly articulate discourses. Harré has in fact had to reintroduce a distinction between the expressive and the instrumental in an attempt to make room in his theory for all those aspects of social activity that fit awkwardly on the verbal map. In this respect, social constructionism is in danger of reproducing an epistemological hierarchy which subordinates emotion, gesture, and the body to dispassionate, verbal, reasonable discourse (compare Seidler, 1989). Social constructionism has rushed into the intellectual vacuum left by the supposed demise of Marxism, and its lack of attention to the more obviously material aspects of life is part and parcel of its formation.

My other reservation is connected to the first. It is that social constructionism has inherited from Foucault and Althusser a preoccupation with power. True, this orientation has been very useful in directing attention to the struggles for influence and standing that run through human communication. Such approaches foster necessary awareness of the relations of power inhering in discourses both official and unofficial. But on the other hand, this preoccupation leads in the end to a one-dimensional quality, a reduction of the infinitely rich social and interpersonal domain to a terrain of power struggle. It isolates in not-so-safe havens solidarity, intimacy, affection, reciprocity, and in doing so unwittingly reveals the ability of a patriarchal narrative of combat and conquest to mould the thinking even of those taking up an oppositional stance.

In what follows I want to relate an account of narrative to a performative theory of knowledge and identity and to the theme of gender which runs through this book. In doing so, I shall spell out the presuppositions upon which rest the analyses conducted in the following chapters. While this section may appear in some ways abstract or schematic, the points made will be substantiated or developed in the more specific discussions that follow.

I have been borrowing the arguments of social constructionists to support a theory of knowledge of the world and of oneself in the world as a praxis. Narrative – the telling of stories – is one sub-set of such a praxis. However, to define narrative simply as the telling of stories would be misleading, since the very point of using the term 'narrative' is to direct attention to the formulae, the norms and conventions out of which stories are built and according to which they are told and exchanged. The capacity to tell and to listen to stories is one of what Kenneth Gergen calls 'the symbolic resources necessary for full social functioning' (Gergen, 1989, p. 76). Part of what I want to say is that storytelling is normative (we shall return later to the counter position: that stories may be both told and read in innovative ways). A narrative, even when it is written – or, for that matter, read – in isolation, is a form of social exchange. It takes place between parties to the narrative exchange, it establishes an environment for events, it names heroes and villains, typifies the modes of personality appropriate to the different actors in the tale, and designates certain kinds of actions, responsibilities and outcomes (Tölölyan, 1989; Potter and Wetherell, 1987; Young, 1987; Knights, 1992; Bruner, 1986, chs 1–4). There is an isomorphism – of which it will be necessary to say more later – between the events of the telling and the events 'within' the narrative itself. The 'lodgement of stories in speaking situations' says Katherine Young, 'returns attention to the mutuality of their construction, shifting interest from monologue to dialogue' (1987, p. 14).

Sexual identities in particular must be seen as continuously negotiated through dialogue. 'Some of the primary and crucial codes which construct us as subjects' argue Judith Still and Michael Worton, 'are those which shape our sexual identitifications.' In a useful summary they continue:

> Subjects decipher the world, social situations, themselves, as well as texts in the narrow sense. Simultaneously these interpreting individuals, in making sense of the material which surrounds them, write plots for themselves to figure in, and script first themselves and then others as characters in the scenario. However, it must not be forgotten that these acts of self-script-writing necessarily involve using the language of others and that the scenarios are meant to be seen, transcoded by others. The construction of a subject may well be understood as an aesthetic act. (1993, pp. 6–7)

Narratives are scripts for social encounters where act and actor are linked in a mutual dialectic. It is important to remember that they are discursively organised according to an aesthetic design: that is to say to yield pleasure. But while we should not forget the anticipation of pleasure that propells storytelling, narratives fulfil other functions as well. As Gergen puts it, 'lives are constructed around pervading literary figures or tropes' (Gergen, 1989, p. 154). Gender asymmetry has resulted in a situation where masculine narratives are regarded as normative for all. Masculine stories imbue individual lives with collective significance: narratives are, as Tölölyan argues, both projective and regulative (1989, p. 101). In a similar vein, Harré summarises: 'Lives are lived according to the local patterns of exemplary biographies, creating moral careers, ups and downs in reputation in the eyes of others' (1993, p. 32, and see ch. 8 generally; also Henriques, *et al.*, 1984). Stories orientated to men and men's experience not only articulate for the future what it is to live and act as a man. They also act as blueprints for future stories. As people tell typifying stories about themselves or others ('I never learn, do I?'; 'I've always hated parties', 'let's face it. she's always been a troublemaker', 'of course he would have to go and tell them'); as they tell stories of which they are the triumphant heroes, or where it is demonstrated that some unfortunate 'couldn't organise a piss-up in a brewery', they pass on and revalidate narratives that are collective as much as personal. Those narratives become part of the collective stock of ways of construing ourselves and others.

The hypothesis upon which this book rests is that masculine identities and (stereo)typically male ways of being and acting are constantly being reinforced and re-enacted through social practices of communication among which narratives both oral and written, in speech, in films and on paper, figure prominently. At this point it is necessary to take a further step in the argument, since, as we have seen, a social constructionist argument can potentially lead to a communicational determinism as rigid as any other kind of determinism. If we are constituted as social persons according to prefabricated structures and rules, we have little room for manoeuvre or choice as ethical actors.

As I suggested in the Introduction, the project of this book is not simply descriptive. I have visualised it as a contribution to a practice of change, in particular change in the ways in which men understand themselves and socially act out manhood. The whole project is deeply influenced by a belief in the need for struggle towards social justice. My account of narrative aims to find a way of making room for innovation as well as convention, dissidence as well as conformity, surprise as well as routine. In the chapters which follow, the possibility of innovation will figure in relation both to the production and the reception of narratives.

We might imagine innovation as arising both within texts (for example by the recombination of traditional elements, or the articulation of new styles or subject matters) or within readings (for example by deliberately reading against the grain of the narrative). In practice, this distinction between production and reception will be hard to uphold in the light of the dialogic theory of reading to which I shall return later in the chapter. Since a narrativist or social constructionist account, whether of consciousness or of actions, emphasises the discursive processes of selection and organisation, it must have as its corollary the possibility of an infinity of potentials that were *not* rhetorically foregrounded in any given practice of communication. Just as in perceptual terms a fresh set of schemata will bring out new aspects of reality, so in communicative terms a different story may refigure thought and feeling into possibilities as yet unglimpsed. Social constructionism supplies a parallel with the Lacanian awareness of all that is consigned to the unconscious by the entry into the symbolic order.

> ... I may not be able to find a ready signification for those aspects of my experience that I find inexpressible. My discursive resources are ... constituted and therefore limited by the conventions of the situation in which I live. Were I to be introduced into a different set of discourses, then I would find that my subjectivity became transformed because the vague feelings or intimations of absence were made explicit by becoming nameable. (Harré and Gillett, 1994, pp. 178–9)

The idea that a self has a vast range of latencies and potentials that have never been given discursive space and thus never been recognised is one that represents the often unspoken corollary of constructionist thought, and finds its equivalents in other psychologies.[4] Such an idea lies behind the widespread adoption of the term 'subject' in critical theory. Dormant aspects of the self may be awakened by different circumstances or location in different stories. To see even the inner life as what Shotter calls a 'boundary phenemenon' is crucial from the point of view of this book, since it implies that even something as apparently private and personal as our inner life is 'never wholly our own':

> We live in a way which is both responsive, and in response, to what is both 'within us' in some way, but which is also 'other than' ourselves. Why? Because dialogic inner speech is *joint action*, and joint action always creates that third entity – the context, situation, circumstance, etc. that the action is 'in' and must 'fit in' with. In this *communicational* view of ourselves, then, the current view we have of persons as all equal, self-enclosed . . . atomic individuals . . . is an illusion. (Shotter, 1993, p. 110)

In relocating identity and inner life at the margins, such a theory endorses attention to the multiplicity of voices both of the text and of the self.[5] It draws attention to contradiction, to inconsistency, to puns, to slips of the tongue or pen, to the points where the smooth surface of the discourse is fractured or rough. It draws attention both to the multiple languages and registers that make up both textual and personal discourse and to the regulatory acts through which we attempt to simplify and normalise them. In doing so it could open a gateway to change.

As Scholes points out, it is 'only the multiplicity of codes that allows humans any scope for freedom or choice in writing or reading. . . . In the spaces provided by conflicts of codes we find much of our freedom and our verbal art' (1985, pp. 162–3).[6] This seems to be the point where postmodern theory and feminism creatively overlap, beckoning us towards a theory of the situatedness of identity in actions. Such an assertion of social matrix questions conventional masculinist assumptions about the bounded, questing, combative self as private property. Being a man is stripped of its naturalness and resituated in an interpersonal and moral domain, an arena of choices. Masculinity is in fact an unstable sign. In such an account, being a man is a matter of what you say and do as much as what you are. An analogous argument holds for texts as well: attention to the suppressed, embedded or low status voices of texts, or to fault lines in the narrative, brings new possibilities to life.

In her search for stories that might transform rather than simply reproducing beliefs, Marina Warner reminds us that the 'process of understanding and clarification . . . can give rise to newly told stories, can sew and weave and knit different patterns into the social fabric' (1994, p. xiv). To bring to the narratives we read awareness of the kind discussed here would be a potentially liberating act. To talk about versions of masculinity in fiction is simultaneously to enable talking about masculinity and gender issues outside fiction, but to get at them by an indirect route. Firstly, fictions comprise part of our communal repertoire of narratives, and could potentially, if read with attention to our own productive role as readers, add to and extend that stock. Secondly, critical reading of narrative fictions could enable critical reading of the narratives of daily life. Out of this activity arises the possibility of extending or adding to the scripts which provide us with paradigms for action and being.

THE ABUSES OF ENCHANTMENT

In this section, I shall start to relate the preceding general discussion to some specific texts and themes. While concentrating on the pattern of relations instituted by the text, we need to bear in mind that there is of course no such thing as a text in itself. Although we perhaps inevitably think of texts as having a depth and existence somehow independent of their material embodiment, what we experience as texts are themselves the products of material and social practices as various as the practices of education, of publishing and distribution and the expectations created by conventions of genre and of reading. A text only attains meaning as a result of the process of being read, a process with its own rules and conventions. My focus on 'the text itself' therefore has to be understood as taking place in a conditional mode. This discussion will draw generally upon a whole variety of work which has attempted to identify the ways in which texts implicate readers and readings.[7]

Central to the discussion which follows will be the idea that the fictional text works in two simultaneous and interlocking ways. For my purposes these approximate to the narratological distinction between 'story' and 'discourse'. In one modality a text 'tells a story'. A narrative is articulated involving various 'existents' (characters, places, objects) and a series of events sequenced in such a way as to bring about a dynamic of suspense and resolution. Such a narrative in itself assumes norms which may or may not be those of the cultural environment within which readers encounter it. (Who typically performs actions, who is the subject of actions, what sort of events occur under what conditions, what acts are likely to lead to what outcomes, and so on.) In the other modality, the text addresses itself to readers in a way which attributes to them a hypothetical identity: an identity based on knowing certain things, holding certain beliefs, feeling certain emotions, entertaining common fantasies, or occupying a particular sort of orientation towards the universe. The reader who is thus called into being is, nevertheless, always to some degree an ideal, a hypothetical identity existing in tension with the empirical actuality of the reader who is doing the reading and who may or may not recognise him or herself in the shape proposed. Even where there is recognition (or misrecognition) which enables the 'real' reader to identify with the implied reader, it is likely that there will be some dissonant elements, and that readers will need to negotiate their own accommodations with their ghostly counterparts. Yet the preceding section should have made clear that constructionist theory requires us to view the self not as a stable container full of unchanging characteristics but as a dynamic entity, constantly engaged (whether reading or not) in a process of finding and adapting means of describing itself both to itself and to others.

Viewed in this light, the reading or studying of fictions is one mode (others include conversation, watching soap operas, reading newspapers and magazines, telling jokes, listening to or making speeches, religious observance, counselling, appreciating fashions and buying clothes or furnishings) of the daily business of negotiating and warranting an identity. In each and any of these and many other modes we test out discourses, try on masks, or – in terms of a more stable grammar of selfhood – encounter different, latent, and perhaps repressed 'parts' of ourselves. Some of these styles of being will come back to us validated by the approval or recognition of others. At the same time, none of these encounters takes place within a cultural or historical vacuum. We are written over by histories of gender, class, ethnicity. Nevertheless, since we ourselves embody competing and contradictory histories, we have some leverage for choice and change. The point of analysing literary fictions as I shall be doing here is not that those fictions are the only (or even indeed the main) scripts available to us as models for our own stories: it is rather that talking and writing about texts is a pretext, one way of sustaining a necessary critical conversation about grammars of living and knowing. On that basis, let us zoom in more specifically on the relations between text and reader, and in particular as those concern matters of gender.

Our relationship with a text can be seen as operating on two levels. On one level the text is mimetic (even if what it represents owes more to fantasy than to conventionally normal data). At another level it is performative, conjuring up mental events (and a series of transferences)[8] which to some degree happen again every time the text is read. Between them, these two levels establish a set of norms with which we may or may not conform, and which we may indeed later come to endorse or to dispute if we should go on to complicate our reading by studying that text. One aspect of reading a text is thus to find oneself enrolled as a member of a community of those who agree to read this text according to certain prescriptions. Inevitably, given the probable heterogeneity of the actual readers of a particular text, this imaginary community will be somewhat homogenised.

One of the main axes along which a normative community of addressees may be organised concerns assumptions about the gender of the reader. (Culler, 'Reading as a Woman' in Culler, 1983; see criticisms by Scholes, 1987.) These assumptions are activated through identifiable codes. One of the advantages of talking in terms of 'codes' is that the term draws attention to the productive aspect of language traversed by both reader and text, the sets of shared conventions through which readers collaborate in producing meaning. Much valuable work has been done for example on identifying the cultural codes through which a normative body of knowledge is established.[9] Gender codes, while even at once conventionally more invisible, may be seen as acting in much the same way. They address readers not only on the basis of complicity in knowing, but also on the basis of an imputed understanding about what readers would be like, and what they would desire. It is broadly the case that the dominant traditions in Western literatures have addressed the reader on the understanding that the normal position was that of being a male, in what Clark refers to as 'an implicit appeal for masculine solidarity' (Clark, 1994, p. 32). The ideal community of readers with whom any one individual has been invited into solidarity would be made up of men. Reading as a man has thus been proffered to all, whatever their actual gender, as the neutral and universal position from which other positions are deviations.

One powerful strand in feminist cultural analysis has been to draw attention to and contest this presumption (Fetterley, 1978; Miller, 1986; Pearce, 1991; Reid, 1989; Schweickart, 1986; Nina Pelikan Straus, 1987) Women readers need not, it has been cogently pointed out, feel compelled to accept this positioning of themselves. Women can become 'resisting readers' of the discourses directed to them, reading texts 'against the grain' of the dominant discourse.[10] My intention leads to a different but complementary project. That is to build upon the work of feminist critics to make an intervention from a different direction. While it is true that men have on the whole been the beneficiaries of this identification with the universal, there have nevertheless been misrecognitions here too. The universal male position which men too have been offered may propound or enforce identities and narrative paradigms which – while holding out the blandishments of status and influence – deplete or distort them in other ways.

Inasmuch as masculinity too is a rhetorical construct, our choice of masculinities has been limited by the narratives addressed to us. In this chapter I seek to develop the proposal made in the Introduction that 'reading as a man' is not an inevitable and stereotypical process, but rather that men too can learn to read against the dominant assumptions both of texts and of the institutions of reading and criticism. What I seek to do parallels Longhurst's description of his own objective: 'the objective is to begin to frame, describe and unearth the notion of "men as readers" as a *project* rather than as the usual, unquestioned normative procedure' (1989, p. 5). The comfortable normality of reading as a man is an ideologically induced illusion. I believe (and it is a belief that underpins the argument of this book) that it is both possible and desirable for us to develop what Clark refers to as an avowed gender-specific perspective so as to achieve estranged masculine readings: readings which – while reflexively conscious of the gender identities of those practising them – do not accept a hegemonic masculinity as an inescapable given. Robert Scholes's dictum about the praxis of group study may be applied specifically to the problem of masculine dominance: 'we can examine all our uses of language from a new point of view, not to see what they reveal, but to consider what they conceal, and to ask the question, "What violence is being done here?"' (1985, p. 112). At this point the argument can most helpfully be developed by means of an example.

In what follows, then, I propose to look at a sample of text.

The object of doing so will be to establish some preliminary points about the discursive relation between reader and text and about how the text establishes the position of a 'normal' reader. However seductive a text may be, it cannot coerce us into agreeing to be constructed as readers in the way that it proposes. Our example comes from a piece of fiction which, while widely read, is unlikely to appear in a literature syllabus: it therefore has for our purposes the advantage of not being already the subject of extensive critical commentary. At the same time it is close enough to a popular fictional mode to give the discussion some representative validity. Our quarry here consists in metacommunicational cues: everything that is implied within Connor's helpful discussion of the 'addressivity' of the novel text.[11] If we are to question or to refuse the roles offered to us, we have first of all to become conscious of what those roles are and how they function.

The passage comes from a short story by the popular novelist and story writer H. E. Bates, whose novels – especially his best-selling and televised Pop Larkin series – are constantly being reprinted in paperback. 'The Middle of Nowhere' was collected in *The Wild Cherry Tree* (1968). The story concerns an affair between a woman who has been widowed in possession of an isolated country filling station and a lorry driver. In discussing this story I shall be interested above all in the assumed spatial and ethical position of the reader, and shall draw on Laura Mulvey's pioneering early essay on cinematic voyeurism 'Visual Pleasure and Narrative Cinema'. In this now almost canonised essay, Mulvey explores the relationship between the (male) viewer and the (female) erotic object, and links power over the gaze to power over narrative:

> An active/passive heterosexual division of labour has similarly controlled narrative structure. According to the principles of the ruling ideology and the psychical structures that back it up, the male figure cannot bear the burden of sexual objectification. Man is reluctant to gaze at his exhibitionist like. Hence the split between spectacle and narrative supports the man's role as the active one of forwarding the story, making things happen. The man controls the film phantasy, and also emerges as the representative of power in a further sense: as the bearer of the look of the spectator. (Mulvey, 1992, pp. 27–8)

In examining Bates' story we need to be simultaneously conscious of the erotic objectification of the female and of the occlusion of the male body. If this is an allegory of power, it is power gained at a cost. While in some ways the story appears to offer a critique of the prurient heterosexual male gaze (malicious gossip ultimately destroys the heroine's relationship with her lover), the discourse of the story is too thoroughly implicated in the position of voyeurism to sustain a serious critique of its own premises. In any case, the stories of H. E. Bates are full of women coyly waiting around in remote places to be discovered. Indeed, the loss of her lover releases the heroine to go on being an erotic mote in the middle distance. The implied viewpoint is that of the passing man who catches this poignant and seductive glimpse, a motif which 1970s designers picked up in their cover designs:

> Francie, at twenty-nine, was big too. She was one of those women, fair, steamy-eyed, generous of mouth and with a girth of thigh that recalled a brood mare, who matures at a sensationally early age and often by thirty decays into fat and sloppiness, half run to seed. But at the time Williams [her husband] died her skin still had on it the bloom you see on a plum at the height of its ripeness and there was still a deceptive, smouldering, steamy light in the pair of big violet eyes that were really extraordinarily tender. (p. 158)

At risk of spelling out the obvious, this is not simply a neutral 'descriptive' passage. The reader is positioned as a member of a club of male connoisseurs and commentators on women's physical attributes. It calls for the 'waagh' of male solidarity. The analogy with the appreciation of horse flesh and the speed of the metaphorical move from horse via flower to fruit is so extravagant that one suspects for a moment an element of self-parody. But if this is a parody, it is one that does not unsettle the reader's position. Francie spells seduction, and obviously wants it so badly that the fantasising male need feel no guilt. A woman could only describe another woman like that if she was deliberately adopting a male 'voice'. Next, Francie (herself a plum after all) goes in for selling snacks, soon diversifying the sort of food she offers, discovering 'within herself an untapped capacity for lightness in cooking'. On this basis she starts a restaurant, a restaurant whose similarity to a brothel, the text scarcely bothers to conceal:

It presently began to be clear that many drivers were drawing up not merely to sample Francie's cooking but on the chance . . . of sampling Francie herself . . . not a few were quick to notice that far from shrouding herself in lamentation . . . she appeared rather to have flowered. She was stupefyingly mature but still young. (p. 162)

Even repeating this for the purposes of criticism is to risk colluding at its currency. But I hope it makes the point that the discourse of the story does not simply place before us a selection of neutrally charged objects, but invites the reader into complicity in the framing of those objects. The reproductive system of the story – while superficially it evokes sympathy with the woman who is taken up and then rejected – requires the reader to gaze admiringly upon Francie and then to identify with the lucky man who succeeds in winning her devotion. The male becomes in a every sense a consumer of images of women, and a co-worker within a triangle of energies composed of object, narrator, and narratee.

While one set of reasons to urge revolt against the imperialism of the male gaze has to do with contesting the subordination of women, the logic of this book leads me to a reciprocal set of questions. These have to do with the effect of stereotyping upon men who are the real or supposed beneficiaries of cultural power. The dominant aesthetic of a story like 'The Middle of Nowhere' rests upon the poignant beauty of the glimpsed figure of the woman. That beauty, while ostensibly attributed to the woman herself, is lodged in a narrative process, one composed of the elements of the woman externally viewed, the viewer in the original moment, and the event nursed in memory. The vision tells us as much or more about the subjectivity of the viewer into whom it is incorporated as it does about the object viewed. According to this implicit theory, a glimpse of a woman impressed upon memory provides a sustaining sense of order and beauty in the world. By implication this sustaining sense is absent from the unsupplemented man. Let us go on to explore the structure of this aesthetic and the narratives which it generates.

The figure of the woman glimpsed and subsequently appropriated as a formative moment for male subjectivity recurs so often in literature as to have acquired its own patina of taken-for-grantedness. Such moments encompass Wordsworth's solitary

Highland lass and Tennyson's Lady of Shalott as well as the figure of the adolescent girl on the beach who inspires Stephen Dedalus' climactic epiphany. Moments like these have much in common with the formative 'spots of time' which figure so prominently in the post-Romantic epistemology of growing up.[12] They merit attention in the context of the present argument. I propose to try to scrape away the patina of use and familiarity in order to reveal a strategem that tells us much about the fashioning of male subjectivity.

Let us try to break down the structural elements. The original scene (the locus of infatuated memory) consists of three elements: a viewer (characteristically in motion on his way somewhere else); the woman viewed (preferably endowed with an air of perishability – an adolescent or like Francie an almost overripe sexual bloom); and a setting, often in a remote place or as it were a time-space outside the habitual domain of work, institutions and politics. Next, the relation between these three elements is the subject of processing in the consciousness of the viewer, turning the moment into vision, and the vision into poignant memory. The glimpse has the effect of putting routine or daily worries into perspective, even to the extent of inducing a kind of political anaesthesia.[13] Crucially, the recurrence of this vision is of its essence. Committed to memory it has a propensity to recur, the figure and its lost environment constituting a symbolic geography of desire.

Any attempt to analyse this paradigmatic figure is in danger of plodding seriousness. Yet I hope that analysis of the whole bundle of ideas does in the end say something significant about the structuration of male subjectivity. For the point is that the glimpsed figure (and her recurrence in memory) is not an isolated aesthetic moment. Rather, she, or the event of which she is the epicentre, also signifies an alternative narrative, a narrative in which the unseen observer himself would have been transfigured, would have been able to step out of his dreary familiar identity into a being rich, full of depth, purified. So the memorialised glimpse is an imaginary view of an alternative self and thus of an alternative biography. At the same time, the rehearsal of that possibility, the pathos of the path not taken, rests upon division and upon distance. The very poignancy of the memory depends upon a sense of loss. Distance is crucial to this drama. To have collapsed into intimacy the distance between observer and object would have been to lose the whole point:

the standard set by this vision exceeds local gratification just as its object lacks her own subjectivity.

With this in mind, we shall turn next to a more complex text, one which has in a way achieved a paradigmatic status as a story of male loss and longing, Alain-Fournier's novel *Le Grand Meaulnes* (1913).[14] In this novel – which avowedly lurks behind the hidden domains of John Fowles – the twin themes of the vision of the lost girl and the lost domain itself are inextricably intertwined. There is only room here to pick out what is most directly relevant for our present purposes. In doing so we shall explore the novel as an allegory of male subjectivity and of the nature of the adventure space within which that subjectivity is articulated.

The heroine of this novel, Yvonne de Galais – throughout described as fragile, almost ethereal – does not long survive her marriage to Meaulnes. That she dies pathetically enough in childbirth signifies that she never could have supported the role of a mature woman. For the visionary object is an allusion to a world disappointingly made up of traces, a plenitude for which nothing which fully inhabited the body could possibly be a substitute. She promises to her observer the liberation of dammed-up and wasted energies. The subjectivity nourished from this source is based on a glimpse of something you could never return to, and half of whose attraction is based on the plangency of loss, therefore of a self-conscious and even self-pitiful drama.

It is surely relevant to any attempt to grasp the gendering of the heterosexual romance that this propensity to cherish the figure in memory – even to set up situations in which such a glimpse might recur – appears to be a form of repetition compulsion. It is based on a dialectic of presence and absence. The tantalisingly and movingly attractive thing about its object is precisely that you have it and you don't have it, it's there and not there. As I attempt to connect all this to narratives of masculinity, one link that suggests itself resides in dissatisfaction with the state of being male. This seems to lead to the notion that the state of being male – so far from being self-contained and sure of itself – is actually a state of longing, for transformative contact with an object that would enhance and irradiate your being, assuaging all that sense of loneliness and lostness – not womb envy so much as completion envy. Furthermore, that joined to this object the man himself would have been complete had fate not decided otherwise. A cluster of ideas gathers which have to do with loss, absence, desire, a domain of beauty characterised as feminine and therefore existing in contrast to the world which male self-characterisation occupies. This beautiful domain also tells us in mirror image about the domain which it is not and from which it is separated by a process of splitting. While it represents an unattainable purity and depth of being, its structural complement is pornography.

The glimpsed figure is located within a narrative environment which constitutes a symbolic geography of desire. This pocket outside ordinary space and time is as much an element of the ensuing narrative as the heroine herself. In the following chapters I hope to show that flight is a recurrent element of male narratives, and that rapid passage above the surface of things is contrasted with the heaviness of embodiment. The tendency to etherialise and spiritualise the feminine vision springs from an ambivalence towards location in physical space.

Although it is not possible here to carry out a detailed analysis of Alain-Fournier's richly interesting novel, my argument requires me to sketch in some details. The narration involves a first-person narrator, Seurel, himself one of the characters, who plays a sort of Nick Carraway figure to the Gatsby of Augustin Meaulnes.[15] From the start the two principal male characters represent two different sets of propensities, the one reliable, rooted in place, a stolid, meticulous observer and keeper of the records; the other romantic, peripatetic, mercurial. It is of course to Meaulnes that the defining adventure happens: the fortuitous discovery of the chateau of the 'lost domain', the hallucinatory fête, and the discovery of the enchanting figure of Yvonne. Around the loss of Yvonne and her dream landscape Meaulnes' adolescence and young adulthood is shaped.

The early and central portion of the narrative is predicated upon the always already lost condition of this land outside normal time. In terms of the representation of Meaulnes this means that his narrative force is propelled by loss, and a desire for something that is by definition unobtainable – a kind of longing romantic in at least two senses. But the novel also portrays male subjectivity as split: Seurel, who takes great care of his friend is in turn the observer of Meaulnes. Meaulnes is devoted to the image of Yvonne, and Seurel to the reality of Meaulnes. This gaze upon the male figure is legitimated by the fact that his gaze is in turn fixed upon the elusive woman.

That the visit to the lost chateau and the glimpse of Yvonne constitute a code for (male) subjectivity is repeatedly hinted at in the text itself. As Meaulnes himself says: 'I'm sure now that when I discovered the nameless domain I was at some peak of perfection, of purity, to which I shall never again attain. Only in death . . . can I expect to recapture the beauty of that moment. . . . (p. 148). The condition of being haunted – and haunted by his own past – is one crucial aspect of his formation. This is itself an allusion to a pre-pubescent state. It is as though Peter Panishness is one response to the transitive imperial boyhood of the late nineteenth and early twentieth centuries. In his obsession with his lost vision, Meaulnes (who was thirteen when his adventure happened) is in search of his own pre-adolescent self, a fictive moment before history and adult sexuality took hold of him. This becomes clearer as the story proceeds.

Towards the end of the novel Seurel, in his matter-of-fact way, succeeds in locating both Yvonne and the whereabouts of the now demolished chateau. At that moment the realist strand of the text (with which the narrator is associated) seems to be in the ascendancy: there was never, we gather, any mystery in the first place. Everything is susceptible to a naturalistic explanation. The narrator is proud of himself in setting up a meeting between Yvonne and his friend. However, the obstacle to a happy ending (and a generic lurch towards realism) turns out to be Meaulnes himself. His glimpse of Heaven proves to be a passport to an emotional elite superior to the common herd: 'how can a man who has once strayed into Heaven ever hope to make terms with the earth! What passes for happiness with most people seemed contemptible to me' (p. 147). A purified identity is both the pretext of the protagonist's trauma and proof of his superiority. This ethic of nostalgia is not only (as Bronfen could show us) constructed upon the supposed poignancy of the ethereal or dying woman (Bronfen, 1992). Writing to tell his friend that the adventure is over, and that 'it's best to forget me', Meaulnes slips from his account of waiting for Yvonne to re-appear: 'I'm like that crazy woman at Sainte-Agathe who kept stepping outside the front door and gazing towards the station with a hand over her eyes to see if her dead son was coming' (p. 122). He, too, is the dead son of his own story, and the self-regarding aesthetic of which he is the standard bearer rests upon the narcissistic poignancy of the death of his younger self, an early version perhaps of that self-pity on the part of nongay men of which Sedgwick speaks elsewhere.[16]

Though he does in fact marry Yvonne (a muted affair) as a result of his friend's intervention, Meaulnes remains moody and preoccupied. The actuality of relationship was not, after all, what he was after. It subsequently transpires that during the period when he despaired of finding Yvonne he had a brief sexual liaison with a young woman significantly enough called Valentine. Transfixed by guilt, Meaulnes had been determined to return and marry her. The two women exist polarised in his consciousness, the one representing virgin purity, the other sexuality and pollution. While this splitting of the feminine into the virgin and the whore is a common enough trope, the point for the moment is what it says about the failure to integrate Meaulnes' consciousness: his identity is trapped between his pre-sexual and his sexual being, the latter encumbered by a compulsive need to reconstruct the former. The male hero of romance with whose poignant adventure the reader is invited into complicity is a vehicle for nostalgia, a nostalgia above all for his own former self. He is predicated upon his own narcissism, and upon distrust amounting to contempt for his own sexual being. And yet that is not the whole of the story.

Yvonne de Galais has a brother, called Frantz. It was Frantz whose passion for masquerade, for dressing up and theatre was responsible for setting up the fantastic, Cocteau-like fête into which Meaulnes once inadvertently stumbled. Of this nomadic figure the narrator himself remarks as he sets off on another adventure that 'it was as though he were beginning his childhood all over again' (p. 105). The narrator in fact becomes increasingly critical towards Frantz as a self-absorbed actor in his own drama:

At heart no doubt he was more of a child than ever... But it was hard to accept such childishness in a youth already showing signs of age... Now one began by pitying him for having made such a botch of his life and ended by irritation at the role he still insisted on playing: the young hero of romance. (p. 166)

As he gets older, Frantz turns into a figure we shall meet again later: the adult male child. Yet the overriding relationship of Meaulnes' life turns out to be his all-boys-together relationship with this same Frantz to whose aid he has made a solemn promise to come. In a moment of symbolism where allegory threatens to overwhelm realism, Frantz turns up out of the darkness on Meaulnes' and Yvonne's wedding night and calls his friend away to keep his promise. Obediently, Meaulnes drops everything and sets off. An adult relationship is thus blocked from two directions at once: Yvonne must be preserved as a virgin in amber, and at the end of the day Meaulnes' adolescent compact with Frantz is more important than his marriage.

Desire, according to Girard, is always 'according to another', the desirability of the object in proportion to its desirability in the eyes of some one you admire. (Girard, 1966). More evidence for the closeness of the two young men emerges when it turns out that Valentine is Frantz's former lover, the fiancée whose flight ('I left him because he admired me too much. He only saw me the way he imagined me . . .' [p. 193]) caused the breaking up of the fête. So even this relationship has been anticipated by Meaulnes' bond with his friend. At the level of textual fantasy, she was desirable to Meaulnes because already desired by Frantz.

A recurrent image in the novel is that of the map by which Meaulnes tries to reconstruct his adventure. What do we find if we focus on the map of masculine subjectivity delineated here? To put it in a schematic way, the dominant theme seems to be composed of the complementary motifs of a sense of loss (focusing upon a woman) and a compulsion to reconstruct a prior state. The form of self-consciousness arising from this dynamic is immersed in nostalgia and potentially self-pity. Its outcome is a kind of inconsolable self-regard. A compulsion to repeat seems to be built into this self-defeating search for an ideal.[17] The position for which Meaulnes is the model represents a fixation upon an idealised past so strong as to block off meaningful adult relations with the present. It is autoerotic in its nature. Put back in touch with Yvonne:

> fatally, with an obstinacy of which he was certainly unaware, Meaulnes kept going back to the past and all its marvels. And at each evocation the tortured girl could only repeat that everything had vanished . . .
> 'Ah!' Meaulnes sighed, in despair, and it was as though each item in the catalogue of disappearances added fresh evidence to the case he was arguing against the girl, or against me. (p. 155)

What happens next chimes with Mulvey's argument. The

> function of woman in forming the patriarchal unconscious is twofold, she first symbolises the castration threat by her real absence of a penis and second thereby raises her child into the Symbolic. Once this has been achieved her meaning in the process is at an end, it does not last into the world of law and language except as a memory which oscillates between memory of maternal plenitude and memory of lack. (1992, p. 22)

Yvonne, as already noted, is made out to be an almost ethereal creature, and in keeping with this does not survive childbirth. Her meaning in the process is indeed at an end. It is the narrator who is left with responsibility for the child. Not for long however, as Meaulnes returns once more to bear his daughter away. Later on, we shall find other instances of the narrative which ends with a birth: enough to say now that Meaulnes's adventure will continue its cycle reinforced by a form of reproduction from which the mother's contribution has been eliminated. Father and daughter make up a conflict-free dyad through which to live out a fantasy in which romance perpetuates itself without need of either sex or mature women. But the destructive effects of this triumph of the magic powers of the male imagination are not exhausted by the elimination of Yvonne as woman and mother.

François Seurel has from time to time consoled himself with the thought that one day the little girl will become 'in a sense my own child' (p. 204). When Meaulnes carries off his daughter the narrator will be bereft both of his friend and the child ('the one joy he had left me'). Symptomatically, this narrative holds that the watcher and narrator is sterile. Doomed to look on at the adventures of those he loves, he can befriend but not create. His own intervention in the romance of Meaulnes and Yvonne is disastrous.[18] Leaving Seurel to wither on his vine, Meaulnes' adventure returns recursively upon itself. A little while ago I noted the pattern of masculine sight-lines in which Seurel was watching Meaulnes. If we say that *Le Grand Meaulnes* – along with many other narratives – concerns reproduction, we are drawing attention to overlapping features at different levels of meaning. The question of how the phenomenon we can call 'Meaulnes' reproduces itself is in turn caught up in the relations between the hero and his watchers: Seurel within the framed narrative and his readers outside it. A self-aware masculine literary criticism could do with getting hold of whatever aesthetic it is they are enacting between them. Arguing that the theory of transference is central to a psycho-analytically informed criticism, Peter Brooks says:

> It is my premise that most narratives speak of their transferen-tial condition – of their anxiety concerning their transmissibility, of their need to be heard, of their desire to become the story of the listener as much as of the teller, something that is most evident in 'framed' tales . . . which embed another tale within them, and thus dramatise the relations of tellers and listeners. (1994, p. 50)

The pattern which the novel summons into being concerns the status of male subjectivity and its own power to recreate itself. The narrative proposes a three-way splitting of male subjectivity: Frantz the everlasting boy; Meaulnes, the roving adventurer, and Seurel, the sterile observer. The attention of each of these figures is riveted upon the previous element in the chain. This leads to a form of romance in which the male subject is both his own observer and his own offspring. The time-space he occupies is dignified and aestheticised by touching biological reality at as few points as possible. Its power to enchant resides in is its very elusiveness. As a form of romance, this narrative delineates an erotics of vacancy. If we men who are addressed as readers are expected to be representatives of a universal nature, that nature is posited not only upon the aestheticisation of the feminine, but on the simultaneous denial of the male body itself.[19]

MASCULINITY AND 'ENGLISH'

In the tradition of the new criticism, literary texts were valued precisely for their supposed superiority to abstract ideas. But however apparently concrete and idea-free, any text promotes 'theories in use',[20] implying working theories about, say, what it means to be male, how you should act, what ideals you should aspire to, where you would look to for authority. A text is a blue-print as well as a reflection: as Kenneth Gergen puts it: 'lives are constructed around pervading literary figures or tropes' (1989,

p. 154). Yet at the same time these performative texts themselves are not encountered by solitary individuals in deserted places. Their meanings are arrived at through a complicated series of mediations, among which institutions devoted to reading and symbol-making figure prominently. In this section I shall take up the contentious subject of the gendering of English Studies. In doing so I intend to concentrate on English Literature as a subject in Higher Education. This is not as arbitrary a decision as it may appear. As a former adult education tutor I am acutely aware of the limitations of the assumption that all serious reading takes place within or in association with the academy. If I concentrate upon Higher Education here it is partly because I assume that most of the readers of this book will be staff or students in Higher Education. Nothing I suggest implies that the gendering of the subject in other areas of education would not be an important subject for study also. Nevertheless, in the Anglo-American world, Higher Education English/Literature Departments (along with publishers, literary agents, teachers, professional associations, examination boards, literary prizes, and cultural journalists) occupy a strategic role in the reproduction of literature and literariness, the maintenance of the canon, and the establishment and propagation of canonical ways of reading.[21]

Throughout this book I shall take as a given that practices of reading, appreciation, and study are carried on and reproduced socially within the oral encounters of the subject. No educational subject is composed solely of the written or printed output of scholars and researchers. Each discipline constitutes what Jean Lave calls a 'community of practice' (Lave and Wenger, 1991). It is fashioned and refashioned in all the places (seminars, tutorials, lectures, demonstrations, informal discussions) where newcomers and insiders meet. A good deal of what passes for a 'subject' is made up of the practices by which it reproduces itself.[22] In the case of 'English' (as I sought to demonstrate in my book *From Reader to Reader*, 1992), traditions of reading and reader positions are negotiated within those occasions – simultaneously social, cognitive, and affective – where texts are discussed (Bleich, 1988; Knights, 1992; McCormick, 1994). As those who have been influenced by the recent revival of Vygotsky can show us, learning is as much an ontological as an epistemological process, and to be initiated into a subject is at least partly the acquisition of social competencies in social settings (Shotter, 1993; Van der Veer and Valsiner, 1994). In this specific connection, the subject's norms in respect of the gender and influence of sub-groups of readers will be reproduced or contested in the system of relations negotiated in the classroom (Aaron, 1995; Thomas, 1990; Thompson and Wilcox, 1989; Bleich, 1988).[23]

While it may only be a pious hope that new practices of teaching and learning could lead to new forms of knowledge, it seems that the converse is likely to be true: new knowledges transmitted through unexamined forms of pedagogy will inevitably fossilise and fail to bring about any lasting change. Thus this book is arguing at once for more reflexively aware reading on the part of those who are addressed as men, and in favour of a participative pedagogy which is critically aware of how gendering is enacted in the classroom.

Two major and to some extent contrasting moves available to any attempt to defamiliarise the normal are to theorise and to historicise. While both moves have the goal of reframing what seems natural and inevitable, one takes the route of logical analysis. The other reaches the same destination by the route of demonstrating the contingent processes of origin, implying as it does so hypothetical counter-narratives. Over the last twenty-five years or so, various forms of literary and critical theory have challenged the dominant norms of English Studies. At the same time there has been a complementary movement to reframe the subject's norms by exploring in a detailed way how English as a subject came into being (see for example, Baldick, 1983; Doyle, 1989; Hunter, 1988; Mulhern, 1979). To those histories of the subject have been added the impetus of the feminist movement, and also to some extent, studies of the rise of 'English' in the context of empire (Viswanathan, 1990).

Out of this complex history I shall pick a theme concerning the history of covert gender operations within the subject. Feminist scholars have confronted the effect of male-dominated power structures upon women and the work women could do. I want to approach the issue from a slightly different angle in attempting another reading of the gender struggle within the subject, a struggle which I believe has played a formative part in shaping the subject as it has been taught and researched. The underlying argument of this section is that the struggle for masculine supremacy in 'English Studies' may account for phenomena as apparently diverse as the academic canonisation of (one version of) literary modernism, and much of the practice of contemporary 'theory'. For 'English' is and has from the beginning been a subject closely aligned with modes of being and knowing, with forms of sensibility which are traditionally gendered as feminine. And furthermore it has been a subject whose complicity in the mother tongue has led generations of male scholars and critics to the counterrevolutionary assertion of their own superiority.[24] One secret history of the discipline, I propose, concerns a struggle for mastery not only over the text but more generally over the management of cultural energies. In a curious way, this is a struggle in which both male authors and male critics (whatever inter-group contempt they may have shown for each other in public) have frequently found common cause.

The subject matter of 'English' (unlike, say, the subject matter of physics or engineering) tends to gravitate towards a domain conventionally associated with the feminine. Much of it – preeminently in the case of novels and lyric poetry – concerns emotions, relationships, courtship, the repair and maintenance of family and kin, and the discourses within which such matters may be articulated. Its discourse embraces both intimacy and subjective experience (Bleich, 1988, ch. 5). Despite attempts by such as George Eliot or D. H. Lawrence to fight off the alarming similarity, one of its major staples – the novel – bears more than a passing resemblance to the traditionally feminised domain of 'gossip'. The thread which runs through this section concerns a subject created and administered by male professionals where there has been a recurrent compulsion to assert the subject's masculine credentials, a drive to take control of the subject's affective leanings by insisting upon the superiority of the styles and of the conceptual frameworks through which the affective could be organised and managed.[25] As we shall see shortly, the origins of university English, like those of modernism, lie in a period of gender ferment, and the subject represents the disciplinary adjunct of a campaign to roll back a perceived feminisation of the written word. The 'male novelists and critics who sought to define fiction in the late nineteenth and early twentieth centuries entered a field that was perceived either as gendered feminine or as dominated by women and women's issues' (Pykett, 1995, p. 70; compare Trotter, 1993).

In terms of the gendered connotations of the hard / soft

metaphorical set, it is not surprising that English has battled from the beginning against being classified as a 'soft' option. As long ago as 1921 the Newbolt Report asserted that the man 'who enters an English "School" hoping for an idle or easy time should at once find that he has deceived himself' (*The Teaching of English in England*, 1921, para. 194; see also Baldick, 1983; Doyle, 1989).

It was as a university adult education tutor that I initially became conscious of a gender struggle within 'English' and literary studies. Even if we leave on one side those programmes specifically for women of which English and literature used to form a major component, English in the last years of British liberal adult education was predominantly a women's subject. While, as you would expect, most of the full-time staff were men, most part-time staff in the subject were women, and women outnumbered men students in a ratio of roughly 4:1 (Knights, 1992). This in turn mirrored the general identification of women within the culture as the people who read fiction. Literature groups, when not under the institutional pressure of assessment, commonly form small female cultures. Working as a man with student groups composed largely or entirely of women alerted me to gender issues in reading and drew my attention to how the gender structure of the subject reproduced itself. I have often been vividly confronted with the need to 'read as a woman', thus taking part in a classroom re-enactment of the contest between gendered reading positions. Many of the readings essayed in this book have their origins in such dialogues.

That was a personal way of trying to get hold of something which it is necessary to develop in other ways. University adult education and 'English' were to some degree symbiotic in their origins. One of the principal roots of the new subject of 'English' in the later nineteenth century was the university extension movement (and to some extent other forms of adult education), in which English was widely regarded as a women's subject. As Baldick notes, the healthful value of literary study was 'that it did not seem to involve straying too far from the acceptable staple of artistic 'accomplishments' which made up the wealthier woman's training for the marriage market' (1983, p. 68). In a Ruskinian spirit, the process of civilising the middle classes was to be led by women, and Baldick quotes Charles Kingsley's first lecture at the Queen's College for Women: literature provides an intimate history of the nation's enduring spirit:

Such a course of history would quicken women's inborn personal interest in the actors of this life-drama, and be quickened by it in return, as indeed it ought: for it is thus that God intended woman to look instinctively at the world. Would to God that she would teach us men to look at it thus likewise. Would to God that she would in these days claim and fulfil to the utmost her vocation as the priestess of charity. (Quoted by Baldick, 1983, p. 69)

Over one hundred years later, A-Level and University students of English are still – as they have always been – predominantly women. Into the 1990s the ratio both at A-level and in the 'old' universities remained roughly 7:3 (Protherough, 1989, pp. 41–4; *University Statistics Register*, Table 5).[26] In 1992 in the then public sector institutions, three out of four students of English were women (Evans, 1993, p. 116). In 1995–6, the latest year for which figures are available, the figures for British universities as a whole were still much the same. Out of 18 000 home full-time undergraduates in English, 5532 (30.7 per cent) were men (HESA, Table 2a). English has a higher proportion of women students than any university subject other than Modern Languages. But as is usually the case in a patriarchy, women are increasingly filtered out the further up the pyramid you travel. There has indeed been some improvement since 1980. While I cannot disaggregate the figures, in the Language related subjects women have moved from 4.3 per cent to 15 per cent of professors and from 14.1 per cent to 23 per cent of readers and senior lecturers, while still making up a near majority (47 per cent) of lecturers and the overwhelming majority of 'other' and part-time staff (HESA: Higher Education Resources, Table 16; *USR*, Table 30). Nevertheless, and despite considerable recruitment of younger female staff in the last ten years, this means that a common pattern is still that of young female undergraduates being taught by older men. Of the 100 professors of English in 1993, 15 were women (Evans, 1993, p. 116). This is still (even if decreasingly) a subject where students' subjectivity is as it were coaxed out and then shaped under the tutelage of older males. Indeed, Evans goes so far as to call English a 'female subject dominated by males' (Evans, 1993, p.; and compare Thomas, 1990).

There is of course a corollary for those men who read English and for the regulation of the subject at a disciplinary level. The male student of English is going against the social grain. He is likely to be seen as self-indulgent rather than task-orientated, a throwback to a non-vocational age. As members of a minority within the student body, males have to negotiate their standing, and fend off the effeminacy that may be attributed to them by other students. It is a personal impression substantiated by the interviews conducted by Kim Thomas that in many cases this leads to a high degree of competitiveness, and correspondingly an assumed air of comfortable superiority to women students and staff (1990, for example, pp. 145–56; and see Evans, 1993, ch. 6). So far from feeling embarrassment about being a minority, many of the male undergraduates interviewed by Thomas enjoyed being different, and throve on being provocative or controversial in seminars (Thomas, 1990, ch. 7). In this connection, it is worth reflecting on Viswanathan's remark that it is 'not generally realised how infinitely more binding the tyranny of representation can be on the coloniser than on the colonised' (1990, p. 12). Paradoxically, I hope that one effect of this book might be to make men less rather than more comfortable with their performance in the subject. The covert history of the gendering of the discipline requires bringing out in the open if we are to avoid simply re-enacting old manoeuvres.

Histories of the subject recount its rise in terms both of its kinship with nationalism, especially in the period immediately before and after the First World War, and to the perceived need to maintain cohesion in an era of social conflict through the establishment of a new educational class (Baldick, 1983; Doyle, 1989; Newbolt, 1921).[27] A related and consistent thread is a long-drawn out contest to do with gender. As Doyle has shown, during the interwar period 'English' became established as a masculine profession. Much of this new profession's energy was devoted to achieving respectability through sound literary scholarship, and devotion to maintaining the national heritage. Though the Newbolt Committee's programme for a nationally funded class of missionary English teachers was not in fact realised on anything like the scale intended till after the Second World War, nevertheless by the late 1930s 'the academic English scholar was becoming less of a public policy maker by aspiration, and more of an arbiter and custodian both of literary language and literary knowledge' (Doyle, 1989, p. 75 and ch. 3 generally).

Viewed from whatever position within the subject, its battlegrounds had to do with the canon of great texts, and with its relation to ideas of Englishness and an English sensibility. Given the long-term decline of Classics, another ingredient in these debates was the subject's legacy from the nineteenth-century tradition of 'liberal education' (Knights, 1978, especially pp. 188–98). Within this influential tradition the objective of a liberal education was a form of mental cultivation through which the educated man [*sic*] would rise above specialism and technical know-how to achieve the disciplined, detached consciousness of the ideal gentleman. The goal was a superior form of mental life, the more prized the further it could rise above sensuous, technical, instrumental, and partisan knowledge (compare Lloyd, 1993). Its outcome was a detached mastery, an intellectual condition both rational and above all ironic, in which opposites could be reconciled or held in play. The initiate would learn to embrace the specific only as an instance of the universal. Inasmuch as the text was supposed to address our full humanity, that humanity was seen as transcending the limitations of class or gender.[28] While the whole bundle of ideas radiates class and gender prejudices, its tacit identification of the masculine with the balanced overview was very much part of the Arnoldian inheritance of the new discipline.

Where the Newbolt Committee had argued for the humanising force of English in terms of reconciling the class struggle, the liberal education version located harmony within the individual mind (Newbolt, 1921, paras 232–8). Even the *Scrutiny* school, with its pronounced sense of cultural and social mission, based its vision of social redemption upon the integration of the inner world through the practice of strenuous reading (see for example, Leavis, 1930; Mulhern, 1979).[29] To become qualified as a member of the discriminating minority you must have undergone a process of internal intellectual and emotional discipline by definition unavailable to those who were merely the passive consumers of mass communications. If, as Bernstein and Henriques have argued, educational subjects call into being 'educational identities', these considerations are relevant to any attempt to explore the kind of sensibility, the disciplined and attentive internal condition, which English has sought to instil in its students (Bernstein, 1975; Henriques, 1984). One feature of this condition has been communion with the sensibility of great (male) authors. At times it is hard to resist the inference that the male mind of the author was to fertilise the (?female) mind of the student. In the context of its proposals for re-establishing national coherence in 1919, the Ministry of Reconstruction commented: 'The primary aim of education in literature, so far as adult students are concerned, should be not the acquisition of information, but the cultivation of imagination.' So far so good. But the Report continues as follows:

> The test of its success is not that students should be able to talk fluently, or even intelligently, about literary history, but that they should have been penetrated by the power of some great writer, should have made something of him, at least, a part of themselves, and should have acquired insensibly an inner standard of excellence. (Ministry of Reconstruction, 1919, para. 160)

Within fifteen years what was to become the hegemonic English Studies of the mid-century included among its aims the production of the richly stocked and discriminating mind that could survey and 'place' its objects. Such a mind was above all evaluative, its primary act one of discrimination and 'mature' judgment. The doctrine of impersonality derived from Eliot was among other things a response to the way in which textual subject matter was found to be embedded in the emotions and the unconscious (Ellmann, 1987). Hearn's account (1987) of the control of the emotions within the professions provides a wider gendered context for this disciplined sensibility.

It is a commonplace of any history of 'English Studies' that the discipline associated with the early work of Richards and Empson, of the Leavises and the *Scrutiny* circle drew much of its own intellectual sustenance from modernism and specifically the work of T. S. Eliot and Ezra Pound. Over the past few years, numerous studies have realigned the discussion of modernism and modernist texts within debates about gender (Gilbert and Gubar, 1988 and 1989; Scott, 1990; Huyssen, 1986, for fiction summarised by Trotter, 1993; Pykett, 1995). In the context of increasingly successful literary production by women, argue Gilbert and Gubar:

> we find ourselves confronting an entirely different modernism. And it is a modernism constructed not just against the grain of Victorian male precursors, not just in the shadow of a

shattered God, but as an integral part of a complex response to female precursors and contemporaries. Indeed, it is possible to hypothesise that a reaction-formation against the rise of literary women became not just a theme in modernist writing but a motive for modernism. (1988, p. 156)

Without attempting to summarise those arguments here, I would like to suggest the implications for our purposes of this emergence of a form of modernist pedagogy within literary studies. In a suggestive but in some ways unsatisfactory essay, Andrew Huyssen (1986) follows Adorno's argument that modernism must be seen in many ways as a reaction to mass culture and commodification. He takes the further step of noting that modernism's crusaders from Flaubert onwards tend to identify mass culture as 'monolithic, engulfing, totalitarian, and on the side of regression and the feminine' (ibid., p. 201), with modernism posed within the same dichotomy as 'progressive, dynamic, and indicative of male superiority in culture'. This despite the fact that 'it has always been men rather than women who have had real control over the production of mass culture' (p. 205). Huyssen's argument is European in scope. I suggest however that at a more parochial level the same pattern can be discerned within the foundational texts of new criticism. Thus the account of the new standardised society of 'vicarious living' contained in Leavis's early polemic 'Mass Civilisation and Minority Culture' could be read as an assault on a society seen as infantilised and by implication feminised:

> [The] new forms of recreation in the civilised world [Leavis has film especially in mind] . . . involve surrender, under conditions of hypnotic receptivity, to the cheapest emotional appeals, appeals the more insidious because they are associated with a compellingly vivid illusion on actual life. (Leavis, 1930, p. 10)

One way of reading the formation of a new 'hard' poetry by Pound and Eliot, and the isomorphic formation a few years later of a new strenuous criticism, is as another phase of the male attempt to manage and to police cultural reproduction. But it would be a mistake to think of this gender policing as addressed solely to women, a defence of cultural creation and reproduction against feminisation. It was, argues Koestenbaum (1989), also addressed to other men, and the implicit subject of the address was the dangers of homoeroticism. The formation of a heroic band of critics who study *The Waste Land*, he argues, is partly a product of an acute misogyny, but also a response to an equally acute, even hysterical, sensitivity to the perceived vulnerability of masculinity to itself. The high and difficult curriculum espoused by the foundational new critics we might say enabled a certain kind of argument, a certain kind of combative bonding between male critics, a fact with enduring consequences for the practice of literary criticism in Britain and the USA. Proposed within these new and enthusiastically disseminated practices was a consciously exclusive literary language that involved setting off a new high language, an enclave within the mother tongue – Gilbert and Gubar again: 'these linguistic revolutionaries became latter-day Merlins seeking, through "densest concentration", to regain the mastery lost when male artists were forced by history to operate within the degrading confines of the vernacular mother tongues (1988, p. 259). In Trotter's luminous economic model, a literary language which accretes value through the sheer difficulty of processing it (Trotter, 1993) became the paradigm for a form of study that proposed to guard literary production and transmission against both feminisation and unworthy, because permeable and unstable, forms of masculinity.

This judicious and discriminating function of the trained mind was to be achieved not by a catholic exposure to a wide variety of texts and genres, but by participation in a process of ritual combat. The 'common pursuit of true judgment' was a combative rather than a collaborative procedure. Its aim was boundary demarcation, and the propagation of hierarchy in the service of cultural survival. As the century advanced, much of the oral and written practice of studying English was devoted to learning the moves of aggressive and sectarian condemnation of out-group authors and rival critics. Once again, it is hard not to see this as an attempt to stave off through ritualised aggression the fear of subjectivity and thus feminisation. Thus the sensibility which was to save civilization had to be initiated into authority by learning intellectual sword play, in a form of association which bred in disciples the fear of shame or ridicule resulting from being seen (whether by teachers or peers) to espouse a rejected author or subject matter. Literary criticism in fact accommodated itself to those agonistic procedures which Walter Ong has identitifed as characterising the institutions of male knowledge (Ong, 1981, throughout). Just as a canon was achieved by strict rules of exclusion and status, so homologous rules were by implication applied to the subject's initiates. Great tradition and 'armed and conscious minority' go hand in hand. And in the terms of this agenda, lower status was accorded to those writers who were held to have failed to transcend their gender limitations.[30]

Since the 1970s, feminist scholars and critics in North America and Britain have demonstrated the masculine bias of the canon, and of the critical practice that went with it. They have also, though to a lesser extent, explored the implications for oppositional teaching (Bleich, 1988; McCormick, 1994; Thompson and Wilcox, 1989). Yet it seems to me less well recognised that the internecine campaign associated with the 'theory' movement against everything that 'New Criticism' and 'Liberal Humanism' were believed to stand for – and simultaneously against the 'commonsense' beliefs of most literature students – has (in one of those paradoxes to which opposition movements are liable) in many ways reinforced and perpetuated masculine norms within the subject.[31] One way, for example, of reading the ill-tempered Oedipal struggle carried on in Shakespeare studies since the early 1980s would be as the enactment of homosocial bonding between a new generation of male critics.

My comments here are directed not to 'theory' as a body of knowledge, but to 'theory' as a genre and as a pedagogic practice. Let me make plain that in advancing this argument I do not intend a blanket assault on 'theory' and all its works. For one thing, it would not be possible – even if desirable – to shed so much of the intellectual history of the past thirty years. Further, 'theory' is a plural and heterogeneous series of movements.[32] Cumulatively, these have been enormously influential and productive in developing a rigorous critical discourse and in providing students of Cultural Studies and English with a map of intellectual history, however selective. I am concerned here with 'theory' as a practice, an educational genre, rather than a curriculum. A self-aware gender politics requires us to question the dynamics of the classroom whose paradigmatic procedures include: the compulsive, almost theological allusion to a new canon of patriarchs (Nietzsche, Saussure, Heidegger, Gramsci, Lévi-Strauss, Althusser, Foucault, Lacan, Barthes, Lyotard, Derrida, Baudrillard . . .); a metalanguage characterised by an intimidatingly high level of abstraction; an exaggerated formalism that dismisses the links between text and referent; a symbolic geography of the human body that is reduced to 'phallus' or 'lips'; and a contempt for history other than a highly selective history of ideas. The resulting classroom practice tends to generate a small elite of intellectual heroes bonded to the charismatic teacher, and a large group of the alienated and excluded, those whose role is to embody the commonsense which is the 'other' of theory. Even Jonathan Culler, who has done as much as any individual to pioneer 'theory' has recently remarked that in its endlessness it 'is thus a source of intimidation, a resource for constant upstagings' (1997, p. 15). Patriarchy strikes back, and on this occasion its guise is another kind of idealism, reproducing the mind – body dualism that Seidler has characterised as typifying patriarchal masculinity (1989, pp. 18–22; see also Lloyd, 1993). We seem to be dealing with a parochial variation on a postmodern theme. Speaking of social theory, Connerton notes a

> marked tendency within social history towards the disappearance of the human body from its object-domain. This disappearance results from a strategy of what we might call etherialisation. In the case of certain more recent conceptions of social theory, for instance, the object-domain for social theory is defined in terms of what is taken to be the distinctive feature of the human species, language: this in turn itself being conceptualised by the various Wittgensteinian, hermeneutic, Structuralist and post-Structuralist schools as a set of social rules, or a text, or a system of signs, or a powerful discourse. The human body cannot be included in a domain defined in these ways, at least not when it is regarded as a material thing. (Connerton, 1988, pp. 205–6)

'Theory', like formalism before it, and whatever its avowed intentions or proclaimed materialism, tends to seek purity by interposing a *cordon sanitaire* between idea and the dangerous human earth.[33] An active and high-status explanatory discourse subordinates other discourses to a passive role as those which have to be explained. In contemporary English Studies we seem to be inhabiting a diglossic culture, and one where the 'high' language gestures towards mastery even while simultaneously denying its possibility. There is a parallel with the way modernist poetic subordinated its quotations from women and popular culture to a new high language, a parallel explicitly made by Gilbert and Gubar, who note that much 'recent male theory bears a striking resemblance to some of the masculine linguistic fantasies' of modernism (1988, p. 261).

In imposing a hierarchy of explanation, 'theory', especially in its deconstructive variant, has a a lot in common with other rationalisms down the ages. As Bleich has remarked, it is a form of thought that has no political constituency except the academy from which it sprang: from 'a social point of view, Derrida's work helped to preserve the institution that has historically perpetuated the attitudes of "Western metaphysics" that his intellectual program opposes' (1988, pp. 40–1). To unpick this paradox and continue to work with the enormous productive energies of 'theory', we need to attend to the residual gendering of pedagogic practices.

Socially approved forms of writing, reading and responding to narratives constitute a modality of power as well as a disinterested pursuit of understanding. If a new discourse is to arise, and one in which masculine power is more open to challenge and criticism, it will have to be worked out on the basis of tending and developing the oppositional strands always present within textual studies. Narrative is situated in social and transactional space, and while a story will encode its own means of reproduction, different voices and other codes can nevertheless be enacted in the dialogues that surround the text.

While I seek to offer tentative models for discussing narratives – a contribution to what Sinfield (1992) calls dissident reading – the ideas I seek to promote require for their further development fundamental change in the social practices of education and learning. (Compare Lentricchia, 1983; Scholes, 1985; Thompson and Wilcox, 1989; Knights, 1995.) Narratives make proposals to which it is often necessary to make counter-proposals. At the same time, what Shotter calls the 'retrospective coherency of narrative' requires constantly to be checked against the local and particular (1993, p. 173). Such dialogic processes cannot take place in the individual head only. They require a collaborative and reasonably safe social forum. Speaking as a cognitive psychologist, Bruner identifies those elements of literary discourse which work to enlist the reader. Together, he says, these 'succeed in subjunctivizing reality . . . To be in the subjunctive mode is . . . to be trafficking in human possibilities rather than in settled certainties' (Bruner, 1986, p. 26). In this book I hope to suggest ways of reading that 'subjunctivize' and make conditional the role of male readers and their fabulous counterparts.[34]

In the kind of reading advocated in this book, the cities of texts are peopled, thronged with varied and often conflicting voices. I suggest that this gives grounds for hope rather than despair. In explaining why, I can summarise an argument underlying this section. Earlier on, I noted that to read literature has often in the past been envisaged as a form of intercourse with the mind of the 'great' writer. This idea is based upon a strongly patriarchal account of lineage, a pure, uncontaminated, line of descent from master to initiate. Such is the attraction of this will o'the wisp of the unmediated channel that it turns up even within otherwise conflicting critical schools. The New Critical 'words on the page' fetish was one such influential manifestation. Such a desire for proximity to logos used to lead easily enough to a more or less contemptuous dismissal of mediations: textual scholarship, seminar teaching, the theatre, even – paradoxically – reading criticism. There is a lesson here. Any attempt to enquire what it would mean to go beyond the masculine tradition in reading cannot be carried on in the individual mind alone. Such an enquiry requires us as readers, students, and teachers to immerse ourselves in the anxious, messy, social world of teaching and learning.

2

The Portrait of the Artist as a Man

By intimate association with beauty embodied in his friend, and by keeping him always before his mind, he succeeds in bringing to birth the children he has long desired to have, and once they are born he shares their upbringing with his friend; the partnership between them will be far closer and the bond of affection far closer than between ordinary parents, because the children that they share surpass human children by being immortal as well as more beautiful. Everyone would prefer children such as these to children after the flesh.

(Plato, *The Symposium*, trans. Walter Hamilton, Harmondsworth: Penguin, 1951, p. 91)

Throughout this book we are concerned with communicative scenarios, the use of narrative to enforce or develop gender norms. One focus for acts of formative communication is the situation of the writer, and in this chapter, and by way of laying a foundation for much of what follows, I shall turn to the theme of symbolic mastery through art. The project of the hero as artist or writer may not in fact differ so much as we might at first suppose from that of other sorts of hero. In investigating this claim we shall build on the premise that any novel concerning art and artists, writers, film-makers or musicians is itself reflexive: a metafiction which enacts proposals about creativity, reproduction, and the social and moral role of art (Waugh, 1984). Texts which foreground the male artist simultaneously reveal assumptions and propagate norms about the nature and social function of fictions. An examination of the topos of the male artist will help to position our understanding of narrative, and the nature of the relations of solidarity (or antagonism) between reader and

49

narrator, narrator and subject matter. Male attempts, whether seen or unseen, to legislate for the symbolic realm are central to the subject matter of this book. Indeed, the theme of the male artist has recurred time and again in fictional texts since that moment around the 1880s when the whole issue appears to have gone critical. Henry James's *The Lesson of the Master*, James Joyce's *Portrait of the Artist as a Young Man*, D. H. Lawrence's *Sons and Lovers*, Thomas Mann's *Doctor Faustus*, Anthony Burgess's *Earthly Powers*, Saul Bellow's *Humbolt's Gift*, Alasdair Grey's *Lanark: A Life in 4 Books*, or Martin Amis's *The Information* are all examples of this abundant narrative genre.

In this chapter I shall concentrate largely on an aspect of the work of the contemporary novelist John Fowles, in particular the novella 'The Ebony Tower' (1974), and the novel *Daniel Martin* (1977). With the success of *The French Lieutenant's Woman* (1969), Fowles triumphantly crossed the line between minority and popular fiction. Much of his output has been visibly concerned with masculinity and male roles. I want specifically to argue that Fowles' work of the 1970s demonstrates a preoccupation with the role of the male artist that is particularly suggestive for our purposes, and which appears to be in some ways a response to 'second wave' feminism as D. H. Lawrence's work was to the first (Woodcock, 1984). Significantly, attempts like Woodcock's to read Fowles' work in the light of gender politics have aroused the ire of critics (for example, Palmer, 1985): the stature of the artist as a spokesman for transcending values is felt to be diminished by being mapped onto issues of gender. On the contrary, I intend to argue that reflection on Fowles' work in the present context offers us a way of articulating the complex relationships between artists, readers, and subject matter in a way that I hope will demonstrate the importance of taking gender into consideration in what might otherwise be ostensibly gender-neutral discussion about art and 'the artist'. I intend to begin by looking at 'The Ebony Tower', and then move on to *Daniel Martin*. The discussion of both will, I hope, radiate outwards into developments of the general argument.

To put it briefly and provisionally, we find in masculine narrative a recurrent ambivalence towards the figure of the male artist, who is at once envied for his direct contact with a highly charged and precious domain, and also despised as not altogether a man: the object of admiration as well as of revulsion. Such a figure is divided where a man is conventionally supposed to be unitary. His symbolic field of operations marks him out as a passive viewer rather than an active doer, and thus as someone who lacks control over the boundaries of his own identity. (See Habegger, 1982, for a discussion on Henry James in this light.) In his propensity to contemplate himself he can be identified as narcissistic, and self-absorbed. In colonising creativity he is aligned with the 'feminine'. Representations of artists and writers have to negotiate both these positions. One traditional way of rescuing the split male artist from suspicion is to play up his patriarchal attributes: his dominance over women, and his superiority over subaltern men. I hope that the detail of this chapter will add substance to this bare assertion.

THE EBONY TOWER

'The Ebony Tower' develops a group of interconnected themes which counterpoint the argument of this book as a whole. The story concerns a young male painter and critic called David Williams who makes a trip to Brittany in order to visit Henry Breasley, a famous painter now in his old age living in seclusion in a converted manor house in the forest of Paimpont. David needs to interview Breasley for the biographical and critical introduction he is writing to a major book on the artist.[1] There is thus an implicit contrast set up between painting (a form of iconic representation which is seen as in some way primary), and words (seen as secondary or derivative). The story covers the two days of his stay at Coëtminais and the unravelling of the relationship between the two men and the two young women with whom Breasley turns out to be living. The whole story is an elaborately realised metafiction, in the sense that it refers constantly to the making of art and thus to its own fictional status. The register is one of rich painterly detail, a code by which to allude to its own subject matter in the detailed representation of the scene, and its metafictional resonances include having one of the characters reading a novel of Fowles' own.[2] Breasley is himself in some ways a reworking of the magus figure, and his domain parallels in its warmth, sexual exoticism and seclusion the island of the previous novel. It is also a place where the young initiate's manhood is put on trial (a 'kind of ordeal', p. 62).

Let me try to orientate this discussion. First of all, Fowles' stories are not univocal. They do not argue only one case or represent only one position. 'The Ebony Tower' is, however, certainly exploring arguments about representation and art, and near the end its hero, appalled by what he has come to see as the emptiness of his own generation and its 'surface liberties', reflects that perhaps 'it was happening in the other arts – in writing, music' (p. 111). One reading of the text would be to take it as a coded diagnosis of what was missing in the novel of the early 1970s, and a proposal for return to a more masculine form. Yet I must make clear that I am not seeking to take to task the figure of the author ('John Fowles') for his imputed views on gender or the subordination of women. One reason is that blanket accusations of 'sexism'– in this case by no means accurately targeted – represent an impoverished form of critical discourse. But another reason should be apparent from the course of the argument so far: the communicative dynamics involved are more complex. That is to say, that in talking about or writing about Fowles I may myself be drawn into a transferential relationship already mapped out in his story: playing on a small scale Williams to Fowles' Breasley, coming to analyse but remaining to pray. The younger follower of the great man could turn out to assume the cloak of the disciple. That is to say that the novella has already mapped out one model for the relations between a younger and an older man.

The story is focalised through David Williams, and he with his narrator is a variant on the figure of the male messenger or go-between. Such a narrator-intermediary (of which Conrad's Marlow in 'Heart of Darkness' is an outstanding example) shuttles between the central symbolic terrain of the narrative and its readers. In some sense, then, this messenger, like so many other interpreters within texts, acts as a surrogate not only for the 'author' but also for the reader. He is an outsider who assumes the role of insider and returns bearing news from the interior. In sustaining the illusion that he has been in the vicinity of the truth, he dramatises presence. He has gone back to origins, even if he now, like Marlow, reports merely to a profane audience. He is the exemplary interpreter, or translator, and the impact upon him of what he has witnessed prefigures its impact upon the reader. David, like Marlow, has made the journey to a remote place and into the presence of the central enigma of his own narrative. He returns transformed, having glimpsed his 'lost true self' (p. 111) but unable to speak fully of what has happened to him, or of the loss implicit within his return to normality. At the end, when he meets Beth, his wife, at Orly Airport and she asks him how he got on, he 'surrenders to what is left: to abstraction: "I survived"' (p. 115) – a summary of whose inadequacy, mendacity even, the reader is by now well aware. Beth must be protected from the truth. That this intricate modelling of the reading process is not gender-neutral will be a theme of this chapter as of the discussion of Conrad that follows. First we must turn to the time-space in which the core of the narrative is embedded.

Like Meaulnes' lost domain, of which it is acknowledgedly a descendant, Breasley's estate at Coëtminais is another variant on the enchanted kingdom. ('But Henry's got one rather extraordinary quality. Apart from painting. A sort of magic . . .', p. 68). Like the 'green world' of pastoral, it stands outside ordinary time. 'Once more he had that uncanny sense of melted time and normal process; of an impulsion that was indeed spell-like and legendary' (p. 98). Celtic myth, Fowles has elsewhere hypothesised, occupies a key place in the genealogy of the novel, and in that sense both David and Daniel Martin return to source in Brittany and Devon respectively.[3] In any case, Fowles's mythological allusion locates the genealogy of his own text in 'the green source' and a larger cultural history. The motif of the old artist as sorcerer has returned elsewhere, for example more recently in Iris Murdoch's oddly similar *The Good Apprentice* (though there the old man appears to be more the prisoner of his women than vice versa). In terms of this book the enchanted domain has functional similarities with the island, and in the next chapter I shall speculate whether the island may be colonised as a code for male subjectivity. What relations does the island have with the outside world? Who is the ruler of the island? What is the nature of the commonwealth established on the island? Where does Caliban fit? And where Miranda? Where the old witch who was there first? In this case the old caretaker (who is in Breasley's debt for taking him back after he had been imprisoned for murder) constitutes a sort of Caliban figure. And a Miranda actually has by this time already turned up in Fowles' work as the young woman imprisoned and killed in *The Collector*.[4]

Into the triangle of the old man and the two young women (one chaste, one promiscuous) comes the young male artist with a mission to understand his senior and reduce him to the printed word of art criticism. The point of the story is that his mission is subverted, and by the old man himself. The story suggests that the old man really is in touch with some quality (wickedness, amoral energy, true creativity, the phallic centre of his male self?) which the text holds up as admirable, but which the younger man, straightjacketed by politeness, deference, and a suburban morality, has lost. 'Henry knew sin was a challenge to life; not an unreason, but an act of courage and imagination. He sinned out of need and instinct; David did not, out of fear' (p. 108). True art, the narrative seems to be asserting, is produced out of wildness:

> What the old man still had was an umbilical cord to the past . . . That was the real kernel of his wildness. David and his generation, and all those to come, could only look back, through bars, like caged animals, born in captivity, at the old green freedom. (p. 110)

Although the past is apparently identified with the mother, the artist's wildness is visualised very clearly in masculine terms. Its converse is the loss of manhood in domesticity: 'He felt a little bewitched, possessed; and decided it must be mainly the effect of being without Beth. They lived so close, one had forgotten what the old male freedom was like . . .' (p. 75). In the last chapter we noted ways in which male modernism was a reaction to a perceived feminisation of culture. Here, the triumph of abstraction and cerebral art with which the fleeing David taxes his own generation is not a matter of 'jettisoning the human body' in some gender-neutral way. It is also 'Castration. The triumph of the eunuch.' Breasley's courage to throw himself into life is, it appears, all a matter of spunk. Recklessly, he can take charge of women where David defers to them. Notable about this colonisation of creativity by the male is that it rests upon a kind of reversed fertilisation, whereby Breasley's uninhibited relations with women seem to be if not the source at least the condition of his creativity as artist. 'Why I have to have women round me. Sense of timing. Bleeding and all that. Learning when not to work' (p. 29).

Despite the element of affectionate mockery, Breasley's voice is the privileged voice of the text, and to take up a critical stance towards that voice is to ally oneself with the forces of superficiality, mediocrity and mere words. (The story has pre-empted you.)

He has a grounding in his own male physicality which is simultaneously the masterful access to the physicality of women. The male reader who objects is probably a bumboy, and certainly a humourless and uncreative little grumbler. (I am not sure whether the text is actually endorsing Breasley's casually homophobic outburst: but the outburst is there for all that.) It is Nietzsche's genealogy of morals rewritten in terms of art: the lesser have no right to judge the great in terms of their own petty morality. '[One] either had the temperament for excess and a ruthless egocentricity . . . or one didn't. . . . Coët had remorselessly demonstrated what he was born, still was, and always would be: a decent man and an eternal also-ran' (p. 113). This may lack unambiguous narrative endorsement (it occurs in David's bitter self-flagellation at the end), but it is a powerful voice within the text. Its message is not just that great art stands above morality, but that it is supermoral in a specifically masculine way.

The making of art (and by implication the making of literature) is not, however, grounded solely in the relation between Breasley and his women. As I have already noted, the story, like so much of Fowles' work, evinces a highly visually realised surface; painting is simultaneously subject and metaphor. The women compose themselves under the male gaze not only of the painter (as in the bathing scene) but of the writer and the reader as well (pp. 74–7). What sort of magnetism, what sort of seduction does the story represent to the male reader? One sort of seduction is presumably constituted by the appeal to heterosexual voyeurism in which the reader is expected to be complicit with the two men. At times this verges on the whimsy pornographic, so much so that one looks around for an implied narrator (another, even more knowing man?) to 'place' this: 'He felt a kind of mental . . . randiness; a sinuous wave of the primeval male longing for the licitly promiscuous . . . ' (p. 76). Once again we return to the subject of the foothold that a text has in 'male' identity and consciousness, a foothold that is in turn part of the subject matter of this story.

Let us, then, note that in this 'déjeuner sur l'herbe' there are three figures grouping themselves around the old artist. One of course (also subsequently challenged to undress) is David himself, who is thus part of Breasley's view as much as are the women. It is indeed his relationship to Breasley to which we need to return. There is a form of homosocial bonding (Sedgwick, 1985) enacted not only in the relation between Breasley and David, but between text and putative male reader. In a sense, David is a surrogate for the reader as he tries to piece together the scene at Coëtminais, and in his unfolding relationship to the old artist. He is both initiate and heir, the one person in whom the old man can confide. During his brief visit he has glimpsed an alternative, wilder, probably – the text implies – more creative self, but is condemned at the end to being 'an eternal also-ran'. His glimpse is focused through his attempted liaison with Diana 'the Mouse', yet his brief and unsatisfactory relationship with her is conducted under the old man's auspices, and effectively at his instigation ('pity you're married . . . they need a good fuck' [p. 61]: simultaneously an acknowledgement of his own failing prowess). Prospero, so to speak, makes Miranda available to Ferdinand but ensures that their relations shall be chaste. Structurally, the characters enact Girard's case that desire is focused on the object which has been validated by the figure of the mediator. It is the wanton old patriarch whose vision transforms and sexualises what the younger man sees. In this relationship the latter is also a surrogate for the male reader, invited as it were into the presence for a private view (an image made irresistible by Breasley's collection of famous painters). The sorcerer's island fastness (like Seegard in *The Good Apprentice*) is a magnet for sons and would-be sons. In turn David's relationship to Breasley is mediated through the two women (who quite literally act as interpreters and go-betweens). The fascination Breasley holds for him is partly the fascination of a model of male identity which, while that of an artist, is nevertheless depicted as at home in its own sexuality, unconstrained by petty rules and inhibitions. It is also the desirability of sharing vicariously in the triumph of one who has attained fame and sway over his island. The implied desirability of being close to the patriarchal Breasley organises the energies of the novel.

Part of Breasley's attraction is his fame. He has had the courage to voyage into his interior world and return to make art which has both drawn to him the attention of the *cognoscenti* and enabled him to surround himself with women. This very masculine conception of artistic success has pronounced affinities with Freud's notorious passage on the artist from the (1916–17) *Introductory Lectures on Psychoanalysis*. There Freud argues that the path of art leads back from neurosis to reality. Yet the artist (naturally a man) is not your average neurotic who has the good fortune to find the right kind of therapy. He

> understands how to work over his day-dreams in such a way as to make them lose what is too personal about them and repels strangers, and to make it possible for others to share in the enjoyment of them . . . Furthermore, he possesses the mysterious power of shaping some particular material until it has become a faithful image of his phantasy . . . If he is able to accomplish all this, he makes it possible for other people to derive consolation and alleviation from their own sources of pleasure in their unconscious which have become inaccessible to them; he earns their gratitude and admiration and he has thus achieved *through* his phantasy what originally he had achieved only *in* his phantasy – honour, power, and the love of women. (*Introductory Lectures*, pp. 423–4)

Triumphant return from the voyage into the interior brings a man tangible benefits, through the medium of fame. Fowles' text follows Freud closely. He was 'impossible'

> so one believed in him. And now even those many who had refused to believe had been comforted: he had come through to this, reputation, wealth, the girls, freedom to be exactly as he always had been, a halo round his selfishness, a world at his every whim, every other world shut out, remote behind the arboreal sea. (p. 57)

There is another element in this masculine constellation of voyage into the interior, leading to fame and female admiration. That is the bond of solidarity with a male audience which is forged through the communicative dynamic of the novel. We must next turn to a novel in which the figure of the male artist is developed further.

THE WOMAN IN THE REEDS

A preoccupation with male creativity appears to run through Fowles' work of the 1970s. This phase seems to reach a climax in the long novel *Daniel Martin*, published in 1977. *Daniel Martin* is the story of an Oxford-educated playwright who graduates into writing film scripts, and eventually into writing his own novel. Daniel himself is perpetually exploring ways of transmuting his own experience into art. As he pursues his career of self-observation, there is a further hint that behind the figure of the eponymous protagonist lurks the figure of Fowles himself. The authenticating master thus perpetually recedes even as the reader is promised plenitude. The novel is elaborately self-referential, its subject (writer and subject matter) divided as the text moves between first-person and third-person narration. The novel, which takes the form of a *Bildungsroman,* alerts us to its own status as commentary on cultural production, one of its discourses taking the form of reflections on art, the making of art, and on the 'symbol industry'. My account of it will draw on both Eve Kosovsky Sedgwick and Elisabeth Bronfen, and will inevitably reflect some of the unease expressed in writing about 'The Ebony Tower'.

One way of starting would be to recall Fowles' early novel *The Collector*, a parodic *Tempest*, the story of a man who, longing for a relationship with a beautiful young woman, imprisons her in his cellar, where ill and lonely she eventually dies. I am far from wanting to accuse Fowles personally of being in favour of imprisoning women in cellars. Nevertheless the novel must raise questions both about the meanings inherent in the choice of subject matter and its illocutionary force. For the purposes of my own argument, the point is that the symbol of the dead woman seems to play a crucially formative role in much of Fowles work ('I have a dead weasel on my conscience; and deeper still, a dead woman.' Introduction to 'Eliduc').[5] I am not hoping to explain this one way or another in relation to Fowles' own biography. The point is that the figure recurs in the texts, and in doing so indexes a productive mystery that lies always behind the text. The reader is positioned as wanting to know more in order to complete the meaning, a meaning that is always tantalisingly hidden away in the implied consciousness of the artist. The artist is both the subject of the narrative and the enigmatic source of meaning. A text as elaborate and in many ways 'realistic' as *Daniel Martin* nevertheless proposes enigmas that invite readers to take part in complicit archaeological activity – an activity which the text's own structure of archaeological moments both prefigures and validates. The effect of metafictional devices in Fowles is paradoxically to confer heroic status on the figure of the author who plays puppetmaster to the competing fictions, and who is the implicit locus of a deeper, integrative knowledge.[6]

The narrative's originary occasion (though not in fact the beginning of the discourse) is the account of finding the body of a woman in the reeds. This discovery turns to horror the quiet revision outing on the river on which Daniel and Jane have been engaged, and leads indirectly to the two of them returning together to Daniel's digs and completing the day by making love, thus setting in motion the main armature of the plot. (The novel is at one level the long-drawn out story about how nearly thirty years later the two get back together.) The body remains nameless and enigmatic to the end, but is a presence repeatedly alluded to. The reader's attention is drawn to a possible pun by the fact that the surname of Daniel's first love, Nancy, is Reed. The Reeds own the farmhouse which Daniel subsequently buys and does up: '[the] ghost of that one carnal knowledge of [Jane] . . . did still haunt the air, as the Reeds would for evermore haunt the house we sat in' (p. 422). Is the woman in the reeds at the same time the woman in the reads: that is, the woman who is read? Whose anonymous death is the precondition of all the cultural activity which follows? Nameless ('some tart'), and very dead, she is yet at the same time the starting place – the mother perhaps – of the story. This figure comes almost to play the part of Daniel's muse. Or, to take a different mythological tack, and one to which Fowles' epigraph from George Seferis lays a trail, she plays Eurydice to Daniel's Orpheus ('You know I love a woman who's gone away perhaps to the nether world . . .'). In Fowles' text, as in the Pre-Raphaelite canvas, the image of the drowned woman seems to hold a peculiar attraction, and the finding of the body to constitute a starting place for what follows.

In her fascinating chapter on the death mask of 'l'inconnue de la Seine', Elisabeth Bronfen (1992) notes that the cult of the feminine corpse:

> may well have flourished because it tacitly involved and implicitly invoked the paradoxical status of femininity in Western representational discourse. Woman, Teresa de Lauretis argues, is the very foundation of representation: its object and support, its telos and origin. At the same time Woman 'is nowhere' as reference to her image. Western representations work as texts telling 'the story of male desire by performing the absence of

woman and by producing woman as text, as pure representation.'
In this sense also, death is at work in the cultural construction
of femininity. (p. 208)

In more empirical terms, there is a possibility that the dead woman
provides a preserved image which encapsulates the relation
between artist or beholder and his subject matter. At the end of
the section on Conrad we shall see how Lena has become an
immobilised aesthetic image of 'transfigured beauty'. To turn a
human object into art represents a heightened version of looking, epitomised in the relation of the male artist to his female
model. That aestheticising gaze transmutes the object of vision
into an artistic object.

Living motion is immobilised into tender memory, the difference of the other submerged in the subjective requirements of
the observer. This recurrent theme has, as Elizabeth Bronfen has
shown, implications for an understanding of the relations between
male artist and female subject matter. Thus of Rossetti's relationship to Elizabeth Siddall she notes:

> Rossetti's images of the fading Elizabeth Siddall, beautiful in
> her dying, signify the virility and immortality of his art and
> by implication of himself as artist. The construction of mascu-
> linity and of the masculine artist is made not only in opposition
> and in precedence to a feminine body caught in the process of
> fading, but also in opposition and precedence to absent femi-
> ninity, because the feminine functions as a sign whose signified
> is masculine creativity. (Ibid., p. 174)

One variant on this aggrandisement of the male artist (as Fowles
spotted in *The Collector*) is for the voyeur to carry off his object
to his island. As a fictional procedure there seems here to be a
connection with that magisterial distance between the artist and
his object to which we shall return towards the end of this chapter.

Daniel's progress is built upon relationships with a succession
of women, some single, some doubles. Married for some years
to one twin sister (Nell), he ends up married to the other (Jane),
for whom he has been searching among his other conquests, and
whose partner, we understand, he ought really to have been all
along. At one point in the text he has a simultaneous affair ('not
in some odious male chauvinist sense . . . the indulging in the

old harem fantasy', p. 269) with twin sisters. That Daniel surrounds himself with doubles and actors is at least as significant as his surrounding himself with ghosts – indeed the phenomena may be complementary. His later actor girl friend Jenny, let into the secret that he is leaving her for Jane, pertinently observes that 'I can see there were always casting problems. With us pale shadows who offered for the part' (p. 663). But this novel is more than a psychological study in Don Juanism. The narrative of the search for the ever-receding right woman among actors and ghosts seems to be deeply implicated in the metafiction: the fact that this is simultaneously a novel about writing ('The story of writing as much as it is the writing of story', Waugh, 1984, p. 136); and not of course just in some neutral sense a novel about writing, but a novel about a man writing. The women are at once his subject matter and the source of his inspiration, his need for them itself the subject of metacommentary within the text itself:

'I wish you'd get us all together. Then we could swap notes.'
'I have got you all together.'
'Like Bluebeard.' (*Daniel Martin*, p. 663)

One senses that this covering of the tracks, this insistence on the part of the narrator that he is self-critically aware of what he is doing, itself flagrantly foregrounds the novel's reigning dynamic, and even sanctions it in its hero's eyes. Bluebeard's women – like the woman in the reeds or Clegg's butterflies – were dead. The most powerful woman in the text is the dead woman, or the woman returning (like a ghost) from the deep past.

Another formative element – not surprisingly in a novel which mimics autobiography – is Daniel's own view of himself. It is his own past with which he is in love, and his women insofar as they signify his own self-development. Daniel's narcissism is signalled early on, in the description of his undergraduate digs:

The most striking effect was of a highly evolved (if not painfully out-of-hand) narcissism, since the room had at least fifteen mirrors on its walls ... no other room in Oxford can have provided such easy access to the physical contemplation of self. (p. 58)

A student magazine (fame among a gossipy in-group sets in early) has, we are told, referred to him as Mr Specula Speculans, a sobriqet to which the narrator later musingly returns. The effect of the novel as a whole is one of Daniel watching himself and devotedly recording his own movements and the minutiae of his relationships, triumphs and follies:

> He divides conversation into two categories: when you speak and when you listen to yourself speak. Of late, his has been too much the second. Narcissism: when one grows too old to believe in one's uniqueness, one falls in love with one's complexity – as if layers of lies could replace the green illusion; or the sophistries of failure, the stench of success. (p. 18)

The narrator enjoys a complicated relationship with his subject as they bandy first and third persons, nominative and accusative, between them. The effect of this (as of all the other metafictional and self-referential devices the text employs) far from defamiliarising the narrative in a formalist sense, is to strengthen the circle in which the consenting reader is included, since as a reader you are not only party to the illusion of the story, but also, on the next level, party to the illusion of the making of the story. These are concentric circles: even if you step outside the plot as such, you are then an insider to the domain of story-making, just as Dan in California becomes inward with the making of films, rubbing shoulders with the stars who act the films whose scripts he writes. Further, the discursive movement between persons not only creates a three-dimensional effect in deepening the illusion of Daniel's reality, but also has the effect of moving the implied sightline from self-knowledge to self-conscious knowledge: the sort of quasi-personal understanding that an involved outsider might have. The narrative thus acts to legitimate the male reader in his self-observation. The implied position of the reader is as a party to insider gossip, a member of the various sets to which Daniel at one time and another belongs. Like 'The Ebony Tower', *Daniel Martin* proposes to its (male) readers membership of a world organised by the master magician who is the storyteller. Recursively, one of the tasks of the denizen of that world is (re)telling the story of Daniel Martin. As of course I am now doing.

The world into which the reader of *Daniel Martin* is invited holds out the benefits of insiderliness. It is a little like the Catch-22 of some of Donne's love poems: both pretending to conceal your love-making from 'the laity' but also wanting them to watch. It extends to its model reader the lure of being privy to glamorous activites and situations (Hollywood, showbiz, TV talk shows, a celebrated mid-Atlantic set). Even as the narrator cogently criticises the symbol industry, the text proposes the allure of being in a position to talk as an insider. It endorses admiring observation of the primal scene where culture is conceived. In a world where culture is a commodity for those with the right sort of consumer power, the desirability of your contacts resides at least partly in other people's admiring glances. ('He saw one or two covert glances towards them from the group of young people who had just come in – towards Jenny of course; success. . . .' p. 659.) Like Saul Bellow's contemporaneous *Humbolt's Gift* (1975), the whole novel puts the making of cultural text on display and in doing so stakes a claim for the primacy of the male as originator. At the same time, and in an uncanny enactment of Freud's account of the artist, the text operates as a machinery for seduction.

There is more to this than glimpses of what it might mean to mix with movie folk or be on first-name terms with the fictional counterpart of David Frost. The novel resonates with the poignancy of longing and nostalgia for a heightened past. As always in Fowles' work, there is a richness and density of detail which is not purely referential: we need to ask what this abundance means in itself. It seems to be a code which positions the reader as co-legatee of the prehistory of the novel's present. That is to say that the novel enacts its own world in its very length and internal allusiveness. The reader acquires a vicarious memory for what happened before, and a fictive nostalgia for Daniel's past. That process does not in itself distinguish *Daniel Martin* from any other long novel.[7] My point is, however, that here we have a performance of the drama of belonging, of the attractiveness of being an insider to cultural production. The reader is treated as belonging, as positioned somewhere close to the aesthetic centre of things – a bit like having been a model Oxford student, in fact. At the same time, the novel has pre-empted the academic critic: Dan's old friend and Jane's first husband, Anthony, the philosopher and Pluto of Jane's underworld, commits suicide having once admitted to the sterility of his life. Daniel's relationships with men do not in fact yield nearly so much for his inner life or his art as do his relationships with women. His relations with men are distant, oblique, or competitive in a way that his relations with women are not. While this line of thought might be pursued in terms of psychological commentary on male relationships, here I shall look at it in the light of the novel's account of male creativity. One route seems to lie through Daniel's relationship with his father, an Anglican country clergyman.

FATHERS AND GODS

Before embarking on a reading of Daniel's relationship with his father, I would like to gather up some themes that run through these three opening chapters. Through the weakening of boundaries intimacy (even intimacy with symbolic material) threatens identity even in the moment that it holds out a promise of vicarious fulfilment. To write about the specificities of human affairs is to risk being fragmented by the very material the writer aimed to place and reorganise into a stable whole. The micro-processes of libidinal investment either elude the grasp or swamp the spectator. One of my recurrent themes has been the way in which the paradigmatic male writer seeks to exercise border control over the boundaries between his own identity and his subject matter. Let me be clear that here, as elsewhere, I am dealing not with the empirical facts about a given author so much as with the patterns laid down in textual relations. Given the traditional concern of the novel with persons, relationships and the interior world of persons, symbolic proximity to others seems to present a problem which the paradigmatic male novelist has to negotiate.

Conventionally, as too in the discursive asides of male and mock-male narrators, gossip is a form of communicative practice associated with women. Not only is it stereotyped as malicious, but it is also conceptualised as bogged down in the detail of persons and relationships. On this account, it is ill-formed narrative as well as defective in its choice of subject. Worst of all, its pragmatics are those of physical proximity. Thus in arguing that the novel represents a superior and sympathetic form of knowing (and a narrative grammar adequate to such a task) the voice of the book also proposes that the novel has attained a distance from the subject matter and from the audience that the purveyor of gossip has not. The male paradigm (whatever the actual gender of the writer) tends to *éloignement*, to ironic or judgmental distance, to positive and judicious knowledge, to the overview – in the end to mastery of a subject matter, or even to Olympian detachment. As a novelistic creed this set of beliefs parallels the patriarchal version of knowledge and mental activity in general as disembodied contemplation which Marx's theory of knowledge as sensuous activity set out to challenge.[8] In the novel it leads towards the magisterial, even where magisterial figures within the text are ironised. Such novel discourse permits itself intimacy with its subject, provided that intimacy is purified, 'placed' within a framework of explanation and control. Part of the attraction of a Henry Breasley is that he has attained the stature to be permitted an encompassing vision. As so often, Thomas Carlyle seems to have beaten a trail for male heroes. His affectionate representation of Goethe, even his humorous play in *Sartor Resartus* with the idea of Olympian detachment, provides a model of male relations with the male artist:

For if I have been delivered from darkness into any measure of light, if I know aught of myself and my duties and destination, it is to the study of your writings more than to any other circumstance that I owe this; it is you more than any other man that I should always thank and reverence with the feeling of a Disciple to his Master, nay of a Son to his Spiritual Father.[9]

If you cannot *be* Goethe, you can at least be his translator, interpreter, and emissary, constructing as you do so an idealised son–father relationship.[10]

The normative position of the narrator and of the implied figure of the male author behind him is thus one from which he exercises discriminating power over both subject matter and reader. The pay-off to the reader is membership (at least in fantasy) of a club made up of those who share superior vision. The position of narrative superiority is one from which the aggrandised figure of the implied author organises not only the subject matter of his text but also establishes the ground rules for the acts of reading which the reader will perform. He takes authority to stabilise the fissiparous symbolic universe upon which his writing rests. In so doing he occupies a position of centrality which can be admired or envied by the congregation of readers. His implied presence underwrites the fictional universe, and guarantees the reader access to the value system of the text. In overseeing his creation, the author has achieved in fantasy a position in which he is safe from the turbulence (whether of emotion or of language) below. In their analysis of the metaphor of writing as paternity Gilbert and Gubar note 'another implication of this complex metaphor:

> For if the author/father is owner of his text and of his reader's attention, he is also, of course, owner/possessor of the subjects of his text, that is to say of those figures, scenes, and events – those brain children – he has both incarnated in black and white and 'bound' in cloth or leather. Thus, because he is an author, a 'man of letters' is simultaneously, like his divine counterpart, a father, a master or ruler, and an owner: the spiritual type of a patriarch. (1979, p. 7)

That he is watching is a guarantee that some measure of justice will be done, and that the narrative will close in the end.

If all this seems familiar, there is, I speculate, a reason. In a monotheistic or post-monotheistic culture, males who make public claims to authority over symbol systems find themselves occupying a cultural space of ancient antecedents.[11] The trace of the watching god can indeed be found in our text: watching from above the episode of the tramp and the policeman, the narrator notes that it 'leaves our hero caged behind his window above, obliged to smile to himself, like an inefficient god who sees a lapse in his own creation repaired by what he had forgotten to institute' (p. 247). But to occupy this position brings in its wake its own perils. Even in thoroughly secular fictions, the puritanical and superstitious horror inspired by masquerading as the creator means that the Promethean author will be stigmatised as a danger to himself:

> the most refined stages, as well as the most perilous are those of the mystic ('I am what I believe') and of the poet ('I am what I make') – perilous insofar as they encroach on the qualities of godliness, and invite retribution on a Promethean scale. (Woods, 1987)

Yet paradoxically the terrible danger in which the artist stands adds to his romantic appeal. His skirmish with damnation signifies the danger into which he might lead us all. Daniel's formative move after his novel has been given Jane's seal of approval is to walk into the orchard to dispose symbolically of his own guilt. One way out of the Oedipal bind is to attribute the origins of the artist's power to an alternative source.

Guilt and the consequent dread of terrible vengeance, remain powerful materials in the hinterland of creation. In reworking aspects of the Faust myth, novelists as different as Thomas Mann (*Doctor Faustus*) and Anthony Burgess (*Earthly Powers*) have witnessed to the enduring fascination of the idea of the pact with the devil as the originary act for an artistic career. Male creativity can thus be framed not as originating in a return to your own inner space but as taking place in a diabolic liaison with the rebel who would be king. Even suffering, the direct result of the initial breaking of a taboo, is self-aggrandising: marked out for horrible retribution, the rebel become the hero of his own transgression. The paradigmatic route of male artist or novelist necessitates a skirmish with Oedipal terrors.[12] A variant is represented in Harold Bloom's model of the 'strong poet' who has the 'persistence to wrestle' with his (male) forebears (Bloom, 1973). A less exposing strategy is to undermine the ancestor, exposing his spiritual power as a an empty show. If the patriarchal emperor was naked all along, then the strong son has committed a lesser sin.

In the history of the novel, issues of cultural authority may be represented in terms of the dramas of spiritual authority. Charlotte Brontë's 'abundant shower of curates' (*Shirley*) stand for a spiritual and cultural authority no longer adequate to its task. Again, D. H. Lawrence's clergymen (for example in 'The Virgin and the Gypsy' or 'The Daughters of the Vicar') are characteristically etiolated and emasculated. They represent, I suggest, a decadent form of authority, and one ripe for replacement by the prophet-novelist. In the same fashion, Daniel's father is portrayed as weak, and his beliefs as pitiful. (One 'born into a vicarage and its divine simplicities can never see a priest without seeing an adult child as well' [p. 228].) He is therefore not only inadequate as a father, too distant and other-worldly to give his son the example and guidance he needs. He is a spiritual and cultural failure: a counterfeit patriarch who has no legitimate foundation (moral, religious, or aesthetic) on which to build his authority. Male fiction is littered with the relics of inadequate fathers and exploded patriarchs, a fact likely to be as promising to young male readers as it is undermining for readers who are themselves fathers. Given the reputation of patriarchy as an organising principle, this bad press for fathers needs some explanation.

My tentative suggestion would be that such fiction dramatises the failure of omnipotence. It would be impossible for fatherhood to live up to the demands culturally placed upon it: the condition of patriarchy may be to aspire to an unattainable plenitude. Another and complementary suggestion is that for the male text to negate the father is a way of creating more space for itself. The unfortunate Revd Martin is the object of nothing but contempt. He even fails as an actor (a serious failing in the book of Daniel). By contrast Mr Reed the grandfather recites the Bible 'with a simple conviction I never heard in my father . . . or in many far more accomplished actors in later life' (p. 369). His patriarchal authority is underlined by his unforced ability to read from the ultimate authoritative book. The question therefore arises as to where authority comes from if, for one reason or another, the son cannot take his rightful place in the patriarchal line. This as we shall see is the reciprocal of Heyst's problem. Carrying his father's baggage around with him, and so no longer believing in himself, the latter lacks the inner authority which would enable him to fight back against Ricardo and Jones. His father's omnipresence has hollowed out the son. Daniel, by contrast, moves freely, unencumbered by paternal luggage. Yet – since fathers are clearly held to be necessary to the cultural process – even he needs to find a new spiritual authority.

This is the moment to glance across to the argument proposed in 'Poor Koko', another story from *The Ebony Tower*. ('The working title of this collection of stories was *Variations*.') Here the theme intertwines access to language and culture with the relationship to father and father figures. The narrator hypothesises that the secret that the young man who robs him and burns his manuscript wants to possess is his access to words. Robbery and the burning of the manuscript constitute an act of revenge upon the world of the fathers which has impoverished him. The sequel surfaces a page or two later: Koko 'is a Japanese word and means correct filial behaviour, the proper attitude of son to father. . . . My incomprehensible epigraph shall have the last word, and serve as judgment on both father and son . . .' (pp. 186–7).[13] In view of the dire outcomes of failure as portrayed in this relationship, the search for an authentic cultural father and authentic lineage is all the more pressing. Nevertheless, the underlying dynamic propelling the aspiring male artist would appear to be the search for an ideal father rather than simply making do with whatever father you find yourself landed with.[14]

We might capture this in an image: in Conrad's *Victory*, as we shall see, Heyst's last years are lived under the eyes of his father's portrait. Daniel always remembers how his father told him that the eyes of Christ's picture follow you around. That image is recalled in the climactic epiphany of the novel when Daniel, bereft more than he has anticipated by parting from Jenny, strays into Kenwood House. There he finds himself looking at Rembrandt's late self-portrait:

> The sad, proud old man stared eternally out of his canvas, out of the entire knowledge of his own genius and of the inadequacy of genius before human reality. Dan stared back . . . The supreme nobility of such art, the plebeian simplicity of such sadness; an immortal, a morose old Dutchman; the deepest inner loneliness, the being on public show; a date beneath a frame, a presentness beyond all time, fashion, language; a puffed face, a pair of rheumy eyes, and a profound and unassuagable vision. (pp. 666–7)

The absence of a main verb seems to signify 'pregnant' sentence: here stylistically enacting that 'presentness beyond all time' of which it speaks. Consequently, the suggestion seems to be that under the eyes of Rembrandt, Daniel has at last found his real father. Rembrandt is the 'formidable sentinel guarding the way back'. That he is an artist rather than a clergyman is a local re-enactment of the romantic cultural trajectory from religion to art. This revelation, this moment of recognition, heralds Daniel's re-birth in a new medium as a novelist.

However, this re-birth requires a mother as well as a father, and the epiphany that Dan experiences at Kenwood has to be carried back to be validated by Jane. The great picture

> lived, it was timeless, it spoke very directly, said all he had never managed to say and would never manage to say – even though with the abruptness of that dash, he had hardly thought this before he saw himself saying the thought to the woman

who would be waiting for him on the platform at Oxford that evening; telling her also what had gone before, a girl and a past walking into winter trees, knowing she would understand. (p. 667)

Daniel, sustained and fertilised by Jane's approval, has given birth to himself as a novelist. In doing so he has climbed up the status hierarchy of cultural forms proposed within the novel to a superior and lasting form of art.

Daniel's desire to write a novel has grown on him as his eponymous novel has advanced. Since his subject matter is to be his own life, the ambition is itself a metafictional twist upon the idea of a self-portrait. It is associated in his mind with the idea of finding your way back through your own past. 'If you run away, Jenny, you can't find your way back . . . Trying to . . . it's only a pipe-dream. Trying to crawl back inside the womb. Turn the clock back' (p. 21). If Jenny is the novel within a novel's first female sponsor (at the beginning she uses the Los Angeles telephone book to help Dan find a name for his hero), Jane is the second and more important. Significantly, it is when early in the process of their reconciliation she comes to stay at Thorncombe (the Reeds' old farm and Daniel's Coëtminais) that Daniel pushes his thinking on a stage. Jane is an incentive to cultural as well as existential action. 'She was like an old enigma in his life, and she had to be solved; tamed and transcribed' (p. 430). To her he confesses his desire to write a novel, a desire to which indirectly she gives her blessing (pp. 415–18). The resumption of the relationship between the two is simultaneously the turning point in Dan's commitment to writing it. That she is his Eurydice is made explicit later (pp. 588–9), and in recalling her from the underworld he is also confirming his own status as an artist. When at the end of the succeeding section he wishes to hell elitist guilt, that guilt appears to be at once the guilt about writing a novel which dwells on his own experience and about the foreseen necessity of colonising a woman's consciousness. If he is a new Orpheus, he also has to defy another element of Orpheus' biography by daring women to tear him to pieces.

The novel which at this moment Daniel decides to write is of course the novel in which he is himself already a character. The male narrator seeks auto-genesis as a way of symbolically breaking free of dependence on the material /maternal world. That he can symbolically take charge of his own origins is deeply reassuring. This colonisation of the power of giving birth is a subject to which we shall have to return, notably in relation to Ian McEwan's *The Child in Time*. Structurally, the sign consists in the return of the novel to where it began:

> That evening, in Oxford, leaning beside Jane in her kitchen while she cooked supper for them, Dan told her with a suitable irony that at least he had found a last sentence for the novel he was never going to write. She laughed at such flagrant Irishry; which is perhaps why, in the end, and in the knowledge that Dan's novel can never be read, lies eternally in the future, his ill-concealed ghost has made that impossible last his own impossible first. (p. 668)

That first sentence, presumably, is the opening sentence which follows the quotation from Seferis: 'Whole sight; or all the rest is desolation . . .' (p. 7), a sentence which in itself anticipates the role sight and looking will play in the novel which follows. In reclaiming the woman from the underworld Dan has simultaneously managed symbolically to sever his links with the messy business of being born from a woman.

This chapter is not intended in any sense as a polemic against a specific male writer or the male artist/writer in general. It does, however, seek to interrupt that familiar slide by which discussion of the particular problematics of the male writer turns into a normative, universalised account of literary creation. This pattern, with its preoccupation with fathering the work, moves, as Nina Baym has pointed out in relation to American fiction, to exclude women writers or reduce their activities to a lower status.[15] Nor are the effects limited to writers or to the perception of literary tradition. In his 1971 essay 'From Work to Text' Barthes provided a postscript to *S/Z*. One aspect of his account of the movement from 'work' to 'text' is quite explicitly gendered. The 'work' he suggests 'is caught up in a process of filiation'. The author is reputed the father and owner of his work (Barthes, 1977, p. 160). By contrast, 'the Text . . . reads without the inscription of the Father . . . [I]t can be read without the guarantee of its father. It is not that the Author may not 'come back' in the Text, in his text, but he then does so as a 'guest' (ibid., p. 161)'.

Patriarchal theories of the author direct us back, I suggest, to the 'work'. That portentous centrality of the work and its author impacts upon the economy of reading. 'The metaphor of the text', says Barthes by contrast, 'is that of the network.' In terms of this fundamental distinction, Fowles' own metafiction means that his novel is by no means unequivocally devoted to the search for the 'work'. As Barthes has it in a slightly later essay: 'the Father is the man of statements. hence, nothing is more transgressive than to surprise the Father in the speech-act . . . The one who shows, the one who states, the one who shows the statement, is no longer the Father' ('To the Seminar' [1974] in Barthes, 1986, p. 340).

On the assumption that the shift of emphasis from work to text has radical gender implications, the next chapter will explore how the self-referential dynamics of male literary production may shape but also be subverted by the dynamics of reading.

3

Fictional Forefathers: Conrad and Lawrence

What a dread he had of mankind, of other people! It amounted almost to a horror, to a sort of dream terror – his horror of being observed by some other people. If he were on an island, like Alexander Selkirk, with only the creatures and the trees, he would be free and glad. . . .

> (D. H. Lawrence, *Women in Love*, Penguin edn, 1995, p. 108)

[The] movement by which each opposition is set up to produce meaning is the movement by which the couple is destroyed. A universal battlefield. Each time, a war breaks out. Death is always at work.
Father/son Relationships of authority, of privilege, of force.
Logos/writing Relationships: opposition, conflict, relief, reversion
Master/slave Violence. Repression.
    And we perceive that the 'victory' always amounts to the same thing: it is hierarchised. The hierarchisation subjects the entire conceptual organization to man. A male privilege, which can be seen in the opposition by which it sustains itself, between *activity* and *passivity*. Traditionally, the question of sexual difference is coupled with the same opposition: activity/passivity.

> Hélène Cixous, *Sorties*, in Elaine Marks and Isabelle de Courtivron (eds), *New French Feminisms: An Anthology*, Brighton: Harvester, 1981, p. 91)

In this chapter we turn to the work of two authors who are still widely seen by readers and syllabus-makers as pioneers of twentieth-century fiction in English: Joseph Conrad and D. H. Lawrence.

Both, in their complicated relations to literary modernism, represent triangulation points for the received map of twentieth-century literature, and part of the reason for choosing them is to review the idea of the canon in the light of the preoccupations of this book. Both are still widely read and taught, and Lawrence in particular has entered into the wider culture through film and television adaptations. Both represent points of departure for the readings of more recent novels which will follow.

Any one writing about Lawrence or Conrad (let alone presuming to roll them together in one chapter) must be uncomfortably aware of the sheer bulk of criticism and commentary that their work has attracted. If I turn out to have anything to say that is new or valuable it will have to come from placing them within the framework of this book's subject, rather than from anything approximating to Lawrence or Conrad scholarship.[1] And in placing them together at all I am partly influenced by canonical tradition: Lawrence and Conrad are two of the most prominent names engraved over what most of those exposed to a literary syllabus enter as the gateway to the twentieth century. The terrain of twentieth-century English literature – at least as mapped at nodal points in higher education – is overlooked by these patriarchal figures, rather as the portrait of Heyst's father broods over the action from the bungalow wall. So I am talking about traditions of reading as well as about the work as such. But there would, I think, be reasons even in the work 'as such' – as approached through the preoccupations of this book – to group them together for expository purposes. Masculinity, Walter Ong has mused, 'is difficult to interiorize, a kind of stranger to the human psyche' (1981, p. 98). While we should be cautious about the corollary (that 'each woman is her own secret society', p. 90), both our writers might be seen as rising, as it were, to Ong's implied challenge. Both are working within a cultural environment registering the colossal impact of the feminist movement. By implication the work of both men insists that possession of an identity is a process, not a state: it is enacted through a structured sequence of events, and there exists the corresponding possibility (at once appealing and threatening) that you could come to be the object of someone else's story. For both, masculinity and male identity have come to seem problematic rather than assumed and natural. Being male is only partially to be accounted for by the occupation of a particular sort of body: it is also to talk and be talked about in ways which neither Lawrence nor Conrad could straightforwardly assume would persist without the polemical support of writers.

The argument of this chapter has to allow both for the emergence of recurrent themes and for the specificity of the texts under discussion. I do not wish to reduce the historical particularity of either to a homogenised argument about masculinity. I am conscious of the arguments of – for example – Alistair Davies (1984), Hilary Simpson (1982), or Lyn Pykett (1995) that Lawrence demands to be read within his historical context. David Trotter has demonstrated the misreadings that occur if Lawrence is read outside the context of contemporary fiction writing (Trotter, 1993, for example, ch. 13). In turn it is hardly possible for any reading of Conrad (however unspecialised its context) to evade the paradigm shift brought about by post-colonial readings of his work. I intend to discuss texts by both Conrad and Lawrence in relation to constructions of masculinities within the framework provided by the general argument of this book. To do so I intend to explore them as discourses: as specifications for acts of readership, interpretation, and storytelling. In the previous chapter we explored the figure of the male artist as a paradigm for the management of symbolic operations. In doing so I sought to extricate discussion of art and the artist from a debate conducted according to spurious norms of gender neutrality. This account of two classic fictions rests upon the assumption that the deeds of the story teller themselves constitute a prescription for future stories.

In framing and organising their subject matters these texts simultaneously locate and position readers and in so doing compose instructions for future productive acts of narration. We cannot avoid reading Conrad or Lawrence referentially for their subject matter and overt argumentation. Whether critics approve or not, readers will read authors for ontological insight, for insight into 'life' and life's dilemmas. Indeed both invite reading in terms of presence: of the interiority both of text and of psyche. Yet at the same time we need to acknowledge that their texts are performative: acts of communication which in themselves provide models – one might say a genetic code – for other such acts to follow. Texts are orientated to the future as well as the past, and the act of reading is a productive as well as a retrospective process. This orientation does not simply derive from my own interpretative preoccupations – the result, perhaps, of paddling too long in the tidal pools of post-structuralism. On the contrary, the texts of both authors repeatedly foreground communicative acts: narration, persuasion, interpretation, misrepresentation, and the social occasions on which persuasion and interpretation take place. Many of Lawrence's major characters are, like Birkin in *Women in Love*, voices striving for symbolic mastery. As they harangue their audiences, they pose questions about who is to take control over the articulation and promulgation of values, and through what kind of acts such mastery would be achieved. Such acts may themselves flow with or against the currents of their culture, reinforcing or contesting dominant norms, or seeking didactically to replace dominant norms with new ones. In neither author can an understanding of the articulation of masculinity be separated off from an understanding of the pragmatics of the discourse in which it is encoded.

I shall start by considering a short story: Lawrence's 'The Primrose Path', written before the end of 1913 but not published until the collection *England my England* (1921). By giving a brief account of this story I hope to focus some key issues of the chapter. The story concerns two men, both called Daniel, a nephew and uncle. This coincidence of name itself signals a splitting within a masculine identity into the watcher and his fated object. They meet as though by appointment, though the younger man, who has come to town on unspecified business, says that he believed his uncle was still in Australia. The structure of the story is a remarkable series of boxes within boxes: the younger man is watching the older, and both are in turn watched by the narrator. The older Daniel (the 'black sheep' of the family, now returned to England and running a small taxi business) becomes as it were the text which his nephew and the narrator between them try to decipher, a model of male textuality He is 'a chaos of a man', a man 'quite stupefied with fear, fear of life, of death, of himself' (pp. 430–1). Repeatedly, the eye of nephew or narrator watches him:

> Sutton put down his glass. The publican renewed it with a sure hand, at ease in whatsoever he did. Then he leaned back against the bar. He wore no coat. He stood with arms folded, his chin on his chest, his long moustache hanging. His back was round and slack, so that the lower part of his abdomen stuck forward, though he was not stout. His cheek was healthy, brown-red, and he was muscular. Yet there was about him this

physical slackness, a reluctance in his slow, sure movements. His eyes were keen under his dark brows, but reluctant also, as if he were gloomily apathetic. (p. 433)

Daniel Sutton is both the subject matter of the story – one of those Lawrentian figures who draw disaster into his own orbit – and simultaneously an object lesson in the problems of watching and describing a man. As his nephew puzzles to decipher him, the narrator works to find an appropriate register for watching and reporting on a male object and the symbiosis of his inner and outer life. Both detect the pattern of repetition that runs through Sutton's life, and at the end concur in their prediction about the uncle's latest partner: '"That girl will leave him," he said to himself, "She'll hate him like poison. And serve him right. Then she'll go off with somebody else." And she did' (p. 440). The younger man's prediction is retrospectively endorsed by the narrator's authoritative knowledge. The two interpreters have concurred in being right.

In observing his uncle, the younger man has to manage the contrary forces of attraction and repulsion. At one extreme, he might after all succumb to the identity hinted at in the coincidence of name and in the half-expected nature of the two men's meeting: 'I might be like him if I went down a certain road'. Readers find themselves positioned in this sequence of observation and interpretation: thus in commenting on the story I too am drawn into a set of relationships which centre on the elder Daniel, and through which I seek to puzzle out the meaning of his life. The two Daniels, the narrator, and, by extension the reader, are caught up in a web of male relationships blending rivalry, affection, and detached knowledge.

Yet even while the text holds out to us the promise of knowledge, knowledge is subjected to a recurrent critique within the Lawrentian canon. To know, Lawrence tended to argue, was to possess, even to destroy: 'It is easy to see why each man kills the thing he loves. To *know* a living thing is to kill it . . .'[2] For Lawrence, to be known resonates with the Authorised Version: it is to be penetrated. Male members of his casts tend to resist being known by others or indeed even touched unless they themselves wish it.[3] There is thus a curious dialectic going on in a story like this between what is posed as the need for a man to preserve his own inner core from intrusion, and the narrative compulsion to expose and explain; between intimacy and distance. This generative tension exactly parallels Lawrence's epistemological dialectic between valorising unconsciousness and the articulate knowledge of the novelist. The distinction in Lawrence's work between warranted and unwarranted intrusion, I shall argue, resides in the gender identity of the watcher: male watchers and knowers may have special privileges not accorded to their female counterparts. Linda Ruth Williams (1993) has given us a subtle exploration of the gendered role of sight in Lawrence's work, demonstrating how he both associates sight (contrasted with the more fundamental sense of touch) with the female but is at the same time tempted to occupy the position of watcher himself. I would add that women in Lawrence typically want to put men to use. Only a man can see another man in his non-instrumental integrity. Yet to watch may in turn be to risk feminisation.

At a crucial moment in 'The Primrose Path' the narrator leaves his place at Daniel Berry's side, and follows Daniel Sutton as he goes upstairs to the bedroom to visit his separated first wife who is dying of consumption. The narrator does what the nephew cannot and enters for a few paragraphs into Sutton's consciousness. For this few minutes, Sutton's consciousness (which before and after this passage is a subject for speculative reconstruction from without) is exposed to us. Here, while Sutton's own gaze rests on the dying woman, there is a tentative re-adjustment of the relationship between proximity and distance. To be inside Sutton is also to seek to be party to his experience, and later we shall have to ask what the relationship is in Lawrence's work between different kinds of 'being inside'. Does association with a character (simulated or actual) imbue you symbolically with their power? Or conversely render you liable to be sucked into the vortex of their fate? This story, like so much of Lawrence's work, displays elements of an enquiry into what it means to think about or to tell stories about men and male subjectivity. That enterprise is governed by the construction of maleness within the bonds of solidarity formed between narrator and reader. The subject matter is at once both dangerous and seductive. To that extent, the story's subject is as much how you manage your observation of Sutton as it is about whatever it is that drives him. Further, there is an instructive parallel between the situation of one male observing another and the self-knowledge of a man, a parallel intriguingly drawn out in the novel *The Good Soldier*, by Lawrence's friend Ford Madox Ford. The self-observer is, as it were, in both his own nominative and accusative case. For a novelist so much of whose work consists in the mining of auto-biographical material, the split subject, the anticipated watcher of the same sex, assumes acute form. Before this comes to seem like yet another contribution to more or less glib psychoanalysing of Lawrence (of the kind perhaps now unrepeatably if amusingly essayed by Angela Carter [4]), let me emphasise that my subject is not 'Lawrence' the married man and author, but 'Lawrence' as metonymy for a body of work, work which among other things promotes ways of handling masculinity in narrative form.

In the rest of the chapter I propose to work mostly with two novels, novels written (though not published) within two years of each other, Conrad's *Victory*, and Lawrence's *Women in Love*. I hope that the differences between the two texts, once viewed through my proposed lens, will prove mutually illuminating.

BECKONING SHADOWS DIRE

In an illuminating article, Nina Pelikan Straus (1987) has demon-strated how the narration of 'Heart of Darkness' builds a homosocial bond between its male readers, excluding as it does so women readers from its heroic quest. 'The Horror' is a code for something only men can share, the mystique of unsayable knowledge (compare Roberts and Easingwood, 1997). Like so many of Conrad's novels, *Victory*, too, foregrounds the processes of narration, problematising as it does so the relations between narrator and subject matter, narrator and audience. Male rela-tions are enacted at the level of discourse as well as that of story. All the narrators and storytellers – the anonymous 'I', Davidson, Schomberg, the gossip community of the far-eastern ports – are male, as is their object, the point where their sightlines converge, the enigmatic figure of Heyst. In varying ways these overlap-ping narrators manage their relations with each other through the enigma of Heyst and in doing so model the relations the novel establishes with and between its readers. Throughout this chapter we shall be concerned with narrative as code for repro-duction, as mapping the terrain (the geographical metaphor is irresistible) upon which future interpretations may occur. What of course they cannot predetermine is the resistance that the alerted reader may oppose to incorporation in the narrative community.

Conrad's choice of an epigraph from Milton's *Comus* poses the wilderness as the stage for a struggle between the temptations of sensual indulgence and spiritual rectitude. At the same time, this novel, its central figure a man living on a cusp between action and withdrawal, activity and passivity, evidences a notably self-deconstructive streak. The narration exhibits a marked ambivalence towards both conscious thought and articulate language: that is to say, towards the very media which make its own existence possible. Heyst's father – who we understand has exercised a profound influence over his son's life – was a philosopher, a Schopenhauerean who, disillusioned and sceptical, undermined action with irony. As the novel moves towards re-immersing the fastidious Heyst in the world of action and events, the narrator anticipates a thread from Conrad's own introduction and engages in a positively Carlylean diatribe against conscious thought as being the enemy of action:

> The young man learned to reflect, which is a destructive process, a reckoning of the cost. It is not the clear-sighted who lead the world. Great achievements are accomplished in a blessed, warm mental fog, which the pitiless blasts of the father's analysis had blown away from the son. (Pt II, ch. 3)

Frederick Karl reminds us that Conrad is a contemporary of Kafka, the poet of the 'son made impotent by the father's memory' (1983, p. 39). Specifically, it is, we gather, the paternal habit of analysis which has sapped Heyst Jr.'s capacity for unpremeditated action, and which will render him in the end unable effectively to defend himself or Lena against the depradations of evil. (Such rhetorics would soon be well to the fore in the debate about what moral characteristics would enable nations to defend themselves against international bullying.[5]) Yet just as the text shows no sign of following its own logic to the point of forswearing articulate analysis, so it continues with passionate curiosity to unpick the fortunes of a man in whom the 'unmasculine' traits of passivity and withdrawal into seclusion are highly developed.

The novel works with an antithesis between word and deed, conscious and unconscious, which we have traditionally known as 'romantic' but which I now want to re-frame as in some respects 'male' as well. Thus it appears to me that that element of Victorian thought (of which Carlyle may stand as emblematic spokesman) whose ambition is to repudiate consciousness and articulation in favour of 'strong silent action' is also asserting that self-knowledge (the self as object of its own gaze) leads inevitably to inertia, eating away luxuriously at its own ability to act. There is a curious and perhaps indicative parallel with the contemporary holy war against masturbation (See for example, Mason, 1994a, b Hyam, 1990, ch. 3). The male self should be a platform for goal-directed action, not simply a pleasant spot to be. It appears that one of the recurrent projects of masculine-orientated narrative may be to ward off the foreseen danger of succumbing to narcissism. And for that to be felt as a real danger, the narcissistic desire must be strongly felt as well as taboo.

The project of *Victory*, I suggest, is to re-align two sets of oppositions both of which have traditionally been involved in the definition of masculinity: activity/passivity and act/word. In contemplating Heyst, the reader has to look to his own situation among these multiple dichotomies. Might not he too be incapacitated or even emasculated by the thing he contemplates? 'Perhaps we cannot at present' says Andrew Michael Roberts:

> imagine the absence of masculinity without evoking ideas of lack or loss, a formation which leads only back to the phallus . . . When the male critic's acts of seeing, examining, representing is so firmly trapped in the sexualisation of the aesthetic, how can he claim to see, or try to reveal, an alterity in masculine discourse? (Roberts, 1996, p. 167)

And he goes on to wonder whether the Conradian abyss was 'an alterity of the masculine, even if that alterity was for Conrad, and remains for many men today, unspeakable' (Ibid.).

I have already drawn attention to the figure of man watching man, and Heyst is the object of a multiple gaze: a figure who looks up from reading his father's book to see the eyes of his father's portrait upon him, he is under observation at different times not only by the narrator (explicitly male), but also by the community of white male gossip dispersed through the ports of the Archipelago; telescopically by Captain Davidson, whose testimony to the listening 'Excellency' completes the tale, and in due course by his male readers. As Leslie Heywood has pointed out, Heyst as well as Lena constitutes an 'unreadable' text, whose detachment 'necessitates his renunciation of masculinity as a final determinable quality' (Heywood, 1994, p. 15). All his puzzled viewers have something to add to his story, and the story which between them they transact is one which repeatedly seeks to resolve the dilemma posed by the relations between contemplation and action. Can you retreat into seclusion and still be truly male? In the context of the versions of male heroism propagated in the heyday of British imperialism, Heyst, like most of Conrad's protagonists, is virtually an anti-hero (Bristow, 1991; Dawson, 1994; Middleton, n.d.). His anti-heroism is located by the narrative in his self-consciousness and his immersion in words. He suffers in fact from a form of paralysis which the novel in the hands of a Conrad or of a James might almost be calculated to bring about – of seeing so many sides to each question that choice becomes practically impossible. An aesthetic attention to nuance and complexity undermines ethical praxis.

There is, however, one domain in which Heyst not only acts, but acts decisively. In rescuing Magdalen/Lena from the dubious concert troupe and the predatory Schomberg, Heyst re-immerses himself in the world of action with consequences which provide the denouement of the novel. In fleeing with Lena back to his island, Heyst proposes to share with a woman a domain which has in a sense up to now been conterminous with his own mind. (We shall repeatedly notice ways in which islands constitute a code for male subjectivity.) His control over his own inner space is thus subverted by a being who in her gender and her sexuality signifies the creatural world, and whose presence metaphorically gives birth to a new reality:

> 'I only know that he who forms a tie is lost. The germ of corruption has entered his soul.'

> . . . that human being so near and still so strange, gave him a greater sense of his own reality than he had ever known in all his life. (Pt III, ch. 3)

The woman returns to Heyst the inner reality of which his father has deprived him, his own subjectivity mediated through the female. At the same time, as so often in Conrad, the protagonist's entanglement with a woman (for example in the story 'A Smile of Fortune') is an entanglement which seduces him from an apparently straightforward life which was nevertheless itself becoming insupportable.[6] Lane, who notes that Schomberg's obsession begins well before Lena appears on the scene, makes the further suggestion that Schomberg and Heyst are also in some sense paired: 'each wards off actual and imaginary obstacles to identification by adopting a strategy of evasion – abstinence and retreat, denial and projection – that devolves the entire problem onto one woman' (Lane, 1995, p. 117). The process of Heyst's entanglement has of course already been prefigured in the rescue of Morrison. To understand how it is that Heyst's inner gain is simultaneously a defeat, we need to revert to the subject of names.

In referring to Heyst and Lena, I have been using the nomen-clature insisted upon by the text. The text precludes thinking of its hero as 'Axel', and never attributes a surname to Lena. (The father who would have signed her is another one of those male failures who will return in these pages and by the same token has no name to pass on.) In giving currency to a surname and a given name, the text neatly aligns Axel Heyst with the name of the father. But *heissen*, notes Lane, connotes 'to name' as well as 'to mean' (1995, p. 118). Lena's name is 'given' in a quite specific sense – by Heyst himself. She is 'the girl – to whom, after several experimental essays in combining detached letters and loose syllables, he had given the name of Lena' (Pt III, ch. 3).

Lena is now named both with an allusion to her original name Magdalen – a name which seems to ally her more with the whore in the virgin – mother – whore triad – and as Heyst's project. Under this name she is simultaneously pure and corrupt. She is starting her story again, this time under Heyst's authority. Like Conrad himself, he is in a sense both her author and her father.[7] Following the bestowal of this name, the two go on an expedition into the interior of the island, to be precise to the boundary of the area occupied by the indigenous population which, like so many other indigenous populations, seems to have been pressed into service as an objective correlative for the European conscience. On this expedition into the interior the two apparently make love for the first time. This inference is derived from the significant gap between Part III, chs 4 and 5, and substantiated by Karl's analysis of the MS text (Karl, 1983). This silence corroborates a sense that there is in Conrad something both erotic and unspeakable about missions into the interior. At all events, Heyst, who has previously professed a dualistic cosmology – 'all action is bound to be harmful . . . that is why the world is evil upon the whole' (Pt I, ch. 6) – has now well and truly fallen, the island Eden of his inner world subverted.

Now the barrier is breached, another invasion from the outside world is inevitable. Immediately in the wake of this capitulation to the creatural the villains arrive. 'I am the world itself, come to pay you a visit' says Jones (Pt IV ch. 11). In doing so, they enact what amounts to a parody of masculine assertion: melodramatic villainy is a code for criminality and thus an isomorphism of all that is prized about the male propensity to bend the world to its will. Once they have arrived, Heyst, with the object of protecting Lena, finds himself propelled into assertive activity. He is liberated from paralysing self-regard:

> The vague apprehension of a distant future . . . the sceptical carelessness which had hitherto accompanied every one of his attempts at action, like a secret reserve of his soul, fell away from him. He no longer belonged to himself. (Pt III, ch. 8)

Ricardo and Jones have (as the former realises) a curious affinity with Lena in also being emissaries of the material world. Evil arrives along with sexuality in Heyst's inner domain. To develop further the role of Ricardo and Jones in this drama we need to revert to some of the antitheses set up by the narrative.

I have already suggested that much of the narrative of *Victory* is generated by a structural tension between action and passivity, a tension marked out on the very first page, where a key lexical set consists of words like 'inertia', 'inert', 'immovably', 'passionless', 'inanimate', and 'indolent'. The moral economy of the plot is moulded by attempts to mediate between these implicit structural poles. While the novel is simultaneously negotiating issues of class and ethnicity, the narrative so generated (including its silences and evasions) can best be understood as a dialogue concerning forms of masculinity. It may be further, that the shift Karl (1983) has noted from the more 'Victorian' realist manuscript to the 'obliqueness and symbolism' of the published version is itself connected to this negotiation. To explore these claims further, we need to look again at some of the pairings the text throws up.

Insofar as they are realised in discrete characters, the key pairings are those represented by:

Heyst–Jones
Davidson–Schomberg
Wang–Pedro.

Jones, who makes a great point of being a 'gentleman' (and is so
lumped together with Heyst by Ricardo), may be seen as in some
sense Heyst's shadow. Davidson, the reliable storyteller, sympathetic witness, and good solid Englishman, contrasts with Schomberg
who (as well of course as being German, not in 1914 a respectable choice of nationality in English – let alone Polish – eyes) is
represented as an unreliable because self-interested witness
and purveyor of malicious gossip. Wang and Pedro as 'exotics'
offer contrasting images of the under-race as servant – the one
dispassionate and wily, the other physically terrifying, man as
brute. These pairings, which at a descriptive level register psychic
splitting, simultaneously constitute templates for forms of action.
If action is to be precipitated into closure it would have to be
through the performance of these antagonisms at the level of
plot. Action in Conrad, noted Frederick Crews in his Freudian
days, is an antidote to depressive passivity (Crews, 1975). However,
Crews' own illuminating reading needs to be read as itself taking
for granted a masculinist position. His fertile observation that
'his [Conrad's] characters cannot involve themselves emotionally
because they suffer from fixation; they are too busy fending off
resentments and longings towards the departed elders to permit
themselves anything more than the most furtive encounters with
their contemporaries . . .' (p. 47), needs to be understood itself as
tacitly referring to Conrad's male characters. It is Heyst's relationship to his father that saps his life, and Heyst Sr. whose portrait
and books perish in the same fire as the bodies of his son and
his son's lover.

As Jameson has noted, Conrad occupies an interesting place
on the cusp between 'high' modernism and the traditions of
popular fiction (1981, ch. 5). It is the convergence of Lena and
the villains that propels Heyst into action, simultaneously transmuting the novel into a sort of thriller. And it is at this point
that an attempt to subject the novel to an estranged masculine
reading becomes most fruitful and most difficult, precisely because
of that descent into melodrama to whose logic Leavis long ago
objected. I cannot agree that 'the antithesis of lust in Ricardo
and woman-hating in Jones on which the *dénouement* depends

has no irresistible significance in relation to Conrad's main theme.'[8] If melodrama *is* what occurs, that is in itself significant. To attempt to explain this, I want briefly to take up all the intruders, focusing first on Jones and Ricardo, then on Lena.

I suggested above that crime and villainy represent a sort of isomorphism for the kind of actions that are conventionally approved of in men. I believe this to be true in many sorts of discourses as well as the novelistic or dramatic discourse of villainy. If, however, we limit our view to the sort of pantomime villainy represented by the Ricardo–Jones duo, we can see that one element in their story is the magnetism of Heyst. The 'rational' explanation at the level of plot rests on Ricardo's belief in the existence of the baron's secret wealth, and Schomberg's desire to have the pair of them out of his hair. At another level, it appears to me that in the intrusion upon the island we have a variant on that dynamic which – whether in Jacobean tragedy or in the career of Paul Scott's Colonel Merrick – propels a 'villain' (himself a vehicle for projections of evil) into the path of those who seem to hold a power in which he wants to share. That is to say that within the narrative hierarchy the hero occupies a place close to the normative centre to which the villain also aspires. There is so to speak a symbiotic relationship between villain and hero not only on the grounds that one represents the shadow of the other, but also because the villain seeks to occupy a form of intimacy with the hero. The former's crimes are committed in the interest of achieving proximity to the hero and the hero's allotted position of centrality and influence. Such proximity may extend to killing the hero if need be: murder is after all a perverse form of physical intimacy.

The trio of Jones, Ricardo, and Pedro itself represents a series of split potentialities. Propensity for action is here organised on class and ethnic lines, with Jones the white gentleman in a perpetual state of sinister languor (a hyperbolic version of Heyst's own condition); Ricardo, lower-class and uninhibitedly capable of action, as the servant who finally deserts him to strike out on his own behalf; and Pedro as the sub-human recruit from the third world. In that order, the trio represent a descending hierarchy of physical inhibition. (Jones' preferred weapon is the gun, Ricardo's the knife, and Pedro's his bare hands.) Jones also exhibits in an exaggerated form a horror of the feminine which seems to underscore the whole novel's search for a way of managing relations to the female. Andrew Michael Roberts notes that the Jones-Ricardo duo appear to be a 'relatively overt' reference to homosexuality, but homosexuality read through a homophobic screen 'which can represent same-sex desire among men only as misogyny and a male couple only as a criminal partnership' (1996, p. 162). Repeatedly described as a 'spectre', Jones seeks limited contact with the physical earth. It is his relationship to Heyst, brought to a head in Pt IV, ch. 11, and underpinned by his belief that both are gentlemen united against the common herd, which acts as a pivot between the two plots.

If Mr Jones' party of adventurers represent one form of intrusion upon Heyst's domain, Lena represents another, but one which – even if we are apt to treat ironically Davidson's report of Heyst's final words – the narrative movement of the novel seems to propose as a positive force. Her ambiguity as a figure – the unreadability of her text – I would like to examine not in relation to a speculative reconstruction of Conrad's own unconscious, but to the public domain of masculine narrative. The secret sharing between narrator and listeners, observes Roberts, may be based upon 'male ignorance, a covert fellowship of fear and desire in relation to the feminine' (Roberts, 1993, p. 97). I have already noted that Lena is represented ambivalently as both pure and tainted. She also embodies traditional 'feminine' characteristics, significantly framed within a tension between precision and vagueness. As she prepares for her heroic moment: 'A great vagueness enveloped her impressions, but all her energy was concentrated on the struggle she wanted to take upon herself, in a great exaltation of love and self-sacrifice, which is woman's sublime faculty . . .' (Pt IV, ch. 5).

To be a woman, in this scheme, is to be in touch with the sources of your own strength, indeed of your own anger, in a way that Heyst with his hyper-developed mental facility cannot. There is a curious parallel with the uninhibited (because unreflective) strength attributed to the villain. As the action moves towards its crisis, Lena (paralleling Ricardo) decides to act in her own right, disobeying Heyst's instructions so as to save him by appearing to give herself to Ricardo. The point I am making is not one about the more lumpenly Freudian resonances of the scene where she wheedles the knife from Ricardo and secretes it in her skirt. Rather, it is a point about her structural role in the ending: the fact that it is through her superficially gratuitous death that Heyst and the novel attain their final shape. Heyst and Jones have overseen the climactic moments with Ricardo. In turn, over her dead body set in 'transfigured beauty' (Pt IV, ch. 12), Heyst and Davidson, the normative narrator, meet once more. She has become an immobilised aesthetic image of feminine beauty and courage rather than a continuing actor in the plot. The violent crisis and Lena's ensuing death have preserved Heyst from being sucked into the ordinariness and domesticity of a prolonged relationship. Her death is in fact the precondition of 'victory'. If, as I think the text hints, she is also pregnant, then symbolic reproduction – the retelling of Heyst's story to His Excellency, or to the readers – has been substituted for physical reproduction.

At one level *Victory* has to do with an attempt to dramatise and resolve problems about masculinity as a praxis and a subject of narrative. Yet the point of my reading of the novel is certainly not to castigate Conrad the author for his lack of success in this project, for having had to take the melodramatic road in killing off both hero and heroine. Much of the continued interest of the novel resides in the nature of the attempt and the nature of the contradictions that it in turn generates. In Conrad's account action and contemplation are irreconcilable, and both lead to dead ends. Future and past (including the father's portrait and his books) perish on the pyre. But I have access to no superior position from which to write off the result as evasion or failure. Rather, the evolution of new masculinities requires us to question and talk to those evasions and failures if such they are. Conrad's attempt to create space for male protagonists is undertaken in the face not only of the unreadable feminine but of all too readable patriarchy.

WOMEN IN LOVE

Lawrence is an author to much of whose output the term 'phallogocentric' can appropriately, even exactly, be used. He is the most avowedly 'phallic' of our authors, developing during the early and mid-1920s through novels and polemical writings an hysterically male (and white) supremacist programme, and a theory of phallus worship into the bargain.[9] One is left wondering why (if the phallus is naturally so dominant) it requires a polemical campaign to assert its claim to supremacy. Part of the answer lies in the subject matter of this book. We are dealing with what on the face of things anyway appears to be a paradox: that one of the most avowedly phallocentric of writers is in fact engaged in a critical account of masculinity which inevitably raises questions about the nature of male being and of male power. Lawrence's own phallic programme is a direct consequence of the interrogation to which he himself had subjected masculinity. Read in this context, his work is far more interesting than a reductive account of his sexual politics could allow, necessary corrective though that may have been to 1960s mystifications. As Jonathan Dollimore has nicely put it:

> there is much more to be said about Lawrence; much more than was usually said in the days when he was celebrated as a prophet of straight liberation, and more than is often said when he is castigated from the vantage point of contemporary sexual politics. (1991, p. 269)

To set about rewriting male narratives was to risk rendering the whole subject unstable, so Lawrence's later programme was not simply a performance of a script supplied by his own neuroses, but a response to problems he had himself courageously opened up. To be a man in Lawrence's book was to be both more various and more vulnerable than had traditionally been asserted.

The nature of Lawrence's fiction poses problems to the male reader and teacher. To launch into a critique of Lawrence's theories is in a way to collude with the script in engaging in male combat with the patriarch.[10] There are plenty of critiques of the grisly masculinity of *The Plumed Serpent* or *The Woman who Rode Away* (Millett, 1971, ch. 5; Pykett, 1995, ch. 7). To round up all the usual suspects would be in a sense to pay perverse homage (if from a self-congratulatorily enlightened point of view) to their centrality. For the purposes of this book, we are better off approaching by a more indirect route. In Barthes' terms, we need to talk not so much about the work with its affiliation to the father but about the interactive process that is the text.

The title of Lawrence's novel – originally *The Sisters*, from which *Women in Love* was quarried – in a way provides me with my starting place. Not, indeed to dispute its appropriateness to its subject matter – the novel begins with Gudrun and Ursula, and they and their own relationship remain central throughout – but rather to suggest that the framing given by either title is in commonsense terms at least a little misleading. The title signifies that for the male narrator to fix his gaze on men may require a pretext, a feint in the direction of something else: looking at women for example. Male desire, as Sedgwick or Williams would show us, is here mediated through women. Gudrun and Ursula are indeed more than a pretext. But the novel which goes under their title is also the story of men in love. An attempt to explore Lawrence's work in relation to masculinity certainly cannot simply by-pass those issues about his treatment of female characters so vigorously raised by Kate Millett a quarter of a century ago. Yet if we were to look for the signs of a gender programme simply in terms of its oppressive effects upon women, we would in effect be reproducing the distraction of attention from the male and masculine subjectivity which is going on in Lawrence's text.[11] Much of the story revolves around the impact upon the male cast of the liberation of female erotic and cultural energy, for which it simultaneously calls.

Earlier in this chapter, I suggested that Axel Heyst had been rescued by the death of Lena from a condition of domesticity and its associated feminisation. Much masculine narrative can be seen as an attempt both to define the arena of domesticity as an enclosed and claustrophobic space organised under the sign of the woman, and, having done so, to propose escape routes into another domain where being and action could be more authentic.[12] Heroic transgression (even if leading to catastrophic results) is contrasted with conformity within a gendered set. Perhaps I could get hold of this by briefly referring to another and very different novel.

There is a sense in which George Orwell's *Coming up for Air* (1939) represents a paradigmatic male fiction in its positioning both of its subject matter and its reader:

> Hilda is thirty-nine, and when I first knew her she looked just like a hare. So she does still, but she's got very thin and rather wizened, with a perpetual brooding, worried look in her eyes. . . . Butter is going up, and the gas-bill is enormous, and the kids' boots are wearing out and there's another instalment due on the radio – that's Hilda's litany . . .

Do you know the road I live in . . .? You know how these streets
fester all over the inner-outer suburbs. Always the same . . .
what, after all, *is* a road like Ellesmere Road? Just a prison
with the cells all in a row. A line of semi-detached torture-
chambers where the poor little five-to-ten pound a weekers
quake and shiver, every one of them with the boss twisting
his tail and the wife riding him like the nightmare and the
kids sucking him like leeches.

I sometimes think I'd like to have the Hesperides Estate surmounted
by an enormous statue to the god of building societies. It would
be a queer sort of god. Among other things it would be bi-
sexual. The top half would be a managing director and the
bottom half would be a wife in the family way. (Chs 1 and 2)

It is not, I think, enough to protest that Orwell 'knows what he
is doing' and has undoubtedly taken pains to create this voice of
the harried lower-middle-class male – or to object that the enemy
is managerial capitalism as much as women. Hilda (objectively
at least as much a victim of the system as George) is represented
as symbiotically in league with the bosses. Nor is it adequate to
point out what is also the case, that George Bowling, the narrator of the novel, feels almost as much disgust towards himself as
he does towards Hilda. Part of his disgust arises from his sense
of having capitulated to Hilda's world. Real men don't commute,
and the plot concerns Bowling's futile attempt to break out of a
round whose signature is feminine tyranny. I have cited this novel
as a reminder of how time and again the narrative of male autonomy and self-discovery is couched within a misogynist rhetoric:
how from Twain's *Huckleberry Finn* to Updike's *Rabbit Run* the
assertion of male freedom is achieved in opposition to the strait-
jacket of the feminised domestic sphere.

Now self-evidently Lawrence was not Orwell, and I am not
trying to imply guilt by association. Indeed, the point of this book
as a whole is not simply to adopt a superior position in ranking
male authors according to an abstract measure of whether or not
they have succeeded in overcoming masculine prejudices or
assimilating a feminist agenda. As Clark, speaking of T. S. Eliot's
early poems, puts it:

Writing Masculinities

In so far as I understand these 'thousand sordid images' . . . I am implicated in and indicted by them. They are, as Eliot reminds us, that out 'of which your soul was constituted'. But I think that any useful response to feminism must involve acceptance of this double-bind: reading more forthrightly, in a sense more culpably. (1994, p. 219)

It is in these terms that we have to take and work with as part of our material the recurrent narrative trope of flight from an allegedly feminised sphere. And indeed flight is a recurrent feature of *Women in Love*, as it is of most of the other novels we shall look at. One way of thinking of these novels, indeed, is not only in terms of tension between centre and margin, but also as working out a relation between interior space and flight. As we saw in the previous discussion of *Le Grand Meaulnes*, an ambivalent relationship to space and consequent valorising of flight seems to characterise certain narratives of masculinity.

The motif of flight recurs in *Women in Love*: Birkin's trips to the Continent culminate in the whole foursome's excursion. Birkin flees after Hermione attacks him. Despite their jobs, both Gerald and Birkin regularly take themselves out of the way for varying periods of time. 'He was not very fixed in his abode' (p. 53); 'He did not write, nobody heard anything of him' (p. 244). It is as though being in one place or settling into an interior space stands for everything that is opposed to fluidity and process:

> the thought of love, marriage, and children, and a life lived together in the horrible privacy of domestic and connubial satisfaction, was repulsive. (p. 199)

> 'One should avoid this *home* instinct. It's not an instinct, it's a habit of cowardliness. One should never have a *home*.' (p. 352)

This is a trope which recurs again and again in Lawrence's work. Thus in *Aaron's Rod*, Aaron Sisson explicitly sets out to escape the domestic world which is choking his art, and launches into a peripatetic life first in London and then on the Continent under the general mentorship of his friend Lilly. Lawrence's characters flee from jobs, careers, and routines as much as they flee from settled habitats: 'better die than live mechanically a life that is a repetition of repetitions' (p. 192). Unlike, say, his contemporaries

Bennett and Wells, he adopts on behalf of his characters a sort of rentier freedom more akin to that enjoyed by the expatriate cast of Henry James, figures whose goal (even when thwarted) is self-realisation rather than mere material survival. The novel, like its characters, is straining after an unconditioned selfhood. Though Birkin is a school inspector (admittedly with a private income) and Ursula a teacher, they both apparently find it quite easy to throw off the shackles of work and launch into freedom. Gerald would appear to be facing a promising career in the family firm as a captain of industry (a type much in vogue in the social commentary of the period);[13] he would, thinks Gudrun, 'clear up the great muddle of labour and industry' (p. 417). But driven by his demon he goes instead to the Alps and his death, stripped of his economic and social armour. The result of all this mobility is a representation of identity – both male and female – in a singularly naked condition, decontextualised, the opposite of the selves rooted in locality and the earth of the early chapters of *The Rainbow*.[14] As in different ways both Pittock and Lodge have noted '[l]ittle attention is given to the practical problems of life in *Women in Love*' (Lodge, 1990, p. 97). Further, Lodge notes:

> One of the most striking and 'experimental' features of this novel is its foregrounding of debates, arguments and moments of spiritual or erotic crisis and illumination, by relegating or deleting the kind of detail that we expect from the 'social-psychological novel of everyday life'. (Ibid.)

I hope to show that this detachment is at least partly produced by the attempt to re-align masculine narrative.

One might reasonably suppose that the lives of both men and women would require rhythmic movement between phases of development and of consolidation. The search for autonomy and horror of possessions and routine might be and has been experienced – not least in the moment of the late 1960s – as a campaign against the suffocating spread of bourgeois material culture. If that is the case, then it is the women in Lawrence who seem to act as the advance agents of consumerism. So Birkin broods: 'But it seemed to him that woman was always so horrible and clutching, she had such a lust for possession, a greed of self-importance in love. She wanted to have, to own, to control, to be dominant . . .' (p. 200). Lawrence seems to propose that you can align stasis and claustrophobic enclosure with the feminine, and escape and life-bringing movement with the masculine. Gerald, for whom marriage 'is like a doom' finds that

> Marriage was not the committing himself into a relationship with Gudrun. It was a committing himself in acceptance of the established world, he would accept the established order, in which he did not livingly believe, and then he would retreat to the underworld for his life. (p. 353)

Women in Love is full of houses of greatly varying dimensions, carefully and lovingly described. Yet repeatedly we find the house interior is an emblem for claustrophobic horror. In the chapter aptly titled 'Flitting', the sisters revisit the house from which the family has moved. Gudrun cries: 'How I lived here a day without dying of terror, I cannot conceive!', and the narrator comments:

> The sense of walls , dry, thin, flimsy-seeming walls, and a flimsy flooring, pale with its artificial black edges, was neutralising to the mind. Everything was null to the senses, there was enclosure without substance, for the walls were dry and papery . . .

> 'What *must* we be like, if we are the contents of *this*!' cries Gudrun. (pp. 372–3)

When Lawrence said in *Psychoanalysis and the Unconscious* (1923), 'We are too mentally domesticated' (p. 57), he could be sure that the word would carry the right ring of enclosure and loss of wildness. If interior spaces threaten female characters with deathlike stasis, they threaten male characters even more. For one thing women in Lawrence are eligible to be rescued from claustrophobic situations by the undomesticated energy of the male (for example, *The Lost Girl*, 'The Virgin and the Gypsy', 'The Fox', *Lady Chatterley's Lover*). Such an intruder is not the reflex of her own desire, but a plenipotentiary of a higher power. At the end of *The Rainbow*, Ursula, who has now shed much of her worldly self, waits to

> recognize a man created by God. The man should come from the Infinite and she should hail him. She was glad she could not create her man. She was glad she had nothing to do with

his creation. She was glad that this lay within the scope of that vaster power in which she rested at last. The man would come out of Eternity to which she herself belonged. (p. 494)

The passage finds its parallel in Ursula' rediscovery of Birkin after their argument on the drive ('Excurse'):

> It was here she discovered him one of the Sons of God such as were in the beginning of the world . . . This was release at last . . . it was the daughters of men coming back to the Sons of God, the strange inhuman Sons of God who are in the beginning. (p. 313)

No such avatar is available to men, who have to pull themselves up by their own bootstraps or not at all.

This propensity to flee from domestication which provides Lawrence with one of his most familiar narrative germs, involves us in a complicated negotiation with Millett's contention that 'patriarchy's chief institution is the family' (1971, p. 33). What are we to make of the sight of all these patriarchs in the making in flight from their base institution? One element seems to lie in a sense that the home ground has been taken over by women (see Simpson, 1982, throughout). To allow yourself to be domesticated is to capitulate to feminine desire. Backed by the narrator, Birkin struggles with Ursula's desire for a home and possessions (ch. 26, 'A Chair'): 'The thought of a house and furniture of my own is hateful to me'. In turn the dialectical theory of growing up outlined in *Psychoanalysis and the Unconscious* seems comparatively to be organised on a male–female axis, with the struggle into autonomy identified with the male. But there is a further twist in that the home is also identified by Lawrence as much as by Millett as the terrain of the patriarchal father. Heyst, we have seen, becomes a 'waif and a stray' (Conrad, *Victory*, Pt II, ch. 3) and travels the world in the attempt to escape his father's influence. Birkin's advantage in familial terms is to come out of nowhere, self-fathered – if anything the end of *The Rainbow* identifies him as the son of God rather than of a human father. Gerald, by contrast, is deeply oppressed by the familial set-up at Shortlands. It is quite literally the father's business he is about, though he intends to run it in a less benignly paternalist fashion. In turn neither of the friends will become fathers, the role too dangerous to take up; as though you could negate patriarchy by refusing to participate yourself. In contrast to the narrative of the high Victorian novel, the courtship procedures of Lawrence's novel do not lead to biological reproduction: the Criches and the Brangwens have a past but not, apparently, a future. While this is, as Trotter has demonstrated, an aspect of the workings of the 'degeneration plot' (1993, pp. 188–93), it is a plot which impacts differently upon female and male characters.

This dialectical tension between conditioned enclosure and unconditioned flight does not operate alone at the level of story. It is also an underlying feature of the structure of the discourse of Lawrence's novels which seeks to enact the dialectic of fluidity and repetition at every level.

DISCOURSE AND KNOWLEDGE

Let us go back to certain surface features of the text of *Women in Love*. This is a text of many voices and many registers (Fleishman, 1990; Lodge, 1990). While the same could undoubtedly be said of most if not all novels (the novel is the least formally pure of genres), the heterogeneity of Lawrence's registers is significant here. The novel moves – often abruptly – between different centres of focalisation. The primary voices of the text – Birkin, Ursula, Gudrun, Gerald, and the narrator – are engaged in a free-flowing and often repetitive argument which frequently (as in a novel of ideas like Thomas Mann's near contemporary *The Magic Mountain*) moves into an expository and didactic register. The narrative forward motion of the novel is propelled as much by a sequence of almost symbolist images as by a plot of suspense and resolution. Episodes loom into the foreground and recede again into a penumbral zone while characters as well as readers ponder their significance.[15] Time is fluid and the precise temporal location of events often unclear ('One morning . . .'; 'About that time'; 'The days went by . . . And then . . .'). Precise temporality is apparently as constraining as is fixation in space. As a novel, this one is both highly articulate and silent or elusive about matters that a different kind of novel might have explained. The narrator is both knowing and ignorant, the tissue of the plot full of holes. The discursive level, in short, has an oblique relationship with the level of story as the reader attempts to reconstruct it.

While these are phenomena of which any reader of Lawrence must be conscious, I want to elaborate their significance to the present argument. When Birkin tells Gerald that 'you've got to admit the unadmitted love of man for man. It makes for a greater freedom for everybody . . .' (p. 352), he is offering a textual as well as an existential programme: the text is articulating a freedom which has as yet no material enactment and is to that extent utopian.

Lawrence's novel enacts in its very structure beliefs about the nature of knowledge and about the relationship between the conscious and unconscious minds. This discursive enactment has implications for the maintenance of cognitive hierarchy which Lawrence has to find ways of solving. The textual dynamic and its tentative solutions are deeply embedded in arguments about gender and the nature of the male self. In particular, these narrative procedures throw into doubt the location of authority, and pose questions about how to manage the turbulent and fissiparous energies (especially associated with the female) which Lawrence is simultaneously finding ways to represent.

To establish the next stage, I need to touch briefly on Lawrence's attitudes to the body as the site of knowledge. He was working in a tradition and an era that was calling radically into question received ideas about the body–mind hierarchy. To do so was a risky enterprise in many ways, particularly in view of the potency of the tradition which identifies the manly with the assured dominance of the rational mind. In asserting the primacy of 'deep' unconscious knowledge, and in disputing the deathly hegemony of the rational, calculating, mechanical mind, Lawrence was bidding farewell to the security of the traditional gendering of cognitive hierarchy. It is necessary here to plunder a highly complex field for relevant detail.

In his late essay *Psychoanalysis and the Unconscious* (1923), Lawrence, pursuing his quarrel with Freud, developed a number of theories which he had been working out for years. One productive rhetorical gambit was to take a binary metaphorical hierarchy of terms and invert it – thus for example, and centrally, in valorising darkness as a category.[16] In inverting this hierarchy, Lawrence was of course carrying on a campaign on behalf of the unconscious mind as being the core of human creativity. One of his key complaints against Freud was that the latter's version of the unconscious reduced it to the status of a bin for repressions and neurotic garbage, rather than the deep centre of human existence. But to invert the traditional mind–body dichotomy was another and analogous act. The effect of Lawrence's analysis in *Psychoanalysis and the Unconscious* was to devolve thinking and knowledge into what he saw as body knowledge. This had the dual effect of reintegrating the divided human self and simultaneously unseating the mind from its traditional position of rational dominance. Lawrentian cognition is quite literally de-centred. At times it seems as though the object of Lawrence's erotic and cultural programme is the loss of consciousness. At all events, he is setting about redrawing the boundaries between the conscious and the unconscious. While all this is well known, his complex and decentred account of the articulate self has particular implications for masculinity. Homologously, it has implications for the form of the novel, and *Women in Love* represents a laboratory in which to enact the ecology of uncentred identities, identities dispersed among their own and others' unconscious forces. A novel or a body (corpus) of work may metaphorically represent a body, and this one in particular seems to represent a body where knowledge, instead of being the prerogative of the mind (or of the rational mind's surrogate, the narrator), is dispersed throughout. The erratic and allusive relations between discursive and story levels, which I noted above, are the result.

Lawrence's deeply ambivalent relationship to the rational mind is enacted in his narratives. As a move this in a broad sense aligns him with a powerful strand in the intellectual history of the turn of the century. It is also a move with a number of consequences of which we only have room for a few here. It throws up problems at both the ontological and epistemological levels. What would a post-rational life (or society) be like? And how will language and thought stretch to represent such a condition? We need to remember that Lawrence's case is both descriptive (human beings are in any case lived by forces they only partially understand) and prescriptive (we are living inauthentic lives which we need to change; we need to loosen the bonds of mechanism which lead to death). He has on his hands a struggle to represent his subject matter in the words and narrative structures available to him. From our point of view here his argument bears directly on what it would mean to be a man, given that traditional maleness has rested upon a hierarchy in which rationality oversees and disciplines both body and unruly passions, and where the paradigmatic position was one of dispassionate management of emotion and of those (like women, children, or lower-class men) held to be governed by their emotions.[17]

MEN IN LOVE

Human identity as it is represented in Lawrence's writings is the site of turbulent and conflicting forces. Some of these forces are given their head, others denied and thwarted. Some of his most powerful passages represent characters in the state of interior deadness brought about by denial of true inner needs. (See for example ch. 15, 'Sunday Evening'; or the discussion of the 'tortures of psychic starvation' in *Psychoanalysis and the Unconscious*, p. 117) Against certain promptings we have, the argument runs, become so armoured that only prophetic vision can recall them for us. One of Lawrence's recurrent motifs is the visit of strangers:

> What is that knocking?
>
> . . . it is the three strange angels.
> Admit them, admit them.[18]

In calling us to release conscious control and attend to the return of sacred forces, Lawrence finds himself in the company of a mixed band of twentieth-century religious and secular thinkers from Eliot, through Jung to Eric Berne. If men need to attend to promptings from outside the sterile clearing of the conscious self, then in doing so they are in danger of opening themselves up to forces over which they have no control and thus of losing their mastery. Much of Lawrence's work can be seen as an attempt both to decentre the male self and in turn to deal with the consequences that ensue. While we may justifiably deplore the irrationalist and phallic programme to which that attempt led, we should not in doing so write off the critique of masculinity which preceded it, and to which it is itself a response.

Earlier on I argued that many of Lawrence's men are represented stripped of the economic, social and familial roles which might give at least an exoskeleton to identity. This process is made explicit in the case of Gerald, who is held up against one definition of masculinity which emerged from the nineteenth century, the role of the 'captain of industry', the man defined through his work and his triumphant assertion over both the physical world and over other men. The text leaves us in no doubt that this extrovert self organised towards performance and success would have been one of Gerald's options. Typically, he is viewed by the voyeuristic female:

> She thought of the revolution he had worked in the mines in so short a time. She knew that if he were confronted with any problem, any hard actual difficulty he would overcome it . . . He had the faculty of making order out of confusion . . . As an instrument . . . he was marvellous . . . He would be a Napoleon of peace, or a Bismarck . . . (pp. 417–18; and see the description of Gerald's reorganising work in ch. 17)

These images of acceptable modes of male triumph are put before us only to be ironically snatched away. The text offers a critique of that phallic instrumentality in the moment that Gudrun admires it: 'He was sheerly beautiful, he was a perfect instrument. To her mind he was a pure, inhuman, almost supernatural instrument. His instrumentality appealed so strongly to her she wished she were God, to use him as a tool' (p. 418). But not Gudrun, God, nor the narrator can so use him. The narrator can no more take charge of the novel world than Gerald can of his. Indeed the denial of instrumentality is precisely the point. The vulnerability that is the chink in the armour of the captain of industry lets in the forces which destroy him. One route for the male is to deal with his unconscious by projecting it upon the world. To go unarmoured, to expose himself to his own unconscious forces is to court destruction. Birkin (perhaps because he has seized the discursive high ground, and because his father is safely off-stage) survives his nakedness, but Gerald loses his will to live.

To return for a moment to the strangers. Birkin and Gerald represent two versions of identities whose boundaries have become fluid and dangerous, and whose attempts at mastery (through physical intimidation or through discursive overkill) represent the need to maintain control and dominance over selves and others become increasingly polymorphous. In perpetually haranguing Ursula and others, Birkin is usually taken to be a persona of

Lawrence himself. His punitive didacticism is a way of warranting his own identity as a master of his own fate where that mastery is insistently called in question by invasion from outside the conscious domain. One of the invading forces (and one from which as I have already suggested the title of the novel or the asymmetry of the chapters 'Man to Man' and 'Woman to Woman' provides a distraction) is Birkin's reciprocated affection for Gerald:

> It was always the same between them; always their talk brought them into a deadly nearness of contact, a strange perilous intimacy which was either hate or love, or both . . . they really kept it to the level of trivial occurrence. Yet the heart of each burned from the other. They burned with each other, inwardly. (p. 33)

In courageously developing this relationship at length, Lawrence found himself having to invent a narrative structure that would cope with the strain.

That novelists in many ways as dissimilar as Forster and Lawrence were seeking to find narrative modes for reintegrating compartmentalised male passions is evidence of a contemporary ferment over gender that went beyond 'the relations between the sexes'. And that males were emotionally 'ungrown' by comparison with women was commonplace in the gender debates of the 1890s and early 1900s:

> Perhaps (speaking broadly) all the passions and powers . . . are really profounder and vaster in Man than in Woman – are more varied, root deeper, and have wider scope; but then the woman has this advantage, that her powers are more co-ordinated, are in harmony with each other where his are disjointed or in conflict.
>
> . . . the point is that Man with his great uncoordinated nature has during these later centuries dominated the other sex, and made himself the ruler of society. In consequence of which we naturally have a society made after his pattern – a society advanced in mechanical and intellectual invention, with huge passional and emotional elements, but all involved in whirling confusion and strife – a society ungrown, which on its material side may approve itself a great success, but on its more human and affectional side seems at times an utter failure.

This ungrown, half-baked sort of character is conspicuous in the class of men who organise the modern world – the men of the English-speaking, well-to-do class. (Carpenter, 1896, pp. 27–8)[19]

It appears that for Lawrence (as perhaps for Edward Carpenter) the road to male emotional maturity would lead through close, even passionate, male friendship. The story of the comrades that is written under the story of women in love is one for which the text has to find a narrative register. The suggestion is that in male friendship it might be possible to find that relationship of equality, that 'strange conjunction . . . not meeting and mingling . . . but an equilibrium, a pure balance of two single beings' ('Mino', p. 148) that Birkin despairs of in his relationship with Ursula.

Birkin is not alone in watching Gerald, who is viewed at different times not only by the narrator, but by Gudrun ('there was something northern about him that magnetized her' [p. 14]; 'he should have all the women he can' [p. 413]), and Minette ('Gerald was what she called a man' [p. 81]). However, where the women want to put Gerald to use, Birkin is represented as seeing his friend whole. Birkin repeatedly takes the initiative in their relationship, and his attempt to move their relationship on to a new stage occurs in the context ('Man to Man') of his feverish broodings about women and the kind of relationships he believes women to require. Gerald 'really loved Birkin' but would not by himself have attempted to carry their relationship into the physical domain. The next phase, the naked wrestling match ('Gladiatorial') follows immediately from the fiasco of Birkin's attempt to propose to Ursula. The physical intimacy of this scene is represented as healing for both of them, and as grounded in another kind of knowledge, a knowledge about which the text is imprecise while being apparently specific: 'He seemed to penetrate into Gerald's more solid, more diffuse bulk, to interfuse his body through the body of the other . . .' (p. 270).

It appears that for Lawrence the search for male emotional maturity would lead through male friendship. Yet their love for each other rests upon Birkin's unreciprocated knowledge of his friend. As is abundantly clear from the cancelled 1916 prologue, a great narrative energy is invested in the erotic nature of the relationship between the two ('It would seem as if he had always loved men, always and only loved men' [p. 505]).[20] Yet this is an intimacy that signally fails to grow. Hammond (1996) observes that at the discursive level Birkin and Gerald 'seem to accept their intimacy without relating it to the vocabularies and definitions current in contemporary society. In this respect, Lawrence makes them inhabit an hermetically sealed linguistic world' (p. 193). At the level of story, the relationship may paradoxically be safeguarded by the anticipation that it is doomed. Birkin is maddened by the sense of limitation in Gerald even as he makes his proposal of blood-brotherhood: 'the man himself, complete, as if fated, doomed, limited . . .' (p. 207). It appears that the relationship is made possible by the narrator's knowledge (which Birkin shares) that Gerald is programmed to autodestruct. In having accidentally killed his brother, Gerald is identified by Birkin with Cain (another wanderer), and the blood-brotherhood of the two men will be ended by Gerald's own death – 'He did not believe there was any such thing as accident. It all hung together, in the deepest sense' (p. 26). There were of course many reasons in 1916 why Lawrence and his Birkin should be preoccupied by the propensity of male stories to end in disaster. That the trenches of the Western Front represent another kind of male intimacy and a male world legit-imised by the ubiquity of mutilation and violent death, is the argument of Paul Fussell's chapter' Soldier Boys' (Fussell, 1975, ch. 8).[21] Within *Women in Love* the oncoming disaster provides a legitimating framework for an experience for which Lawrence offers us only an interrupted, oblique and heavily edited text.

ART AND ITS INTERPRETERS

Works of art, their contemplation and interpretation, constitute a recurrent motif in *Women in Love*. The text's propensity to free space for interpretation is complemented by its own essays in interpretation as a social act, and one which it may at times seek to control. The enquiry into the meaning of art works that runs through *Women in Love* is simultaneously a debate about inter-pretation and about gender. In the end it is a debate over who possesses the right to impose closure. Major examples concern the African statuette in 'Totem' (to which Birkin later returns in memory) and the discussion of Loerke's sketch for a statue in 'Continental'. The deployment of such images in the text involves a dialogue over the sources and attribution of meaning. These

passages provide a paradigm for the reading of art works, including – by extension – novels. The arguments over interpretation are in a sense prophetic, anticipating the acts of interpretation
which take place over Lawrence's own text, and thus a struggle
for mastery over the subject matter. At another level – and for
reasons explored in detail by Williams – the text negotiates a
fear that it is essentially effeminate to practise as an artist. The
role of Gudrun, whom Williams points out 'can be read as something of a portrait of the artist' is clearly once again important
here (1993, p. 51). Lawrence's text is drawn towards what it sees
as the scopophilic propensity of women and thus needs to guard
against the imputation of effeminacy. (Compare his own play-
ground bravado of referring to Chekhov – of all people – as 'Willy
wet leg'.[22]) Gudrun's counterpart as the male artist is Loerke, whose
portrayal exposes the fear that the artist will turn out not to be a
real man at all but a homosexual and a sewer rat. Male
polymorphousness as represented by the artist is both desirable
and horrifying. Birkin and Gerald unite in finding Loerke repulsive: 'He lives like a rat in the river of corruption . . . I expect he
is a Jew . . .' (p. 428). 'What do the women find so impressive in
that little brat?' Gerald asks Birkin. Birkin's reply is couched
in terms of the sinister power of victims. 'He is the perfectly
subjected being . . . and the women rush towards that . . .'

> 'What do women want at the bottom?'
> 'Some satisfaction in basic repulsion . . . They seem to creep
> down some ghastly tunnel of darkness . . . they want to explore
> the sewers, and he's the wizard rat that swims ahead.'

It is as though the novel is alternately attracted and repelled by
its own voyaging, as though the exploration of masculine empathy and the male gaze in which it had engaged is at the same
time deeply repulsive. 'It sounds a rum sort of desire' says Gerald,
and Birkin replies, 'I suppose we want the same . . . Only we
want to take a quick jump downwards in a sort of ecstacy – and
he ebbs with the stream, the sewer stream.' The two friends' discussion occurs shortly after the passage where Birkin and Ursula
engage in anal sex, an activity which has an almost sacramental
status here, as in *Lady Chatterley's Lover*. As the imagery of the
passage suggests, the horror of the taboo is loaded upon Loerke.
By contrast, Gudrun is fascinated by him – the watcher is watched:

But also, she knew what he was unconscious of, his tremen-
dous power of understanding, of apprehending her living
motion. He did not know his own power. He did not know
how . . . he could look into her and see her, what she was, see
her secrets. He would only want her to be herself. He knew
her verily, with a subconscious, sinister knowledge. (p. 427)

The gaze of the male artist can penetrate a woman's secrets, know
her hidden desires. And to know those desires might be to occupy
them. The corollary of this sinister knowledge is an uninhibited
narrative form. It is such multivalency, this polymorphous refusal
to settle on a single narrative voice, that is the source both of
the novel's strength and its vulnerability. And beset by the dangers
of symbolic collapse, the text twists and turns in pursuit of an
order of meaning that offers stability. But even the attempt to
stabilise Gerald within a supposedly archetypal dichotomy of
northern and southern races will not survive the chronic instability
of the text.

Power relations between men and women and men and men
are realised in *Women in Love* in the power to make representations and attribute meanings. While in one sense the text is 'about'
relationships, my point is that it is simultaneously 'about' the
destabilisation of the gender system through discourse. The modes
of Lawrence's discourse are reflexively foregrounded in his texts.
Within them, artists and audience, viewers and the viewed, struggle
perpetually to take command over the making of meanings. The
discursive system of this novel is perpetually at the point of collapse, and this collapse is visualised as likely to drag manhood
with it. While Loerke may have been able to discipline his young
model by smackling her and subsequently dumping her, the lurking
possibility remains that the unguarded man may be swallowed
whole by that which he looks at, whether it is a woman or another
man. He is likely to be emasculated in the very act of looking.
The ambivalencies and obliqueness of the resulting narrative can
be seen to be grounded in the instability of the male subject,
and its foreseen aptness to turn into that upon which its gaze
rests. Attempts to rework and retell masculine narratives inevitably lead to instability. How to manage that instability in turn
becomes part of the story, a story which in its attempt to impose
'strong' readings on fluid material stakes its own claim to manage
the reader's participation. As the addressees of narrative we are

invited to participate in a textual utopia perpetually threatened by dystopic forces. In looking on at the story of Gerald and Birkin we might, as it is repeatedly suggested Gudrun subliminally has, kill the objects of our gaze. The promise of symbolic power held out to the reader represents an ambiguous gift. Masculinity disperses under its own gaze.

4

Male Narratives

Flee from the wrath to come, boy, that's what I always say. Seen it on a sign one time. Flee from the Wrath to Come. Crazy guy goin' down the street holdin' this sign, see, flee from the wrath to come, it tickled me. Went round for days sayin' it out loud to myself, flee from the wrath to come, flee from the wrath to come. Couldn't get it outa my head.

(Donald Barthelme, 'A Manual for Sons', in *Sixty Stories*,
Minerva, 1989)

The theme of this chapter concerns the performance of masculinities through narrative means. It will differ from the chapters on either side of it in not being based upon a reading of two central fictional texts: rather it will touch on a number of texts in an attempt to theorise and generalise about the narrative construction of masculinity. By concentrating on and developing the subject of narrative in this context, I hope both to consolidate a central part of the argument, and continue to demonstrate the principle of self-conscious masculine reading.

I have been arguing that one implication of the idea of literature as performance – the idea that a text promotes ways of being and acting and in doing so presupposes readers and reading habits – was that the bond of readership could extend to a form of solidarity: an implicit community of those who would accede to read a text in a prescribed way. Admittedly, there must be debate about how far that imaginary community is prescribed by the text itself, and how far it is the creation of social practices of education and reading. Such arguments can probably only be resolved if at all by close attention to cases, whether by genre or by individual text. In any case, no text or genre *could* entirely enforce a single and unitary mode of reading. Readers and communities of readers clearly carry out their own negotiations as they read. However, the reason for returning to this point here and now is that the idea of the implied community of readership provides us with a bridge into the subject of this chapter. That is because a narrative is a social and discursive act which constructs a relationship between a teller (real or implied) and an audience. Even at the formal level, it is never simply a sequence of represented events: narratives possess shape and valency as a result of innumerable tacit social agreements. Further, narrative texts often themselves foreground issues about readership and interpretation, issues which transmute in turn into matters of belonging and estrangement, watchers and watched, insiders and outsiders, guardians and flock. Texts contain within themselves a genetic code, so to speak, for their own reproduction. The narrator who mounts guard over the revelation of meaning bequeaths to his heirs a like responsibility. This positioning of putative audience in relation to knowledge is acted out in the text itself. I would like to start by developing some thoughts about insiderliness and outsiderliness, but first a general word of warning will be necessary.

One of the endemic dangers of a project like this is that of seeming to essentialise and universalise its own themes. In talking about masculinity and masculine narratives I do not mean to imply that some narrative forms are intrinsically and inescapably male, or that even if they were they would always remain reliably so across the boundaries of cultures and histories. That certain kinds of narrative are addressed to men and clearly associated with dominant masculine norms ('high' epic, thrillers, war stories, much pornography) does not lead to the corollary that such forms proceed directly out of and go unerringly back to an unproblematical version of male identity or behaviour. Even where a biological grounding for narrative difference seems at least plausible (for example in the contrast between different ways of handling suspense and climax), we are still talking about forms constructed and understood through layers of culture, not derived directly from some essence of male being. And a central argument of this book is that narratives and narrative genres do not simply reflect given cultural (let alone biological) norms: they also play their part in propagating and reinforcing them. That indeed is one major reason for studying narrative in the first place: so that we may learn to question our own implication in or distance from the narratives addressed to us and those we ourselves address to others.

THE GREAT GAME

The relation between insiders and outsiders is brought to the fore in the corresponding relationship between watchers and watched. One form of insiderliness is to belong to a community of knowers who observe and explain the world around them. And one way of bonding a community of knowers is likely to be through a common interest in managing or legislating for that world: creating and propagating an authoritative version of events. That is to say that the knowledge gained from surveillance is a modality of control. To observe others while remaining unmoved yourself is, as both Bentham and Foucault knew, a way of holding power over them. Further, the role of the voyeur and the role of the narrator overlap and in doing so constitute – as we have seen – a dilemma for the male subject, whether as narrator or as consumer of narrations. Some aspects of a theme running through the earlier chapter on male artists claim our attention now, since they pose questions about the implication of male actors in narrative and in the discursive relation.

In Charlotte Brontë's *Villette*, it transpires that Paul Emanuel (who is a gifted reader of character from physiognomy) is in the habit of observing the girls and teachers of Mme Beck's Pensionnat from a high, concealed window in an adjacent building, as well as entering the garden with a secret key (ch. 31). This figures within a theme of surveillance and spying that runs through the novel. When she finds out, Lucy Snowe taxes him with his 'Jesuit system':

> 'The knowledge it brings you is bought too dear, monsieur; this coming and going by stealth degrades your own dignity ... I tell you every glance you cast from that lattice is a wrong done to the best part of your own nature. To study the human heart thus is to banquet secretly and sacreligiously on Eve's apples.'

He is a consumer of forbidden knowledge, but for that knowledge Eve is still responsible. Monsieur Paul's voyeurism is not a personal hang-up, but is tied up with the political debate going on within the novel. For the moment, however, I want to use this episode to make a different point. As Henry James and his critics knew well, men fit but awkwardly into the spectator role. The male spectator (the novelist, the painter, the spy, the peeping

Tom) is trapped between two traditional but contradictory assumptions about manhood: first that men have a seigneurial right to gaze upon their objects (women in particular), and second that spectatorship as a perceptual and intellectual process is essentially passive, confounding the commitment of the male to activity, to doing rather than being. The male eye is both an organ of control and the sign of a paradoxical stasis. Much narrative energy has been devoted to trying to resolve this contradiction. What narrative could possibly legitimate the male watcher as hero?

As this is a question with a bearing upon the whole subject of the chapter (indeed of this book), I shall attempt to focus it by brief reference to Rudyard Kipling's novel *Kim* (first published 1901; references below are to the Penguin edition).[1] In the last chapter, we noticed in connection with the artist Loerke that metamorphosis or shape changing was dangerous for male actors. There was more than a suggestion that the artist's instability, his suspect empathy with the objects of his gaze, was connected to his Jewishness, his provenance from a group cast as marginal – even Oriental – in terms of a contemporary theory about the European races. Kim, too is a marginal figure, originating from the edges of empire (he is Irish, but brought up by an Indian woman), who repeatedly from the very opening of the novel changes his appearance and language. But the novel works hard to redeem his marginality by locating it within a narrative where marginality and shape changing assume an active political significance. In such a narrative, chameleonism will turn out to be an asset not of ethnography so much as of empire: 'When he comes to the Great Game he must go alone – alone and at peril of his head. *Then*, if he spits, or sneezes, or sits down other than as the people do whom he watches, he may be slain' (Kipling, *Kim* [1987] p. 177).

The apparent instability of Kim as subject is legitimated through his apprenticeship to the 'Great Game', the system of espionage and surveillance by which Britain maintains its rule over India, and keeps at a stand off the rival Russian imperialism. Kim is the spy who came in from the warm. In one sense the novel is another male *Bildungsroman*, the story of the boy Kim's apprenticeship in life and in his own life's work. We are confronted with the process of initiation into a male community, a secret community of people known to each other, and headed by the patriarchal figure of Colonel Creighton who keeps a fatherly eye on the boy's progress. Two ideas merge here: that of belonging

to an exclusive group of men, subject to the approval of a surrogate father, and that of espionage, of passing secretly among others
to find out and relay their secrets. The brew remains potent
through to the Cold War spy novels of John le Carré. And *Kim*
has impacted upon the 'real-world' performance of male roles.
As Bristow has demonstrated, Kipling's novel had a considerable
influence on the early years of the scouting movement and was
quoted at length in *Scouting for Boys* (Bristow, 1991, p. 195 *et seq.*).
The reader of *Kim* is enlisted in the novel's own great game, located
in a sequence of transferences, a progression of surrogate fathers
and adopted sons.

Kim's otherwise mobile identity is warranted by his role in the
exclusively male family of spies and spymasters. His adoption
into this family is grounded upon an essential Englishness. A
revealing example occurs when Kim is being tested by Lurgan
Sahib, the ethnically ambiguous jewel dealer who is in fact a high-
up agent. Lurgan's attempt to hypnotise the boy into believing
that he has seen a shattered vase reform before his eyes fails
because of Kim's inner discipline. That discipline is exercised
through resolutely thinking in English: 'The jar had been smashed
– yess, smashed – not the native word, he would not think of
that – but smashed – into fifty pieces, and twice three was six,
and thrice three was nine, and four times three was twelve'
(p. 202). As elsewhere in the novel, the English language is associated with logic and clear boundaries, Hindi and other Indian
languages with sensation and thus hallucination. There is an exact
parallel with the traditional male–female dichotomy. This inner
Englishness gives Kim a centre defined in terms of mental
distantiation from which he can observe and impersonate others:
as Lurgan trains the boys in practical ethnography ('how such
a caste talked, or walked, or coughed, or spat, or sneezed'), he
finds that by contrast the Hindu child 'played this game clumsily'.
'That little mind . . . could not temper itself to enter another's
soul; but a demon in Kim woke up and sang with joy as he put
on the changing dresses, and changed speech and gesture there-
with' (p. 207).

Marginality and metamorphosis are sanctioned in the male actor
if they can be seen not as narcisssistic or self-pleasuring but as
ruses on behalf of power. In turn, watching and camouflage are
legitimate if adopted as weapons of empire. But the watcher must
not allow himself to be drawn into any relationship of mutuality

with those of whose governance he is an agent. Thus, for example, the apprentice agent will not be led astray by women.[2] Paradoxically, the penis may be the enemy within the phallic narrative. The secret community to which the agent is apprenticed is not only restricted to men, but disciplined to shun the distractions of the flesh. Rewards and punishments are meted out by the senior, inner group. It is in the eyes of the ever-watchful inner elite that the individual gains approbation and with its blessing, if at all, that he gains advancement. The narrative of initiation seems to descend directly from the nineteenth-century fascination with secret societies. At the same time, surveillance and espionage are homologous with the work of the narrator. Growing up into a man's life's work is a project to be supervised by the senior males into whose sanctum the aspirant may one day himself penetrate. The theme of apprenticeship leads us on to the subject of regulative biography.

LIFE STORIES

One function performed by narrative is the establishment of acceptable biographies. Like written biographies, fictions serve as models of how a life may be told and thus in turn of how and with what expectations it may be lived.[3] In this function, fictions are likely to play a normative role, though they may also promulgate biographical paradigms and forms of heroism which counter or question dominant norms. (The autobiographical narratives of Black American women would be a case in point.) It is proposed here that literary fiction, read in a way that contests the assumption that white male identity is universal and normative, constitutes a rich field of study in male plots and the narrative forging of masculine identities. Thus, while there are many ironic and subversive variants, one influential plot – the epic – has concerned the struggle of a man with his environment, the male pitched against adverse forces through which as hero he will attain mastery and emerge as master of his own soul and his own fate. A male identity is, as Gilligan puts it, forged in relation to the world rather than in relation to another person.[4] In such a drama, others figure as helpers or hindrances to the project of self-advancement, and the trajectory towards greater knowledge and maturity is matched by a parallel growth in individuation and autonomy.

Not only can the hero accept or reject others' overtures on his own terms; the centred nature of his identity is warranted by its engagement in effective action, and in being able to know itself and its environment in a way that leads to success. Through a sequence of acts of supremacy the epic hero advances step by step from dependence to autonomy: in a satisfying climax the paradigmatic male hero masters adversity – or at least goes down fighting. He is an agent, a doer; his existential homologue is a responsible adult.[5]

In his chapter on the syntax of seventeenth-century heroism in *Poetry, Language and Politics* (1988) John Barrell demonstrates the pragmatic use of syntax to instantiate a particular kind of male being. Thus in relation to Marvell he describes a syntax which 'asks to be read . . . as enacting the production of a particular kind of character, as enacting the process of a man producing his own identity in resistance to the circumstances that would, in a man less heroic, simply produce him . . .' (p. 57). John Barrell here helps me also to reinforce a crucial point: that narratives of male heroism are not addressed solely (as a schematic gender politics might assume) to men's imperial subjects. Crucially, they are also addressed to men: a constant and intimidating reminder of what you need to do to join the club of those who hold sway over destiny.

In exploring the subject of the relation between the male hero and the domain in which his success (or heroic failure) is won, I would like first to return briefly to the subject of flight. In the last chapter I identified the theme of flight, pointing out that, curiously, given the many stereotypes concerning male consistency and power over circumstances, flight is a recurrent motif in narratives about men. To deal with intolerable circumstances by escaping from them rather than confronting them may turn out to have more in common with the paradigmatic male life plot than we tend to think. At risk of concocting an inventory of overarching, non-historically specific themes, it is worth noting that our texts seem repeatedly to exhibit male protagonists not just on the move but escaping from threat, or fleeing into their own male kingdoms. The figure recurs in Lawrence, Conrad, Gordimer, McEwan, Kelman and Leavitt. From what are such heroes in flight? Domesticity and the family (the 'coming up for air' syndrome) constitute one possibility. We need, Graham Dawson argues, to investigate the relations between the manly world of adventure and the domestic and romantic domains. In this light he sees the 'adventure quest as a strategy for containment for underlying anxieties and contradictions, the key to which may be sought not only in the public world, but in the masculine relation to the domestic sphere' (1994, p. 75).

Thus the boyish tale of adventure, like *Huckleberry Finn*, thematises escape from a feminised enclave.[6] The tradition is still going strong in Updike's 'Rabbit' sagas. It seems there is a long-standing tradition deriving from the succeess of the Victorian male bourgeoisie in withdrawing its womenfolk from the labour market, of associating the angel in the house with conventional, boring, routine servitude. Perhaps the perception of such stifling domesticity is the reciprocal of that domain of calm and nurture, that oasis in a world of unbridled economic competition which someone like Ruskin saw it as woman's role to create within the private sphere. At all events, narratives of male individuation and growing up stress the need to escape both women and the feminised domain. Jane Tompkins (1992) has suggestively developed the idea of the adventure space in relation to the rise of the western after about 1900. We might speculate that flight is in a way the mirror image of quest, the penetration of an adventure world in search of an object or an adventure which will validate the hero's being. If so, then there are both negative and positive impulsions propelling the protagonist into the environment of the defining drama. At the same time, such an attempt to evade the feminine and the creatural may harbour its own bad conscience, and it is significant that E. Annie Proulx's recent recension of the narrative of male flight in *Postcards* (1992) fuses two of our themes, in having the story begin with the murder of a woman whose hastily buried body haunts the protagonist's attempts to escape into new identities and a new life. Read in terms of Bronfen's argument,[7] her novel suggests that the origins of a male attempt to produce an unconditioned culture (writing your postcards home) might lie in an act of aggression not just against the Oedipal father but against women (Bronfen, 1992).

I am suggesting, then, that the narrative of self-making may – at its broadest – be read not simply in terms of the desirability of the adventure world and of the identity to be forged through courageous exposure to that world, but in terms of another represented or implied world which the hero is evading and with which the adventure world is contrasted. This may variously be

the domestic world, the world of work, of the demands of relationships or of routine. If we recognise that, it is open to us readers
to make a perceptual shift, turning into a figure in its own right
the ground of normality against which the figure of heroic
adventure stands out. In highly schematic terms we might say
that the one domain is associated with a conditioned, dependent
and permeable identity, the other with an identity voluntary,
autonomous, and strongly bounded – in fact phallic.

Let us then start from the notion that the adventure world –
the narrative and its narrative environment – tempts both by reason
of what it stands for and by reason of the absence it represents.
Its plenitude is simultaneously a vacuum. In it, as in classical
epics like the *Odyssey* and the *Aeneid*, women and women's cultures
represent spoiling influences which must be prevented from
distracting the hero from his high enterprise. Whether as nurturers
or as seducers, women cannot appreciate that higher forces govern
masculine enterprise, and – even if they are enlisted on the hero's
side – are incapable of keeping secrets because their very propensity
for indulging in language makes them leaky vessels. When Mahbub
the horse dealer and secret agent explains to young Kim that 'it
is by means of women that all plans come to ruin, and we lie
out in the dawning with our throats cut', he is alluding to a
tradition which haunts patriarchal Western culture from the Book
of Proverbs to Ernest Hemingway. Knowing what communication
is appropriate to what circumstances, not grassing, keeping secrets,
is one of many signifiers of an achieved masculine identity and
of membership of the club. The narrator's disciplined and
authoritative control over the flow of knowledge models a widely
acceptable ethic. 'Do not give the vigour of your manhood to
women' (*Proverbs*: 31, quoted in *Kim*) is advice predicated on the
idea that manhood is a fluid substance (oddly similar to semen)
which will drain out if entrusted to the weaker vessel.

Triumphal phallic narratives, I suggest, are not achieved without
cost. We might question indeed whether the simplified phallic
agent is not the victim of a form of ritual mutilation. In these
terms this production of the triumphal hero with his impermeable
body boundary represents an act of cultural circumcision, the
violent cutting away of any trace of soft, enclosing periphery.[8]
Within the heroic perspective, strong boundaries characterise the
male, and the active male self-polices both inward and outward
movement across those borders. The male adventurer and the

adventure world have to be kept as pure as possible. Whatever unspeakability lurks beyond the margins of Marlow's story in *Heart of Darkness*, it cannot be communicated to the betrothed; indeed, such of the story as we are permitted to hear is communicated to a group of male friends. The possession of a grisly secret seals a social bond (Straus, 1987). To that extent the 'facts' of whatever Kurtz has been up to do not matter in the least: the intimidating absence in the middle of the narrative signifies that which may only be approached by those who possess effective inner discipline. Only those whose identities are built upon the necessary internal safeguards can be initiated into the domain of the narrative.

Let us follow up this theme by examining a relatively recent reworking of the narrative of male initiation in the form of Russell Hoban's novel *Riddley Walker* (1980). One context for this novel (as for Graham Swift's *Waterland*) is the proliferation of post-holocaust novels at that chilling stage in the Cold War (Connor, 1996, ch. 6; Schwenger, 1986). Another, however, may be the search for a domain sufficiently removed, sufficiently undomesticated to permit refloating the narrative of male initiation.[9] One advantage of the post-holocaust domain as a narrative environment is that (like other sensorily deprived spaces – space flight for example) it produces fewer obstacles to the fantasy of recreating culture from scratch. This is a kind of literary survivalism: a simpler, more basic society permits a fantasy of man as hunter and adventurer pitched both against nature and competitively against other men. As Schwenger notes, there is a 'recurrent masculine nostalgia for the idea of the male that is simpler, more physical, and larger than life' (1984, p. 102). Such a nostalgia for a mythic simplicity evidently informs the masculine revivalism of Robert Bly and is a feature of the renegotiation of gender attitudes Susan Jeffords has attributed to representations of the Vietnam war (Bly, 1991; Jeffords, 1989).

Hoban's novel can thus be seen in relation both to the simulation of simpler, heroic cultures (as for example in William Golding's *The Inheritors*), and more specifically to the reappropriation of masculinity in the USA from the late 1970s in response both to feminism and to humiliation in Vietnam. There is a fascinating parallel with the rise of the western as documented by Jane Tompkins (1992). The 'structural tactic of Vietnam narrative', argues Jeffords, is 'to create the illusion of a collective experience' (p. 25).

Reality is only available to readers if they participate in the consensus of narrators; 'being there' becomes the central exclusionary category. In the western, Tompkins argues, the violent masculine domain was an answer not only to the domestic novel but to the perceived feminisation of the public sphere in the late nineteenth-century USA (Tompkins, 1992; an earlier version is in Longhurst, 1989). In the western the feelings inspired by work are released from their usual circumstances and 'set in a locale and a set of circumstances that expand their meaning' (Tompkins, 1992, p. 12). Here, action 'saturates the present moment'. The western represents 'not a hunger for adventure but for meaning', a meaning which is guaranteed in a 'genre of death'. *Riddley Walker*, I suggest, represents Hoban's own 'genre of death'.

In the handed-down binary set, the opposition of word and deed are tinctured with a female/male opposition. The western, notes Tompkins, is 'at heart antilanguage' (1992, p. 50). Ambivalence towards the feminising word marks the lore of deeds.[10] Where languages figure in the male epic, they tend to be 'high', esoteric tongues. Hoban's compromise is to invent a dialect unique to his novel. Learning to read any novel is a matter of learning to read its language, and this process is foregrounded in a novel which operates in its own idiolect. To read *Riddley Walker* is to become an honorary speaker of a dialect of English unknown outside the community of readers of this novel. But in a number of other ways too this is a novel about cultural transmission and innovation. Riddley's adventures constitute Riddley not only as teller of his own tale (the world-historical individual in whom his oral culture has moved from a naïve into a self-conscious stage) but as the person whose role it is to assemble and turn into meaning the fragments which come his way. Idiosyncratic as the novel may appear, it is a powerful recreation for the 1980s of one particular masculine narrative. This narrative adheres to the traditional formulae of the male *Bildungsroman*: the loss of the father, exile from the relative comfort of your community, a journey whose rules seem to be established by the elders, a series of encounters, some helpful, some threatening, subsequently coming under the wing of powerful senior males who want to use you for their own purposes, finally emergence after a series of adventures as the reflexive agent of your own story.

At the same time, the environment of the narrative is in many ways as bleak and inhospitable as that of other voyages into an interior designed to test the mettle of the male protagonist (for example, Conrad's *Heart of Darkness*, or Patrick White's *Voss*). The narrative zone consists of a culture eking out an existence both physically and spiritually many hundreds of years after a nuclear exchange. This culture – which is ethnologically perched on the cusp between hunter-gathering and settled farming – draws heavily on fortuitously preserved fragments of the past, weaving them into its own stories and rituals. A vast amount of wreckage of the preceding civilisation is there to be dug up, and new fragments keep coming to light as teams of men sift through the dumps. It is on one of these work parties that Riddley's father is killed, and in the same pit that Riddley himself discovers the relics of the Punch and Judy show which figure so prominently in the story once he has been exiled from his tribe.[11]

The core thematic of the novel seems to have to do with making sense out of the wreckage and fragments of the dumps. To that extent that novel has a lot in common with its immediate ancestor, one of Hoban's books for children, *The Mouse and His Child* (1967). Both take their starting place from the dumps, and concern simultaneously the rubbish which a civilisation throws away or loses, and a male quest in search of integration. Only a growing man, it seems, can grasp the fragments and weld them back into a meaningful whole. This task is given to Riddley himself, both in his hereditary role as 'Connexion Man' (a sort of tribal shaman or seer), and in his role as one who finds fragments and deciphers truths. His difficulties and triumphs of interpretation are re-enacted by the reader struggling with his story. In the end Goodparley and Orffing, the representatives of power, are killed as a result of their own machinations, and there is nothing for Riddley to do but to take to the road with his Punch and Judy show to tell the truth as he sees it. As a bard and teller he is the one who can make sense out of the fragments which come his way. It is a form of heroism different from that of those who rely on their physical prowess. At an early stage in Riddley's alienation from his tribe, Fister accuses him of 'pontsing for the Ram' (the government), and adds 'Leave the telling to the women and connect with a mans doing'. Though Riddley subsequently murders Fister by throwing him into the dump (thereby sealing his own exile), he is himself identified throughout with verbal and interpretative rather than purely physical skills. Yet whatever message Hoban may have been intending to convey about the need for integration and for the abdication of male weapons, it is as though the memory of the epic plot of the man in a man's world has been too much for him. Even if Riddley is going to ascribe to it new, quasi-religious, meanings, the resurrected Punch and Judy show itself perpetuates an atavistic narrative of male domestic violence.

The last temptation of Riddley is to play his part in what is evidently an incipient arms race by abetting those who are trying to reinvent gunpowder. Goodparley tries to use him as a spy to capture the recipe:

I said, 'I don't want to know.'
He said, 'Eusas sake be you simpl or what? The way thingsre going it looks like every 1 in Inlands after the yellerboy and the knowing of what to do with it. Somewl have 1 and somewl have the other and somewl have the boath. And them what dont have nothin will be out of it.'
I said, 'Wel I ben out of it up to now enn I.' . . .
I said, 'The onlyes Power is no Power.' (p. 187)

As Riddley says disgustedly earlier 'Every body juicying for Power 1 way or a nother nor I dint want no part of it no mor' (p. 164). Yet, while foreswearing violent power, Riddley is nevertheless left holding cultural power, a power which is seen very much as masculine and wielded in a world where men have names and roles and women are almost invariably anonymous.[12] Above all, survival (both personal and cultural) is up to him, and though his domain is cultural – even spiritual – rather than military, he has in common with Rambo a personal heroism untarnished by the evasions or deceptions of governments or institutions. If his people are to be saved, it will be through lonely heroism.[13] Yet he has not been driven for ever into the wilderness. At the other end of his formative adventures lies another community which in a sense replaces the tribe of origin from which he has been driven. Riddley as seer and narrator creates around him a new tribe: a community of listeners united by their common interest in what he has to tell them.

Riddley's quest leads to his visit to Cambry, the ruin of Canterbury which is still vested in folklore with a spiritual significance and awe. It is the 'senter' upon which mythology and ritual depend. A pilgrimage to the centre confirms Riddley as himself a central figure to whom messages, like the Punch figure, come and by whom they may be interpreted. Throughout this study the location of the centre and the relations between centre and margins are going to be a recurrent if elusive topic. In the various narratives that form the subject of this book we shall see a variety of ways of defining the centre, and note a corresponding motif of displacement.

Many of the novels studied in this book provide us with representations of men who feel they are not where they ought to be but do not know what to do about it. In some cases the feeling is so strong that it militates against doing anything. The centre, the desirable and influential place to be, can be defined in ways that vary from novel to novel, but we shall find that some common themes concern proximity to the narrator's values, the capacity to be 'heard' by narrator or other significant characters, and approval by father or other powerful figures. We are talking about a place in a cognitive pantheon, a place that functions as a seat of norms in the novel even where, as with the metropolitan seats of empire in Conrad, those norms may be highly questionable. Though the novel may implicitly define a centre, there is a further question whether the protagonist actually wants to be in or near it. Many of our protagonists turn out to prefer to be somewhere else: an island, a remote farmhouse, in flight to the Alps, the flat, or the porno movie theatre. This constant negotiation over centrality has the effect of calling centrality into question, of deconstructing the centre – margin dichotomy. Is the centre after all vacant? And if it is, does that Nietzschean eventuality have different implications for men than it does for women? Does it give growing up a different shape? Has the last generation left you a mess of pottage? Or a collection of nihilistic maxims? If you are in flight, what are you in flight from? Even if the centre is actually vacant, the longing to be home at the centre of things remains a potent legacy of patriarchy to its sons, a legacy reinforced, as Bristow demonstrates, by the simultaneous legacy of imperialism.[14]

The desirability of the centre is a motive which paradoxically both heroes and villains have in common: as I suggested in the last chapter, villainy may – as with the Jacobean malcontent – be a way of short-circuiting the route to the position of centrality of which you feel yourself to have been unjustly deprived. The villain or his substitute is an alternative centre of norms within the text.

If you believe that by rights you should be at the centre, exclusion will seem all the more bitter. (A version of this narrative of exclusion is part of the stock in trade of that 1990s figure, the angry white male.) But the tradition of villainy is only one mutation generated by the dialectic between centre and margins. One of the effects of patriarchy is to create in its heirs the sense of a lack which they are never fully going to be able to make up.

NOTES FROM UNDERGROUND

While narratives of climactic assertion are common enough in the literature of empire and lead a prolonged life in popular fiction and film, the student of literature could be excused for assuming that ironic versions of male progress, or indeed male failures, constitute an enduring subject of texts characterised as literary. The villain is not the only figure in whose progress the dialectic of centre and margin is re-aligned. In this section I shall propose that narratives where male success is ironised provide a way of mapping the norms by contrast with which their own counter-narratives are told. It seems to me axiomatic that any narrative carries around with it the ghostly lineaments of the narratives it is not – the other narratives to which it alludes, and whose difference from it constitute part of its own meaning.[15] Joseph Heller's *Something Happened* (1974), for example, is a pretty pointless chronicle unless we assume that behind it lurks the trace of the tale of male success and self-determination that it itself is not. The anti-heroism of his *Catch 22* is only meaningful against the dual background of heroic war story and the patriotic idealisation of institutions. I shall orientate this investigation by briefly discussing a novella which in some ways might act as a paradigm, Dostoyevsky's *Notes from Underground* (1864, trans Jessie Coulson, 1972).

Writing about Hemingway, Peter Schwenger speaks of a stylistic search for solidity and self-containment, an attempt to become an object in order to evade your nature as a subject (1984, p. 54). By contrast, for many male writers the nature of the man as subject has been an enduring preoccupation. That search is dogged by the anxiety that the more the subject is developed as the site of an inner world, the less effective he will turn out to be in worldly terms – that chilling Carlylean misgiving we have seen at work in Conrad that self-consciousness and action are incompatible, that reflective mental activity leads to paralysis. However, the nameless narrative voice of *Notes from Underground* is resolutely preoccupied with his own subjectivity and obsessed with his own failings, all of them measured against what he supposes a man ought to be and achieve. The dialogic nature of his immersion in discourse spells his permeability to the meanings of others. As Bakhtin notes of him, it is as if 'interference, voices interrupting one other, penetrate his entire body, depriving him of self-sufficiency and unambiguousness' (1984, p. 235):

> After all, to tell a long story about how I missed life by decaying morally in a corner . . . losing the habit of living, and carefully cultivating my anger underground – really is not interesting; a novel needs a hero, but here all the features of an anti-hero have *purposely* been collected. (Dostoyevsky, *Notes from Underground*, p. 122)

As a solitary observer, the underground man envies the successful men he sees around him. But Dostoyevsky's underground man is not simply the representative of individual pathology. His position on the outside, his marginality, facilitates his role as a critic of forms of thought and structures of feeling which the Russian intelligentsia was beginning to import from western Europe. It is many years since John Carroll included *Notes from Underground* among the texts which mounted a critique of positivism and the scientistic belief in progress, and there is much in the thinking of the underground man that anticipates later assaults upon what a rather cavalier postmodern sociology now refers to as the 'enlightenment project' (Carroll, 1974). From the point of view of the present argument, what is significant is that these anticipations of Freud ('Where did all the sages get the idea that a man's desires must be normal and virtuous?' [p. 34]; '[A]fter all, perhaps prosperity isn't the only thing that pleases mankind, perhaps he is just as attracted to suffering' [p. 41]), this tirade against political economy, and against progress, is simultaneously a critique of the imperialism of 'normal' masculinity.[16] As David Trotter shows us, narrative identity can be built out of fear of the abject as much as out of desire, and Dostoyevsky's novella constitutes an inquiry into the figuration of masculine self-disgust (Trotter, 1996, for example, ch. 14 and throughout).

Though strictly we only 'hear' the voice of the underground man, this is, as Bakhtin has shown us, a highly dialogic narrative where others' voices are all the time embedded in the narration. The role offered to the narratee of this story is that of butt, the man over whom the speaker can achieve a simple dialectical victory, and the typical relationship the underground man sets up with his imaginary interlocutor is one where he pretends to believe that his listener is the sort of man who entertains all the usual clichés. By contrast, the speaker himself is by his own account singled out as simultaneously abject and visionary. Like any self-respecting member of an *avant-garde*, he thrives on shocking the bourgeosie. The rational and respectable male reader is the 'other' against which the underground man defines himself. 'I have been listening to these words of yours through a chink for forty years' (p. 44):

> I really was a coward and slave. I say this without shame. Every decent man in this age is, and must be, a coward and slave. That is his normal condition . . . [and] not only at the present time, but at all times, a decent man must be a coward and slave . . . Even if one of them puts on a show of bravery before some one else, he ought not to take comfort from that or let himself be carried away by it: he is only showing off to the other person . . . Only donkeys and mules make a show of bravery. (p. 48)

His contempt for bravery and for respectability simultaneously brings into question the straight male's successful fusion of public and private selves, the idea of a self all of whose attributes are harnessed to social ends, and all of whose motives are available to him for rational inspection: 'there are some things that a man is afraid to reveal even to himself, and any honest man accumulates a pretty fair number of such things. That is to say, the more respectable a man is, the more of them he has' (p. 45). Respectability depends upon the repression of the unrespectable; thus the existence and vitality of the unconscious becomes a stick with which to beat the (supposedly) uncomplicated exponents of manly straightforwardness. The disgusting is within.

The underground man's far-reaching critique of male rationality and the unitary, success-orientated male identity does not arise out of some free-floating metaphysical nausea. Dostoyesky's text gives it a fairly precise aetiology in the protagonist's frustrated longing for relationships with other men. A recurrent feature of his tale is a narrative concerning the attempt to form a relationship with another man, as for example the officer with whom and with whose unforced air of superiority he appears to be obsessed. His obsession takes the form of a long-drawn out rage that he finds himself repeatedly stepping out of the officer's way, and a desperate longing for the man to take notice of him. He goes to elaborate lengths in an attempt to get his own back and to force himself upon the officer's notice, an object in which he fails, as 'my darling officer' goes off to another posting still without having acknowledged the nameless man's existence (p. 58). The motif of attraction to the male caste of officers, and the attempt to force himself upon a man or group of men – even if necessary by fighting a duel – runs through the novella. The narrative foregrounds the desire to be close to other men, and to take part in their bonding rituals. Its protagonist has apparently not realised that conventional homosocial bonding requires him to sublimate his own homoerotic drives:

> I did once make a friend. But I was a tyrant at heart; I wanted unlimited power over his heart and mind, I wanted to implant contempt for his surroundings in him; I required of him a haughty and final break with them. I frightened him with my passion of friendship. (p. 69)

It is his exclusion from the influential male bond that fires the underground man's revenge, and that results in his relationship with the prostitute, a sequence of events arising directly out of his failed attempt to be sociable with men even at the expense of humiliation. In this Girardian triangle, the desirability of Liza is the by-product of her desirability to the men whom he both despises and admires. She is very much a second best, and will become the person to whom to export all the humiliation he has himself suffered at the hands of other men.

This textual figure, the male unravelling under his own gaze, recurs repeatedly in the twentieth century. In his fascination with his own degradation, the underground man's literary descendants include Amis's John Self (*Money*, 1984) and Will Self's Ian Wharton (*My Idea of Fun*, 1993). These narrative acts of self-consciousness are technologised as writing, or in *My Idea of Fun* as cinema:

Now I have become aware – as we all have – of the true Trinity.
God the Father, God the Son, and God the Cinematographer.
And so it is that I await the word rather than the flesh. For only
humungus titles, zipping up from the seam between the sea
and the sky, will convince me that I have really begun. (p. 18)

To contemplate the self, the underlying fantasy seems to suggest,
is to be compelled to tell the story of the self's own debasement:
the disgust once directed outwards upon a man's objects is taken
back within the boundary of the self to become – perversely – a
badge of pride, a sort of heroism of the abject:[17]

> The destruction of one's own image in another's eyes . . . as
> an ultimate desperate effort to free oneself from the power of
> the other's consciousness and to break through to one's self
> alone – this, in fact, is the orientation of the Undergound Man's
> entire confession. (Bakhtin, 1984, p. 232)

In this particular theatre of the masculine subject, a dialectic of
degradation passes back and forth between the self and its objects.
Threaded through the drama of abject manhood is the recurrent
theme of punishment, the expectation that punishment is indeed
central to its own claim to existence. This leads to the consequent projection upon the surrounding human environment of
a malign epic in which (in a reversal of the commonsense hierarchy) retribution invites corresponding transgression. In the final
section of this chapter I shall propose that some sorts of masculine narrative are constructed around the interrelated themes of
humiliation, punishment and revenge.

MORTIFYING THE FLESH

In the final section of this chapter I shall argue that male narratives, with their propensity to violent resolution, and so often
thought of as driven by aggrandisement and success, can as well
be driven by the fear of revenge and humiliation. My argument
will take a rather roundabout route. One recurrent dialectic to
which I have drawn attention in this book concerns the relationship between centre and margins. I would now like to draw
attention to an analogous dialectic between distance and proximity.

Masculine narratives, I have suggested, organise events in a way which permits the subject to move from dependence to autonomy. Such narratives both reinforce and promulgate a normative manhood characterised by a high degree of management over the calls the world makes upon a man's identity and inner resources. They are the narrative enactment of strong boundaries. The corresponding feminine position is one where the subject, having weak boundaries, is not permitted nearly the same level of control over the demands (either physical or emotional) placed upon her by others. We might thus characterise narratives and narrative subjects in terms of how far they adhere to an ideal either of proximity or of distance. To some extent that attraction towards either proximity or distance may also govern the overall shape of the narrative: an ideal of mastery exercised from a distance permits a higher degree of control over the disposition of events. In narratives, as in hierarchical institutions, 'top-down' organisation licenses inattention to the micro-processes of which social life is made up. These rather abstract binary terms proximity and distance can refer variously to the gap between the consciousness and somatic embodiment (real or inferred) of the subject, to the relation between the observer and his subject matter, or, again, and perhaps most obviously, to the dominant form of relations between hero and other narrative figures. In turn, this dialectic is likely to be reproduced in the relations between the text and its readers. Let me now try to put some flesh on these bare abstractions.

Earlier on, we saw that the underground man's attraction towards the prostitute Liza began in his ill-fated attempt to gate-crash the evening entertainment organised by a group of male acquaintances. His desire for their company and their recognition is side-tracked into desire for Liza once they succeed in evading him. Just as he has humiliated himself before them so he seeks to abject himself to her, and his abjection is based upon his own specular view of himself as a physical object. As Liza entered the room, 'I caught sight of myself in a mirror. My agitated face seemed to me repulsive in the extreme: pale, vicious, mean, with tangled hair. "All right, I'm glad of it," I thought; "I'm glad to seem repulsive to her; I like that"', (p. 85). He 'hates his own face,' says Bakhtin, 'because in it he senses the power of another person over him, the power of that other's evaluations and opinions' (1984 p. 235). But inasmuch as your face constitutes your passport to the social domain, it is not even necessary to like it yourself. Narcissistic pride in the revolting nature of the body is the structural complement of a belief in one's irresistible attractiveness. The underground man's conviction that he is repulsive means that his own body cannot be given as a gift to another: all he can do is to use it as a weapon to shock and repel, or even injure. At the same time he is obsessively drawn to his own flaws: his whole monologue – his art – results from a disgusted narcissism.[18]

At its most proximate, proximity equals intimacy. Intimacy is so threatening to the jealously bounded identity that the only way of coping with it is to retain intellectual and emotional distance even while physical intimacy is taking place. As the tale continues, Liza becomes the recipient of all the narrator's desire to hurt someone. With seeming reciprocity he lures her out from behind her own emotional defences in order the better to crush and humiliate her. That he has done so, of course, gives him all the more grounds to lavish narcissistic loathing upon himself. The unfortunate Liza has in fact got caught up in a drama not at all of her own making, a drama in which the underground man seeks to indulge both his furtive and revolted love of himself and his desire for proximity to other men. His only way of striking a blow for his own freedom from this in all senses vicious circle is by casting a woman in the role of object for revenge.

This rather nauseating plot is not confined to the pages of Dostoyevsky. It compels our attention precisely because of its endemic power to mould the male imagination. A potent strand in fiction provides us with a model of a man taking revenge upon women for the insults the world has heaped upon him. Like the narrator of Camus' *The Outsider* (another nameless underground man), the protagonist takes revenge through a form of inverted intimacy, a cruelty evidently reckoned as payment in kind for the vulnerability to which she has exposed him. The hero of Milan Kundera's novel *The Joke* (1967) takes his revenge (again through sexual humiliation) on the wife of the man who some years before got him expelled from the Party. While he fucks her (the word seems appropriate) he cannot resist marking out his own distance by reflecting upon how the male mind is apt to take flight from the act itself even while the body is engaged. The dialectic of proximity and distance could hardly be more clearly instanced, the former identified with the female and the latter – the ground of his freedom – identified with the male. From *Hamlet* to Will Self, this underlying narrative structure proposes that on the female body can be revenged the institutional oppression, the proud man's contumely, all the injustices to which a man has been or believes himself to have been subject. That intimacy leaves you open to invasion, leads to that 'taboo on tenderness' for which Suttie found a memorable formulation (1935, ch. 6).[19] One way of symbolically proving your invulnerability to yourself is to export vulnerability to someone else, preferably someone whom it is culturally acceptable to turn into a victim.

It appears, then, that one simple mutation of the narrative of masculine assertion is into revenge, a way of establishing a pure moral economy of the universe: justice can be obtained by making sure someone is made to compensate for the protagonist's own sense of being wronged. At the core of this homeostatic narrative, transgression is symmetrically balanced with an act of retribution, thereby re-establishing an equilibrium. As an agent of this reordering process, the protagonist of the male narrative turns all too easily into the loner, the maverick, the embittered hero returning to wreak revenge upon those who have humiliated him. At its extreme – and I am not here endorsing the pernicious stereotype about all men being natural killers and rapists – the narrative may underlie the punitive fantasy of the mass murderer. As men we have for too long colluded in allowing ourselves to be scripted by this archaic narrative of punishment and revenge. In the closing section of this chapter I wish to put forward a tentative argument linking the narrative of revenge and punishment to a conception of male identity.

One recurrent motif of masculine narrative is the desire to anticipate the vengeance of the universe by a pre-emptive strike. The victim role in the ensuing narrative is apt to move around, and may even gravitate towards the hero himself. (As suicide figures demonstrate, male violence is after all frequently directed against the self.) The male body, that hostage to vulnerability, when not veiled from sight by the high aspirations of spirit, offers itself as a target for violence.

Ambivalence towards the creatural domain may in fact result in self-immolation, the anticipation of the revenge of the universe by choosing your own time and place. Yet the identity cannot be defended against all eventuality, and the defences themselves may prove more of a liability than anything, an investment of energy which could perhaps have been better spent. Gerald Crich implodes within his armoured instrumentality.

One very specific locus for the narrative of vengeance is the Oedipal dialectic at work between the original and the copy. In Wilfred Owen's poem 'The Parable of the Old Man and the Young' the angel offers the old man a let out from the compact to sacrifice his son:

> But the old man would not so, but slew his son,
> And half the seed of Europe one by one.

Owen visualises an extreme where patriarchy may destroy its own heirs rather than either abdicate power or jeopardise its unmediated forms of reproduction. In doing so he locates vengeance within a relationship which we might see alternatively as that of father and son or of creator and created. For men have attempted to compensate for their inability to give birth by fabricating identities for themselves or for others. However, the creature so constructed is liable to play monster to the paternal Frankenstein, taking on a life that evades its creator, even turning into another enemy against whom to guard (Warner, 1994). Patriarchal norms pit father and son against each other in an armed stand-off, a cold war that perpetually threatens to turn hot. Brief attention to one more text will bring us to the end of this phase of the argument.

Iain Banks' novel *The Wasp Factory* (1984) has some affinities with *Riddley Walker*. Both share a preoccupation with animal totems, in both the narrator is a young person being initiated into adult life, and in doing so taking up the role of interpreter, reader of omens and signs.[20] Both heroes occupy in different ways an impoverished narrative environment in which they believe it is up to them to piece together a new culture. The novel also recalls our island theme, though this one is closer perhaps to the habitation of Dr Moreau than that of Axel Heyst. Frank and his father live on a private island connected by a bridge to the Scottish mainland. This island is a place where both have tried in different ways to project outwards their mutilated internal world upon a culture of their own devising. As much as any of the novels which we shall study in Chapter 6, *The Wasp Factory* concerns the nature and reproduction of masculinity as its performance and its signature in the masquerading male body.

Building on Neale's (1983) insight that violence perpetrated upon the male body derives from repressive homophobia, Peter Lehman has recalled us to the male body as material signifier. He argues that psychoanalytic debate about the relationship of penis and phallus has become obsessive:

> We may learn a great deal by reversing our attention and analyzing the representation of the penis rather than the theoretical purity of the phallus. If we do so, I think we will find the literal male body and the penis lost to us within the symbolic conception of the phallus. And it is lost to men as well as to women. Masculinity is not simply a position of power that puts men in comfortable positions of control. If we ignore studying images of the male body, we are likely to think of masculinity as an ahistoric, powerfully secure, monolithic position rather than one riddled with cracks. (1988, p. 108)

The male body and its vulnerability to abuse are the elements of Banks' drama. Importantly, its male body is – self-reflexively – a fabrication. The proto-culture of omens and grotesque violence which Frank stage-manages is seen by himself as a direct response to his own castration in childhood. In understanding himself as a male, Frank compensates for his mutilation by creating his own culture of ritual and violent death. I referred earlier to an 'erotics of vacancy'. As a way of imposing fantasy upon physical reality, violence can be construed as a means of ridding the physical world of its difference, of its dense local significance in order to impose upon it a tidy schematic order.[21] The island is available as an empty stage, upon which to act out gruesome retributive fantasies. When it subsequently turns out that 'he' is actually a woman and the subject of the father's experiment in disguising her true sex, Frank/Frances reflects upon the children s/he has murdered:

> Lacking . . . one will, I forged another . . . Having no purpose in life or procreation, I invested all my worth in that grim opposite . . . I believe that I decided if I could never become a man, I – the unmanned – would out-man those around me, and so I became the killer, a small image of the ruthless soldier-hero almost all I've ever seen or read seems to pay strict homage to . . . Believing in my own great hurt, my literal cutting off

from society's mainland, it seems to me that I took life in a sense too seriously, and the lives of others, for the same reason, too lightly. The murders were my own conception; my sex. (p. 183)

Self versions have, as Wetherell and Potter remind us, pragmatic force in the world. (1989, p. 207) Here at the end of the novel the narrative voice re-assumes the role of authoritative commentary. Its account of the forging of violent, vengeful masculinity still privileges castration as the origin of the determining 'male' narrative. This is a catch 22, a double bind: Banks' brilliant, gruesome novel both deconstructs and returns to the obsessive power of the Oedipal drama as the source at once of narrative and of masculine identity.[22] At the end of the day, the novel still turns upon a final climactic revelation about masculinity.

There are now many voices calling on us to cease privileging castration and the Oedipal drama as the central cultural formation. Such a move is implied throughout Elisabeth Bronfen's deeply challenging book *Over Her Dead Body* (1992). At the end of his essay 'Fictional Fathers', having explored the paradoxical role of the Freudian father in *Totem and Taboo* where he both triumphs and is defeated, Jon Cook expresses a wish 'to have done with fictional fathers, with that whole tradition of figuring the father as a monster or god.' (1988, pp. 161–2) More recently, in an endearing rhetorical move, Judith Butler refers to the paternal law as a 'perpetual bumbler' (1990, p. 28). Or – to take one more instance – Kaja Silverman explores in detail texts which dramatise 'suspension of masculine belief in the dominant fiction and its injurious binarisms – the refusal to project castration onto the corporeality of the sexual Other, and thereby to secure the phallus as the unquestioned signifier of power, privilege, and wholeness' (1992, p. 388).[23] Seen in this light Banks' narrative is both a diagnosis and a confirmation of the masculine dialectic and the ensuing attempt to export inner horror to the outside world, by making the environment party to the drama of male self-purification.

Even a rhetorical strategy aimed at questioning phallic supremacy, it seems, is liable to be re-absorbed into its own myth. Masculinity hugs to itself the narcissistic wound as a guarantee of its own superiority. Frank/Frances, like the underground man, or the captain in 'A Smile of Fortune', is another example of the dispossession represented by the exclusion from phallic supremacy signified by namelessness. Though she actually has a name, its instability is represented in its uncertain location between masculine and feminine variants. He/she is absent from the record, never registered, with no birth certificate. To that extent he/she is a concoction of her father's, as much as her violent landscape is a concoction of her own. (Or for that matter both of the author's.) Shuffling around with his stick, father, the old trickster, is an ersatz Oedipus who has resolved his own predicaments by trying to create himself a mutilated son in place of a daughter. In turn, his monstrous creation passes on revenge to those weaker than herself who cross her path.

Masculine narratives constitute persuasive systems on which men can draw both for models of identity and models of the sort of lives they expect to lead. While such narratives are by nature heterogeneous, one dominant strand concerns the exercise of authority over self, world, and relationships. The selfhood which is its exemplary protagonist subjects others to its controlling vision, and possesses boundaries secure against infiltration from without. As Rutherford, speaking about the 'solitary male hero', puts it: 'In the absence of sufficient internal boundaries men must substitute them [sic] with external action and control. What is an attempt to hold on to a sense of self is translated into an attempt to master others' (1992, p. 130).

That self moves on an upward trajectory, maturing inwardly through a parallel process to that by which it develops power over its segment of the world. However, as we have seen, this authenticating narrative breeds its own shadows, and can never adequately guard against the threats posed by impurity or diversity. It can never fully overcome the seductive attraction of its own objects, or evade the disintegration resulting from dispersing itself among them. Insistence upon stable unitary identity is a direct outcome of the fear of disintegration represented by the lure of intimacy with other objects. The gruelling symbolic work of producing the male as complete and invulnerable hero is never finished.

One simple way of summarising the argument attempted here is to say with those feminist critics (for example, Butler, 1990) who are engaged in debate with Lacan that no one possesses the phallus. Phallic superiority is a phantasm, an order of aspiration, not an empirical reality. So Banks' text concerned the drama of fabricating a male, a drama scripted by the father. Behind the father stood the figure of the male novelist, and in front, and as it were to one side, the male reader. In the next chapter we shall take a different approach to the theatre of male construction by studying two novels where the male subject is disoriented by the reader's knowledge that the father of the text is in fact a woman.

5

Male Impersonators

Gender ought not to be construed as a stable identity or locus of agency from which various acts follow; rather, gender is an identity tenuously contructed in time, instituted in an exterior space through *a stylized repetition of acts*. The effect of gender is produced through the stylization of the body.

(Butler, 1990, p. 140)

If the pen is a metaphorical penis, with what organ can females generate texts?

(Gilbert and Gubar, 1979, p. 7)

'Whole sight; or all the rest is desolation' announces *Daniel Martin*'s narrator in vatic mode, anticipating as he does so the privilege attached in his novel to sight among the senses (John Fowles, *Daniel Martin*, p. 7). One of the problems Daniel finds most intractable as he contemplates the project of writing the novel of his life is how to get inside a woman's experience (p. 430). To carry out his project, he needs to know what sort of thing a woman knows, what the inner life of a woman feels like. This is indeed for him beyond the limits of sight. At the same time, it is of course the kind of manoeuvre to account for which humanistic accounts of the novel have always drawn on the plenitude of 'imagination': the idea of a faculty which would permit the exceptional being in whom it was well developed to leap the narrow confines of time, space, or gender so as to empathise with another's experience, however different that experience might initially appear from their own.

One of the functions of the novel has traditionally been held to be to extend the imaginative range and sensitivity of its readers. Imaginative empathy has repeatedly been invoked to account for

134

those frequent occasions on which male novelists have preoccupied themselves with a female protagonist. Some of the most famous novels in English and in other European languages have taken this course: Flaubert's *Madame Bovary*, Tolstoy's *Anna Karenin*, Fontane's *Effie Briest*, Hawthorne's *Scarlet Letter*, James' *Portrait of a Lady*, Hardy's *Tess of the d'Urbervilles*, Roddy Doyle's *The Woman Who Walked into Doors*, to name but a few. The manoeuvre has been less common the other way round. Women novelists have been much less forward in volunteering to speak for men's experience. Or perhaps, as Jane Miller puts it, women 'have always written about men, but they have needed to be extremely circumspect about doing so. To read as a woman is to confront that circumspection as a mode of being and a kind of language, which can be powerfully subversive and potentially revolutionary' (1986, p. 9).[1] In this chapter we shall explore the construction of gendered being from an oblique angle: by looking at two novels written by women, Christina Stead's *The Man who Loved Children* (1940), and Nadine Gordimer's *The Conservationist* (1974), which either represent male consciousness or at least give a close-up and detailed account of a male protagonist. In doing so I hope to be able to unpick some tangled but central issues about masculinity and the gendering of representations. My choice of novels is at the same time a conscious allusion to another set of homologies: the complex cultural relations explored by post-colonial criticism. The provenance of both novels is 'post-colonial' in an accepted sense, and both constitute acts of 'writing back' to metropolitan norms, in doing so appropriating the terrain of masculine self-articulation.

Before going further, some more theoretical ground-clearing seems to be necessary. The whole subject of novelistic cross-dressing is fraught with difficulty. For example, the underlying argument of this book – that representations and reader positions are constructed, not natural – would seem to call into question whether the actual sex of the author mattered in the least. Indeed, might not focus on the actual sex of the author open a door to that kind of essentialism which this book sets out to question? Nor of course is this the only theoretical position from which to dispute the relevance of the author's biological (or for that matter historical) reality to the texts which bear his or her name. Repeatedly in the twentieth century the relevance of knowledge about the author to knowledge about the text has been disputed, often for good reasons. (For example, as an antidote to that kind of discussion which reduces the text to an unmediated transcription of the author's biography or neuroses.) The theme was as much part of the various formalisms of the first half and middle of the century as it was of the 'death of the author' vogue of the 1970s.[2] On a parallel track, historians have tended to play down the influence of 'great' individuals in favour of broader social and economic movements. Historicists have shown how the subject positions of 'individuals' may be constructed by social and discursive circumstances, and put forward the scandalous proposal that individualism itself was a temporary historical phenomenon. In turn, postmodernist thinkers warn us against treating 'experience' as an unmediated category, the absolute possession of the autonomous and self-contained individual. At the end of the day, any account of the text as a weave of codes, or as the product of linguistic and cultural practices, is bound to diminish the significance of the individual author.

In this chapter I am not calling for a return to some notion of the supreme imaginative autonomy of the individual author released from biological or historical conditioning. Authors write, as individuals live, under determinate conditions, and their texts are published, distributed and read as a result of complex and frequently contradictory institutional mediations. Secondly, I am not proposing a return to an essentialist notion of gender (masculinity and femininity as sets of universal and internally coherent characteristics instantiated in their entirety by any man or any woman). However, the serious defect of the formalist position (at least as adopted in mainstream Anglo-American literary criticism in the 1940s and 1950s) was its naïvety about its own assumptions: curiously, the impersonality of the author and the priority accorded to the words on the page almost always favoured texts by men, and went along with a canon whose advocates unabashedly overlooked the implicit theories upon which it rested. If the sex of the author really did not matter, it was to say the least statistically surprising that all the authors who were taught at A-level or in higher education (bar the occasional Austen, Brontë, Eliot, or Woolf) turned out to be men. Formalism favoured male hegemony, though whether that was a historical coincidence, or (as I am inclined to suspect) because of an inherent masculinist bias within formalism, remains to be seen. At all events, to be a student of literature was to be socialised into an educational world where male texts (and male teachers) were the norm. It was of course for this reason that feminist scholars, publishers and teachers from around 1970 onwards made a point not only of recuperating lost woman authors, but also of seeking to redevelop the curriculum both in higher education and in schools so as to represent a higher proportion of women's texts, conveniently defined as texts by women authors. Knowledge about the author was fundamental to this enterprise, and the determination and perseverance of women authors as they struggled against adversity was held up as a role model for women readers and students – and in turn for a new generation of women writers.

One solution for this book would simply be to adopt the reciprocal position: that the fact a novel is by a man matters because the fact itself explains features of the text's style or subject matter. There may be textual features which are attributably masculine. But if you can tell by careful reading whether a text is by a man or a woman (and there have been some nasty surprises lurking) what happens to this case? Does it not become circular? What about those stereotyped, stylised genres – Restoration Comedy, some forms of journalism, or romantic fiction are examples – where the genre itself is so formulaic that any one might learn to do it? There seems to be a dead end here. Let us return to the argument implicit in this book that readers can and do learn to read 'as a man' or 'as a woman'. This, as we have been seeing, is in part brought about through the discourse of the text, and the subject positions it offers the reader, in part through educational and intellectual practices. This process is also asymmetrical in the sense that while women have commonly been acculturated into reading as men, on the whole men have not been acculturated into reading as women.

They have however also had to learn to read as men. That is to say that reading as a man does not come naturally to men either, anymore than do playing video games, spitting in the street, or homicidal driving habits. There is no straightforward masculine position which someone could unerringly or instinctively adopt without prolonged cultural apprenticeship. Reading practices are learned, and one of the objects of this book is to propose that men too can learn to re-read their heritage. Into this argument fits the question of women writing men.

I am going to propose, in short, that our knowledge about an author (however minimal or impressionistic) unavoidably leaks into how we read. And as one of the first things that we want to know about people is whether they are female or male, that knowledge (with all the attached presuppositions) becomes part of the framework within which we read. Part of our relationship to a text is our relationship to our idea of the author. Thus the gender of the author matters, if for no other reason than because if the reader does not know, she or he will make it up. As Scholes points out, we do read 'as if', and we all make attributions as we read (1987, p. 205). The inferencing work that readers carry on extends to inferences about the author and the character of the author. Our consciousness that some one called Grace Paley or Edith Wharton wrote the novel we are reading is part of what we know about it, and tinctures our reading experience. If the name of the author presents a blockage to commonsense, if we know (or believe) that a representation of a man's consciousness was written by a woman, that knowledge reframes how we read that text, however much we might in the name of formalist conscience want to bracket off the author from our mind. An author who ventriloquises a member of the opposite sex forces us to re-examine our assumptions about the relations between text and the author's experience. Thus I shall in this chapter adopt the working hypothesis that for our purposes the (supposed) sexual identity of the author does after all matter. The value of the hypothesis is heuristic: it will be established if at all through the insights it enables.

There is a reciprocal in the attention recently given to the phenomenon of male authors writing female protagonists. The point now is not to criticise them for an unwarranted intrusion into feminine experience, but to ask what the attempt means. For a man to take on the part of a woman cannot be a culturally neutral act, just another helping of evidence for the polymorphousness of imagination. The act of doing so is conditioned by the cultural weight attaching to the figure of the male author, by his own and others' consciousness of his gender identity, and by the traditionally subordinated position of the woman. So such a choice, even if taken ostensibly in women's interest (and out of whatever psychic compulsions of the author's own), is akin to an act of colonisation. The specular male gaze crosses the threshold of sight and actually penetrates its object.[3] If a woman takes the much more unusual step of deciding to write 'as though' she were a man, that act too demands attention, though because of the differentials of cultural power it is not symmetrical. In terms of the argument of this book, attention to the results may help us to define further what is meant by representations of men, about the elements of masculinity, and what kind of relations are proposed between masculine text and reader. As Showalter (1986) has pointed out, a lot of male experience may be visible to women precisely because it is couched in the dominant discourse. Or, in Miller's terms, women have always had to be bilingual. What in textual terms does a woman have to do to produce the illusion of writing as a man? What are the necessary representational moves? What codes does she need to employ? Inevitably, a formative tension is set up between the implied author and the narrative voice.

For a male author to write his way into a woman may be seen as an act of colonisation. Conversely, the woman writing her way into a man may be engaged in an activity which has much in common with post-colonial rewriting of traditional power relationships. Just as the exploration of liminality has characterised much 'post-colonial' writing, so these are male narratives reread through the lens of marginality. There are strong parallels between reframing the relations between the former colony and the metropolis and realigning the relations between women and patriarchy.[4] As indicated above, both the novelists whom I have chosen to explore in this chapter emerge from post-colonial environments. The entry of their novels into the realm of novels in English parallels their entry into male experience. Both have been read as part of that new curriculum alluded to above. Both seek to understand not just the power of the oppressor, but how that power is enacted through the rhetorical self-construction of influential male figures. They are interested, I believe, not in character as a given, but in the linguistic and cultural practices through which a man develops and maintains his social power, consolidating an identity as he does so. The polymorphousness of the narrative body acts as a constant reminder that no one naturally possesses the phallus; that apparently stable and authoritative gender identities are constructed like fictions. To purloin a term given currency by Joan Riviere, we are here dealing with masquerade (1929).

THE MAN WHO LOVED CHILDREN

The Man Who Loved Children sets squarely in front of us from its title onwards the relations between the generations, and the figure of a man (like Gordimer's protagonist, a kind of conservationist) whose life project is to mould the future through both biology and culture. At the end of the novel his failure is more evident than his success.

My starting place must be the nature of the text we are dealing with. The initial point concerns the nature of the reading experience which *The Man Who Loved Children* elicits. I believe that, while in some ways *The Man Who Loved Children* has a more conventional structure than *The Conservationist* (for example, in following a linear plot and 'natural' time order), a lot of its features are directly relevant to our purposes. We are confronted with a text that defies formalist purity or internal organisation. This novel is quite definitely not in the highly-crafted Flaubertian or Jamesian tradition. Read in the light of conventional aesthetic norms, the text displays many of the features of an unedited draft: hyper-abundance, repetition, the piling up of parallel scenes, frenetic shifts of point of view. The plot lurches from climax to climax. The reader, like the family member, can never be sure that some apparently ordinary scene, some harmless festivity, will not erupt in high emotional drama. I want to argue that in this novel redundancy has its own semantic force. The sheer volume of rhetoric – generated by Sam Pollitt or in response to Sam – which the novel throws at you is in itself significant, and plays a crucial role in establishing the novel's relations with its readers. It is actually through this hyper-abundance that the novel enacts its own themes. By the same token this feature of the text is difficult to illustrate. Its mode of operation does not lend itself to being economically pinpointed. Exemplification would demand further repetition – more quotation than there could be room for here. The reader has to protect him or herself against this onslaught. So one takes on something of the same role as Sam's daughter Louie, as she tries to defend herself against her father's ubiquity, his prying, his knowingness, righteousness, inexhaustible monologue. There are parallels with reading Lawrence: in the absence of reliable textual boundaries, readers, like daughters, need to establish their own.

The invasive process of this text sets in motion a transference, a form of relatedness that re-enacts its own family dynamic.[5] The Pollitt family theatre continues off the page. While inevitably the reader knows that a process of selection has been at work, the discourse of the text constantly insinuates the superfluity of original oral material over aesthetic and literary secondary process. In turn, the refusal of the narrator as editor to impose her literary control upon the material is itself a political choice. To seek to dominate the material through aesthetically motivated selectivity would be to enter into patriarchal competition and rivalry for mastery with the great Sam himself, to try to play him at his own game.

An examination of the discursive procedures of the text leads me to the transferential relations that it establishes. The politics of the Pollitts are sustained through the pragmatics of reading as much as through referentiality. Stead's textual proliferation does more than simply *represent* the Pollitt family: it reproduces its inescapability, the self-perpetuating quality of its conflicts. This is a text whose main communicative resource taps the semiotic potential of everyday living. In turn, the master trope of the novel is that of the family, towards which all signifiers point. At the core is what Louie, in a melodramatic moment, calls 'the horror of everyday life' (p. 410). The protagonists themselves are adept at reading oppressive sign systems. From near the beginning of the novel it is made clear to us that their shambling house and untidy garden constitute both lexicon and syntax for the relationships lived within it. The lexical items of furnishings and contents of house and garden are strung together in a familial syntagm.

At the beginning of the novel, Henny comes in from town:

> she would sit with her glances hovering round the room, running from dusty moulding to torn curtain frill . . . considering each well-known item . . . she belonged to this house and it to her. She and it were her marriage. She was indwelling in every board and stone of it: every fold in the curtains had a meaning . . . Cells are covered with the rhymes of the condemned, so was this house with Henny's life sentence, invisible but thick as woven fabric. (pp. 44–5)

In an exact homology to Tohoga House (and, later on, Spa House), the text becomes a woven fabric of life-sentences. The role offered the consenting reader is to become an honorary member of the Pollitt family in learning to read the language of their signs. This process reproduces the socialisation process that members of the family themselves undergo. Sam, as the dominant speaker of this language, is offered not only as a text to be read in his own right (the text glosses his language for us), but as an interpreter, someone who strives to impose his reading upon events, the narrator's rival for the position of explainer and judge. Despite the critique which the narrator mounts, the discourse is nevertheless constantly attracted back into his point of view. His tireless pedagogic zeal is at once a form of communication and a form of meta-communication, an attempt to impose on all around him rules by which to interpret what they see and hear. Faced with recalcitrant text, he descends to blustering and threats. A telling example is the incident of Louie's diary (p. 366 *et seq.*).

Sam, who mocks 'poickry and poicks' (for example, p. 430) entertains a positivist model of language. In a scientifically ordered world, it is implied, signifiers and signifieds would be neatly aligned with each other. True to form, he assures Louie (his daughter by his first, romantically remembered wife, and thus in his eyes his channel to true womanhood) that he communicates with her by telepathy, has always since she was a baby been able to read her thoughts.[6] Typically, he is drawn to the idea of a medium of communication against which the supposed interlocutor can maintain no barriers, a medium based upon a fantasy of an ur-language which evades creatural constraints. No corner of Louie's consciousness (according to this fantasy) is safe from the possibility of penetration. She reacts to this assertion with disbelief, and in the argument that ensues, Ernie, her half-brother, reveals the existence of her diary, and fetches it for Sam to read. Sam is, of course, pruriently delighted with this find, and insists on playing to the other children by making the hideously embarrassed Louie translate it out loud from the code in which she has written it. For Sam, part of the amusement value of this is provided by her naïve ideas about reproduction, which (ironically given his persistent lecturing on biological subjects) he has been too embarrassed to explain to her.

The incident stands as a model of the communicative dynamics of the novel. Sam is floored by the fact that his daughter has taken refuge in a language from which he is excluded (the reverse of his telepathic fantasy), and to get his own back he then seeks to manipulate the other children ('his smiles reflected on all the little mirrors round him' [p. 369]), into becoming the audience for a drama in which he will demonstrate to them all his power over her. In this he fails, and is reduced to playing for her sympathy with his recurrent story of how he strives for the good of all, his primary narrative of which he is always the hero and centre of pathos. Symptomatically, it is a story couched in the idea of speaking an unimpeded universal language. Sam's theories will be propagated orally in a way that transcends the divisions of language:

> we both believe that good is paramount and will spread through the nations, perhaps through the help of the radio. I always said that a second Christ could arise with the radio, speaking to all mankind – though for that we need the universal tongue and not cranky Frongsay and guttural Deutsch. (p. 371)

While he lectures her, she is bent over writing notes:

> Shut up, shut up . . . I can't stand your gassing, oh what a windbag.

Hurt and vengeful, his recourse is as usual to overt emotional blackmail. Louie proposes that she needs to be on her own. If she left home, he retorts, he would blame her stepmother:

> I would put all the blame on her shoulders for driving you from home . . . I have always fought for the sanctity of my home. Do you want me to blame her? (p. 373)

The incident encapsulates the way in which in *The Man Who Loved Children* the story of paternal power is told as a story of language and rhetoric strung between the opposite poles of penetrative universality, and resistance through textuality. Patriarchy, Stead suggests, operates through colonising the mental space of others. Its struggle to maintain its legitimacy against the forces which threaten to undermine it is re-enacted for others in their own struggle to resist its intrusion. Sam's need to warrant his own identity leads to a failure to recognise the difference of others, Louie in particular:

'You will be all right, Looloo . . . you are myself; I know you
cannot go astray.'
'I won't be like you, Dad.'
He laughed, 'You can't help it: you are myself.' (p. 164)

Sam may be an extreme example, but his model for language
and education is one which (like a developed capitalist economy)
promotes free trade oblivious of the fact that weaker economies
cannot prevent its more highly developed industry from flooding their markets. The motor of the plot is the struggle of others
– Henny and Louie in particular – to resist this cultural imperialism. Louie's persistent attempt to defend her boundaries leads
to the final disaster of the plot.

Throughout this book I have been concerned with the paradigms for the relationship between consciousness and material
world built into or problematised in male narratives. I have wanted
to find a way of defining the praxis of being a male in relation
to the biological and somatic domain. Biology as an interven-
tionist form of knowledge is foregrounded in *The Man Who Loved
Children*. Sam's self-chosen role as universal educator rests upon
his own professional practice as a biologist working for the US
Federal Government.[7] His knowledge of ecology and natural
history constitute a predominant element in the fabric of the novel,
and are the cornerstone of his mission to educate both his family
and the rest of the world. The text raises awkward questions about
the relationship between ecological awareness and the means
chosen to propagate that enlightenment, questions which half a
century later still face the green movement. Sam's drive to convert
and to achieve a rational world through the spread of scientific
principles, environmental awareness, radio, and a universal
language lead him to the brink of fascism. Indeed, in his espousal
of eugenics and ethnic hygiene, over the brink.

Despotism, the novel seems to suggest, is compatible even with
principles in many ways admirable, and the channel connecting
the two is the pedagogues's self-characterisation as the hero-victim
of his own narrative. Sam's power over his family and those who
come in contact with him resides in his didacticism and his capacity
to script, direct, and act out his own dramas, turning those around
him variously into co-actors and enthralled audience. To that extent,
he has features in common with the artist figures of Chapter 2.
He is represented as a source of perpetual semantic abundance,

an artist of the tongue. His fertility is enacted in spoken language and his rhetorical hold over others. But, as I suggested above, it is not coincidental that his domain is biology and ecology, rather than, say history, or economics. For it appears that his knowledge of biology is predicated upon a compulsion to annexe the domain of reproduction as his own. In this novel 'Sam' is the name for a discourse which strives after an impossible fusion between biology and language. There is more to this than the reworking of biographical themes.

One way of accounting for the ubiquity of Sam and the depth of affect invested in the Pollitt story is through biography.[8] At the same time, Stead has found a way of forging her narrative register in the public domain, and it is there that we must enquire into the meaning of this constellation of biology, language and pedagogic overkill. Margaret Atwood, too, had a biologist for a father, and he is transmuted into the fathers in novels like *Surfacing* and *Cat's Eye*. But a comparison between *The Man Who Loved Children* and *Cat's Eye* would show that the field of forces constituted by the triangle father – biology – children has a different force in each novel. Sam's science, the former novel seems to announce, despite being grounded in a passionate love of the natural world, is a mode of control, a hyperbolic exaggeration of the enlightenment project of taming the world through scientific knowledge. His children, like Elaine and her brother, will grow up with a marvellous knowledge of plants and animals. Simultaneously, the natural world will figure as a central code of both novels. But Sam's project is of an imperial nature.

Emerging from this study of 'women's men' seems to be a common thread to do with the Baconian proposition that knowledge is power. More precisely these novels constitute their own problematic upon the contradictory dynamics of knowledge (specifically here biological knowledge) as socially constituted and reproduced. Such knowledge is, so to speak, both cognitive and pragmatic: simultaneously power over nature and power over other people. Power over others works both through exclusion and initiation. I shall try to define this more clearly by anticipating the discussion of *The Conservationist*.

Mehring's sense of superiority over the land and its other inhabitants is reinforced by his access to ecological knowledge. In his own eyes, his knowledge legitimates ownership (and makes him 'the conservationist' of the title). For example, surveying the farm after the fire he wonders: 'Will the willows ever be the same again? They think if the lands are saved no damage has been done. They don't understand what the vlei is . . .' (p. 97). Just as Mehring's knowledge confirms his belief in the inadequacy of the knowledge possessed by the blacks, Sam's knowledge grants him a superior hold over biology in all senses – a domain in which were it not for his 'science' women might outpace him. Women, he fears, have access to secrets from which he would be excluded were it not for his superior knowledge. To make this point is not by implication to deny men any rights in the matter of biological knowledge, nor to fall back into claiming a mysterious precedence for women in the somatic domain. Rather it is to note that Sam's science colonises biology for the purposes of aggrandisement and the colonisation of somatic territory. The counter-knowledge represented by the narrator is torn between admiration (quoting Sam at enormous length, even to supplying glosses on his Uncle Remus vocabulary), and vigorous critique. Central to that critique is the case that the knowledge he represents is based on the same magisterial distancing from the object that we have seen characterises the male knower as hero: '[N]ever an experiment in chemistry or physics did he perform . . . but only talked with tender abstraction of "great lives" and "great chemists"' (p. 379). Biological knowledge in Sam's hands is a way of having access to reproduction and the inner space of others without extending reciprocal rights to others: knowledge as child abuse.[9] It is a knowledge which, while defending its subject against his disgust and shame at sexuality, is redolent of the Foucauldian account of surveillance:[10]

> he was full of the mysteries of female adolescence . . . He poked and pried into her life, always with a scientific, moral purpose . . . Her speech according to his genteel ideas was too wild, too passionate, too suggestive . . . His nice Louisa . . . intended for the holy life of science, he could see . . . was a burning star, new-torn from the smoking flesh of a mother sun, a creature of passion. (pp. 340–1)

He was

> becoming more horrified each day as Satan's invisible world was revealed to him . . . With the proper training and carefully watched . . . and kept in touch with pure adult minds, she would

pull through ... He would be her constant companion: they would communicate thoughts ... With mental lip-licking, he followed her in her most secret moments.

The Man Who Loved Children enacts a paradigm of knowledge as theatre. That theatre is constituted by the family, whose dynamics cannot simply be described as emotional: at the same time they concern forms of knowledge and access to knowledge. We can read the novel as a parable which goes beyond the account of a local pathology, one dysfunctional family: our attention is drawn to the pun on Pollitts/politics in the text itself, and this household is resonant of a larger economy. The novel figures in this book because its drama concerns masculinity, not as a stable and universal substance, but as produced and producing itself under determinate conditions. Biological knowledge is only one (though important) element in the construction of Sam. We must briefly examine the ongoing performance in which the family actors are caught up.

THE POLITICS OF THE FAMILY

The Man Who Loved Children is a novel devoted to the drama and politics of the family. Sam plays a crucial part in this drama, dramatising himself and attempting to script the drama for the rest of the family. His didactic voice is as pervasive in the novel as it is in his family. It is a voice characterised by consciousness of audience, doing all the voices, putting on his own 'childish' speech, above all performative. The narrative is well aware of Sam as act: 'Now the children had no need of a Punch-and-Judy show as their gifted and possessed father went through his antics' (p. 144). Showmanship is a form of power, and Sam's never-ending act is a mode of control over his family:

> by almost imperceptible noises Sam could tell that everyone was awake now, listening ... 'Womey, Womey, c'mon, c'mon, giddap for your pore little Sam.'
> Evelyn giggled. He heard it all right and insisted, 'C'mon, Womey: come on: do my head, come scratch my head. Come, do m'head: do m'yed, do m'yed.' ... His voice had fallen to the lowest seductive note of yearning. (pp. 62–3)

He is at his most typical at the centre of an activity, whistling and calling the children together, organising his tribe into work gangs, emitting a perpetual stream of whimsical commentary. Another aspect of all this is Sam's persona as another child, enacted in his pretend childish language. In terms of the subject of this book, Sam's enthusiasm for donning a child persona is one of the most important things about him, and one which gives us pause. For Sam both wants to be a child among children and simultaneously to exercise cultural and spiritual power over them. In doing so, he becomes that menacing figure, the adult male child, with disastrous results for those around him. Here is a model of the family as a private theatre in which the actor father can tirelessly re-enact before a captive audience the drama of the 'marvellous child' (Gunn, 1988, ch. 2), a role in which authority resolves into the capricious exercise of power when things fail to go his way.

Late on in the novel, Henny 'saw her husband for the first time: she had married a child whose only talent was an air of engaging helplessness . . .' (p. 336). The figure of the adult male child, the man who refuses to grow up, recurs in fiction often enough to suggest that the phenomenon is one which troubles Western cultures: the figure is the structural opposite of the autonomous and authoritative identity towards which the male is expected to aspire. At one end of a continuum he may be a childlike figure, an innocent whose refusal to be tarnished by the corruption and compromises of the world which interested parties glibly deem to be 'adult' is a standing reproach to those who have sold out their innocence and childlikeness. Examples would be Dickens' Tom Pinch (*Martin Chuzzlewit*), or Dostoyevsky's Alyosha in *The Brothers Karamazov*. Often, however, the figure is represented as something much more sinister, a figure like Harold Skimpole (*Bleak House*) or Old Dorrit, who uses the pretence of inaptitude for survival in a sordid world so as to exploit the gullibility, good nature, and resources of others. William Dorrit's pathos, remarks Jon Cook, 'becomes his privilege' (1988, p. 150). Men who exploit their 'loveable' innocence and incompetence turn up in many novels. This is a figure to which we shall return in discussion of *Child in Time.*

There is a point to clarify here, since it has become part of the conventional wisdom that men need to be more in touch with their child selves. This notion has joined the complementary belief that men ought to be better at expressing their emotions. Reflection on Christina Stead's Sam may suggest at least one caveat to this cook-chill enlightenment. For Sam wants to have it both ways. His power over his children has a fluctuating and unpredictable basis. On the one hand, he wants to be loved and admired as another child, playful, sociable, careless, on their side in deriding the po-faced adults. He even wants to evoke their succouring pity ('your pore little Tad'). On the other hand (and when, as we have seen above, amateur dramatics and cajoling fail of their object), he exerts power by overt manipulation and emotional blackmail. His power over those whom he would control is re-enacted not only in his thrall over members of his family and the neighbourhood children, but the fascination he exerts over the narrator, who follows him around like a delighted child, recording (and translating) his words, even repeatedly falling into Sam-like discourse, as though one source of it were not enough: 'On Sunday morning the sun bolted up brash and chipper from the salad beds of the Atlantic and with a red complexion came loping towards them over the big fishing hole of the Chesapeake' (p. 61).

It is all too easy to moralise about 'failure to grow up' as though maturity was a stable value, achieved once and for all by 'normal' people. Yet we might without falling into such glib superiority, observe that Stead has put her finger on an issue of power that surrounds the man as child. It is a life posture whose claim to radical innocence is discredited by its recourse to emotional (or even physical) violence when the going gets tough. One criticism concerns his capriciousness: he is an unpredictable figure whom his playmates and victims must keep under constant surveillance so as to monitor how the wind blows. Furthermore, it seems to me that the specific critique which Stead articulates is that in acting out his own desire for a perfect childhood (a childhood in which he simultaneously possesses the benefits of adulthood) a Sam expropriates childness from his own children, robbing them of what was theirs in order to feed his own hunger.[11] In this theatre conventional roles are curiously reversed, with the children the sober observers of the adults whom it behoves them to understand: 'They never asked any reasons for their parent's fights, thinking all adults unreasonable, violent beings, the toys of their own monstrous tempers and egotisms . . .' (p. 496). The children are like ethnographers trying to piece together the meaning of a foreign culture:

The children tried to make head or tale of these fatal significant sentences, formed in the crucible of the dead past, and
now came down on their heads, heavy, cold, dull. Why were
these texts hurled at them from their parents' Olympus: Louie
tried to piece the thing together; Ernie concluded that adults
were irrational. (p. 71)

However, as these quotations suggest, the spectatorship of the
children passes over into a role as alternative narrators, storytellers in their own right.

Earlier on in this chapter I suggested that *The Man Who Loved
Children* offered us two opposed models of language. These ex-
tremes were marked off as a version associated with Sam which
proposes that language exhibits an unbroken continuity between
mind and other, and a version (associated with Louie) concerned
with writing, with difference, secrets, and codes. As the novel
proceeds, Louie's role becomes increasingly aligned with the
narrator as an alternative source of language and an alternative
storyteller. In an important sense both Louie and narrator wreak
revenge upon Sam by imprisoning his contextualised oral delivery within the decontextualised printed text. Louie works her
apprenticeship in telling stories to her brothers and sisters. She
is thus constituted as an alternative voice to the dominant voice
of Sam. As the novel proceeds, she is associated with poetry and
plays, both to her father's scandalised disgust: the novel is not
only offering a critique of Sam's discourse, but proposing an
alternative in the form of writing.

In discussing the episode of Louie's diary we have already
become aware of the motif of privacy. Louie's only way, as an
adolescent girl, of escaping Sam's prying and the ubiquity of his
discourse is through secrecy and code. To make that point, however, is in some sense to ghettoise her experience, as though all
she could do is reactively go to ground. But her verbal practice
is not just a personal bomb shelter: it is the basis for a performative role through which she (and her novelist) may possibly
develop a counter-world to that which Sam seeks to rule. Textuality
poses writing as a campaign against Sam's invasive orality. Here,
the episode of the play she writes for his fortieth birthday is
particularly significant, occurring as it does in the context of
the preparations for her teacher, Miss Aiden's, visit to the family
(ch. 9, pt 2). The chapter is in any case climactic, though what

this means in a novel distinguished by its commitment to multiple climax is questionable. Louie's play (*Tragos: Herpes Rom – Tragedy: The Snake-Man*) is written in a language she has invented, and performed by the children in front of their perplexed father. (p. 405 *et seq.*) She has, as it were, sought through writing to appropriate the stage which her father has made his own. Her play concerns a father who, convinced of his daughter's impurity, turns into a snake and strangles her. Louie has given in her drama a succinct account of some of the novel's central themes. But that Sam cannot hear them ('"Why isn't it in English?" asked Sam angrily') contributes to – perhaps *is* – the tragedy of the novel. Louie can only address their common themes in code, while Sam can only hear a language in which he possesses rhetorical dominance. It would not be exaggerating much to say that Sam's implied condition for relationships is that if people want to communicate with him they must learn the language which he already masters: he will not learn others' languages. The failure of the play to communicate in any sense, is emphasised by the 'failed ceremony' of her teacher's visit. Sam simply appropriates Miss Aiden from his grief-stricken daughter, so casually annexing yet another corner of her experience.

As I have already suggested, reiteration is this novel's central mode of operation, an insistence on re-enactment that is thematic as much as structural. The struggle between Sam and his daughter over discourse is renewed a few pages later when Sam finds Louie's poems and subjects them to mockery in front of the other children, who as usual act as half-discomforted, half-hilarious audience for his power politics. By this stage, the older children at least understand that they are being used, and both Evie and Ernie expostulate to no avail that Sam should not be reading the poems. Alerted, Louie, almost dematerialised by the text into a 'large dark shape', bursts in, only to become a subject for Sam's ridicule: 'Looloo . . . is trying to practice poickry without a poick's licence . . .' (p. 430).

My final point about Louie and Sam can be made concisely thus: it is her inability to get her versions heard that leads Louie to her attempt to poison her parents. She acts out in the physical domain what there is no room for in the symbolic order of the family as policed by Sam. Ironically, the idea can in turn be traced back to Sam himself, who has expatiated to her as to others on the beneficial killing of unwanted people ('murder might be beautiful, a self-sacrifice, a sacrifice of someone near and dear for the good of others . . .', pp. 162–3). In the dazed aftermath of Henny's death, Louie sets out on her own for a new life.

The reading I have advanced of *The Man Who Loved Children* in the context of this book may leave the reader with the impression that the novel is all 'about' Sam Pollitt. This is of course far from being the case, and further, as we have seen, new narrators and new narratives are seeded and germinate within the novel. Yet I believe that my reading is not too much of a distortion. Running through and inflecting all the other features of the novel is a study of a man whose appetite for power over his family is based upon an unassuagable appetite for love. At risk of sounding like a paperback blurb, the story of Sam Pollitt is a story of a man whose knowledge, skills, and loveable qualities are all subsumed into a quest for the power that could guarantee him centrality in his own world. This is why Sam's story is in some sense typical or representative. It is a narrative instantiation of one disease of patriarchal masculinity: the futility of his representation to himself is exported as a crushing determination to control the representations of others. The power of this dynamic of representation is written out in the text through the tension between taking the side of Henny or of the children, and the gravitational attraction of Sam's cultural mass. Counter-culturally, the novel associates Sam with the immediacy of speech and Louie with writing and the power that decontextualisation brings. For its author and its readers it is an allegory of the liberating power of writing, an emancipatory politics of textuality.

Both the novels studied in this chapter are concerned to find representations for men slithering from the centrality their culture has promised them towards the perilous margins. Specific as in many ways their stories are, the protagonists are not alone in this. Patriarchal masculinity, we might deduce, is going to have to find ways of living with the experience of liminality. From that experience patriarchy itself cannot emerge unchanged. The struggle of both Sam Pollitt and of Mehring to retain their centrality in their own universe through colonising others, to solve their own contradictions through exporting them is (even in its own terms) doomed to failure. Yet it may well turn out to be a form of failure that unleashes destruction upon all around.

THE CONSERVATIONIST

Let us return for a moment to *Daniel Martin*. Jane, we noticed, was Daniel's Eurydice: Daniel as an Orpheus figure rescued her (in a move simultaneously narrative and ontological) from Hades. The structural motif here is an act of rescue: a woman who has descended to the underworld (an inauthentic and deformed state of being) is rescued by a man who, in undertaking her rescue, is himself restored to his own creativity. The act of rescue through daring the perils of entry into an inauthentic state could be a guiding motif for us in this chapter. A narrator who essays the gender crossover under discussion is much more likely to value their subject than aim to infiltrate as a secret agent the better to condemn from the inside. The implied narrative position is that the figure at the centre of the narrative possesses qualities that deserve respect and understanding: it is desirable to gain knowledge through entry into him even if his life is represented as lived under a false consciousness. The resulting narrator is a sort of anthropologist who – like some of Ursula le Guin's narrators[12] – enters an alien culture the better to understand her own. The protagonist may, in terms of the larger scheme of things, be a representative of a doomed class, but the fact of giving him close narrative attention is to effect, momentarily, a kind of narrative rescue. Indeed, no one but the narrator is there to rescue him. Orpheus ended up being torn to pieces by women, and the accusing voices that surround Mehring at the end are predominantly those of the women he has used or abused ('He tried to interfere with me . . . he propositioned me in a coffee bar' [p. 264]). The narrator stands guard as an intermediary between Mehring, and those who would condemn him out of hand.

The protagonist of *The Conservationist* is, on the face of it, a figure who embodies everything Nadine Gordimer might be expected to distrust, and opposition to which has been fundamental to her novel-writing career. He is a wealthy, white, male industrialist who purchases a farm outside Johannesburg in order to have a *pied-à-terre* in the country ('a place to bring a woman'). Divorced from his wife, and largely estranged from his son, he takes up with a succession of women whom he uses for his own purposes. Like Gerald Crich, he is a male figure who appears to have inherited all the winning cards, but who is caught at a moment of self-destructive implosion. Unlike Daniel Martin, whose

West Country farmhouse is a site of solace and renewal, his attempt to purchase himself a pastoral retreat is doomed to failure. On the face of it, he should have provided a pretty intractable figure for his narrator. It is in the struggle with that intractability that the novel achieves its productive work. The distance between the foregrounded subject matter and the implied position of the narrator generates the current which energises the novel. Throughout, the novel operates at several different levels: as political allegory, as a study of imperialism, and as critique of (white) masculinity. It is a novel whose complexity defies criticism to achieve a neat, logical order, and my discussion of it will inevitably repeat itself and go back over its own tracks. In a sense the very structure of *The Conservationist* deconstructs in advance attempts to reduce it to a neat formula. It sets up a reading experience which keeps attempts at interpretation in constant motion.

Having said this, I propose to start with the structure and discourse of the novel in the hopes of establishing some fundamental elements of the discussion. In engaging with Mehring, Gordimer (like any novelist engaging with their protagonist) is drawing not on unmediated observation or experience ('she must have come across a lot of men like that') but on a repertoire of codes and devices. The novel's work consists in rearranging these with discomposing and defamiliarising effect, managing as it does so the tension between intimacy and distance. (For example, while the narrative voice 'knows' him in an intimate way, Mehring is referred to formally, and thus as it were externally, by his surname throughout. He is never endowed with a first name.) Throughout, the narrative voice manages its degree of distance from its subject.

It is within this context that we can ask the necessary questions about what an implied female narrator makes of the occupancy of a male body, male sexuality, or the male gaze, or more precisely what she needs to do to construct the illusion of such entry. Through what codes does Gordimer represent her Mehring? These questions take us to the brink of issues about the representation of the somatic domain. At issue is a form of masquerade: the act of borrowing not just a male consciousness but a male body. Gordimer repeatedly compels questions about fiction as a somatic domain. Thus in theorising the writing of short stories, she writes:

A short story *occurs*, in the imaginative sense. To write one is to express from a situation in the exterior or interior world the life-giving drop – sweat, tear, semen, saliva – that will spread an intensity on the page; burn a hole in it. (1975 Introduction to *Selected Stories*)

The excluded term here (given the expectations set up by 'express' and 'life-giving') seems to be milk. The author makes a gendered choice of somatic domain to inhabit along with her subject matter. *The Conservationist* is – in more senses than one – about bodies. In getting hold of this, we shall simultaneously need to recognise that the novel's account of male sexuality is at one and the same time a critique of imperialism, part of what Dominic Head has identified as a 'politics of textuality', striving towards a 'decolonization' of the novel's form (1994, p. 99 *et passim*).

The style at which Gordimer was working through the 1970s, the style of *Burger's Daughter* and many of the stories as well as *The Conservationist*, represents a generic cross between naturalism and stream of consciousness. Accordingly, the style that she has constructed for Mehring's story is a form of interior monologue shot through with paratactic detail. His consciousness buzzes with quotations, iconic perceptions, memories, apprehensions, obsessively repeated phrases. Fragments of dialogue with imagined or remembered figures run on in his head. We shall see in due course that it is an indicative pun to say that his consciousness is ungrounded. This style is characterised by weak boundary markers between inner and outer discourse, thus coding the permeability of identity, the breakdown of authoritative control over conscious or unconscious voices. Reciprocally, weak cohesion calls for more inferential work on the part of the reader: chronology and order are in our hands, not in those of the protagonist. Towards the end, this form of textuality becomes a medium for a mind distracted to the point of breakdown

This is a style whose own protocols do not restrict it to the construction of mental processes alone. It is an embodied style, one that seeks to give somatic identity to the figure to whom the narrative is closest. Knowing about Mehring, the novel proposes, is bodily knowledge as much as mental knowledge. In fact the novel seems to aim at the dissolution of any simple Cartesian dualism. By the same token it contests an ancient assumption about the relation between knowledge and soma: that male knowledge was unconditioned, could be physically decontextualised, and was therefore superior to female knowledge which was inescapably confined within the body. While mortality broods over this novel too in the form of another body in the reeds, so Mehring's awareness of himself as a creatural being is constantly alluded to in the text. The rapid and often inconsequential movements of his mind are gestural as much as conceptual. Like Joyce's Leopold Bloom (who may lurk somewhere in his ancestry), he is the both the subject and physical object of his own perception. 'The moment of first sight ... roused an anguished revulsion, an actual physical reaction, as if the python of guts in which his large weekend breakfast was warming uncoiled against some inner wall of his body' (p. 94). In part this represents a complicated game of hide and seek with the reader. The code of verisimilitude employed by the novel demands that its subject be given not just self-consciousness, but an identifiably male somatic self-consciousness. Leaping naked from the shower to answer the telephone, he is nervous:

> Because he is naked, Mehring feels like hopping with impatience. It is born of the nervous apprehension his body feels that someone may walk in: his mind is aware that no one lives in the house, there is no one to enter. Yet while he listens, smiles exasperatedly into the telephone in his right hand, his other hand plays with himself the way a small boy seeks reassurance by touching his genitals – his fingers comb the damp springy hair, draw down the foreskin that has been pushed back during the shower, weigh the uneven balls, absently tender to the one that is smaller and lighter than the other. (p. 49)

In the rhetoric of narrative cross-gendering the circumstantial detail of the exposed body becomes a pledge of inward knowledge.[13] In any case, physically exposing her protagonist to the peeping reader means turning the tables on a male observer who mentally strips (as Mehring himself habitually does) the female object of his attention. While he is afraid some one will come in and see him, the reader of course knows that some one is already and has always been watching. (Prurience is culturally asymmetrical because embedded in differentials of power.) Yet though the narrative proposes to its readers intimate identification with its male subject, intimacy with Mehring is, as we shall see, an ambivalent achievement.[14]

If the sense of touch and physical sensation constitute one strand within this novel, sight, and the erotic eye constitute another. Both promote uncomfortable proximity between subject matter (here Mehring's consciousness and somatic identity) and observer. The reader watches Mehring in the act of watching others. Thus one feature of the mind-style Gordimer has created for Mehring is his sexually alert glance. While entertaining his Afrikaner neighbours he thinks:

> She's a beautiful child as their children often are – where do they get them from? – and she'll grow up – what do they do to them? – the same sort of vacant turnip as the mother. – Sorry, I 've run out [of soft drinks] I've been away. – To go into one of those women must be like using the fleshy succulent plants men in the Foreign Legion have to resort to. (p. 52)

Or he is apt to see both irrigation spray and fireworks as ejaculating (pp. 155, 205). His mind characteristically moves from the details of his surroundings to sexual fantasy and back (pp. 70, 194–5).

I have characterised as both uncomfortable and ambivalent the triangular relationship between narrator, Mehring, and reader. If we assume that the narrator is engaged on a kind of rescue mission, a mission that requires proximity, even intimacy, then how do we as readers handle our complicity in his perception or his actions? In this light, a crucial and disturbing passage, amounting almost to a test of how much the reader will take, is the plane journey when Mehring (who is always trying to reassure himself by entering women) fondles and interferes with the Portuguese girl in the seat next to him, entering her with his finger. The point here concerns the pragmatics of the text: does a passage like this expose the imperial nature of Mehring's erotic colonisation of his world? Is the risk of explicitness well taken? Or does it invite us into unacceptable complicity, and thus risk simply reproducing the power relations it purports to question? I have no convincing answer, but it is clear that such a passage invites readers to make their own choices. The narrative is not going to relieve us of the responsibility for managing our own complicity either with the protagonist or his victims.

To understand the role of Mehring in his novel we need to pay attention to its whole structure as well as to stylistic detail. That structure is in turn integrated with the cosmos of the novel, and it is impossible to talk about structure without considering that cosmos. This discussion will lead us back to the story of Mehring and its outcomes. Throughout, I shall suggest that the novel locates the psyche of its subject within a political and cultural critique, posing its male subject as heterogeneous and increasingly at the mercy of events, rather than as centred and in charge of his own destiny. This means that the narrator (and behind the narrator the author) has to manage the tension between on the one hand intimacy and identification and on the other distance and critique.

Much that is apparent about the local texture of *The Conservationist* applies also to the larger structure. Thus one of the most striking features of the style is what I have referred to as weak markers: the text does not use many of the devices which, like inverted commas, conventionally mark off one element of discourse from another. The effect of this is a polyphony where codes are not hierarchised and readers are invited into inferential activity so as to identify and assign to their place or speaker the elements of the text. The voice of the narrator as manager of this process, guide or friend to the reader is quiet or non-existent. Broadly, this is also the case at a higher structural level. The text is loosely sectionalised into unmarked sections, separated (as though they were chapters) only by blank spaces, and those in turn are subsumed within larger elements introduced with quotations from an early work of anthropology by Henry Callaway. We shall have to return to these in a moment. The time structure is complex, drawing on interlocking analepsis. Chronology is fluid and subservient to the representation of consciousness. There is no clear boundary between prolepsis and analepsis. Thus at every level the text mimes the intertwining of memory and fantasy with the 'actual' moment, the here and now of the plot. In some ways we might see this as a heightened version of realism: since the discourse refuses to break its process up into discrete and clearly labelled units, the significance of events and 'moments' only becomes apparent as they are recontextualised in later phases of the narrative. The overall structure enacts this fluid dynamic at a higher level, establishing an oblique relationship between the order in which the book is read and the implied natural time of

the story level. It is a procedure which, once again, throws weight
onto the diegetic work of the reader, to whom falls the role of
guardian of coherence.[15] That Mehring himself cannot impose
coherence upon his own experience, failing to dominate either
text or reader (or indeed his own career), is a vital element in
the novel's account of masculinity. In literary historical terms we
might say that to put to use for Mehring (a weighty figure in his
own society) a style evolved to represent Leopold Bloom (a marginal figure in his) constitutes in itself a strategy for undermining
his authority. It is almost bathetic in its refusal of a hierarchy of
styles,[16] and this refusal conposes a major element in that 'politics of textuality' of which Dominic Head (1994) has spoken.

Where the chronological and plot structure of a novel has a
low profile, emphasis is liable to be placed on alternative structuring devices. This has always been the case in novels towards
the 'interior monologue' end of the continuum. Typically, such
novels mimic memory in structuring themselves around repeated
motifs, the preoccupations (or obsessions) of the supposed focus
of consciousness. Like the Wagnerian *leitmotiv*, the recurrent image
and the embedded quotation themselves gather cohesive force.
('If I had your money'; 'no ordinary pig iron dealer' . . . the egg
and the egg-like stone . . . earth in his mouth.)

The representation of the male protagonist is therefore produced through the total structure of the novel as well as through
its local stylistic manifestation. The effect of the recurrence of
image, quotation, and motif is to represent both Mehring's memory
and his story as increasingly out of his own conscious control.
His head becomes an echo chamber criss-crossed by remembered
(and imaginary) dialogues with other figures in his life such as
his nameless left-wing lover who has now left the country, but
to whose conversation he repeatedly returns. It is in a way she
who – from off-stage – voices the criticism that we might have
expected the narrator to make her own.

A LOCAL HABITATION

Mehring's farm, as Coetzee has pointed out, belongs in an
anglophone South African tradition that goes back to Olive
Schreiner's *Story of an African Farm* ('White Writing', in Coetzee,
1988). While time is fluid and unstable in this novel, the items

which offer stability to text and to consciousness are spatial. The key events of the novel are located in very precisely realised places, whether the farmhouse, the nearby fields, or the mine dumps where Mehring's story reaches its climax. It is as though place lends a narrative weight and coherence which time cannot. For the next phase of this argument I shall first try to sketch in what I see as the cosmos of the novel, the larger mythology which supports or underpins it. This will underpin the subject of place, specifically the land and the farm. The discussion will then proceed through the complementary themes of belonging, inheritance and flight. Throughout, I shall propose that a reading of masculinity is indivisible from the novel's political and colonial themes.

Let me start by noting that the text itself foregrounds the idea of a sustaining mythology. I referred just now to the quotations from Henry Callaway's book which introduce or act as epigraphs to the main sections. I do not possess (nor presumably do most of Gordimer's readers) the knowledge to weigh up how accurately Callaway and Gordimer are representing the religious system of the Amazulu.[17] But the quotations fulfil at least two functions: they perpetually remind us of the beliefs and rituals of the earlier owners of the land, and they insist upon locating the story within a larger framework of belief and value, a framework within which it is implied that Mehring's story may have other and larger meanings. This strand of quotation establishes a code for the co-presence of meanings to which narrator (and reader) are attuned, but the protagonist is not. We 'cannot avoid believing', says Callaway in Europeanising vein, 'that we have an intimation of an old faith in a Hades or Tartarus, which has become lost and is no longer understood' (p. 163). Perhaps I can schematically represent this cosmos by asserting that the novel has effectively three zones: the earth's surface, above the earth, and below the earth. Further, and relatedly, that the novel adopts as primary signifiers the four traditional elements: earth (ubiquitously), air (flight), water (the flood), and fire. These four elements compose major strands in the discourse. Out of them is woven the cosmos in which Mehring moves. Without attempting a full-scale analysis of the novel, let us try to see how this works. Our first clue is once again a body washed up in the reeds.[18]

Some years before, in the short story 'Six Feet of the Country' (1956), Gordimer wrote what amounts to a cartoon for *The Con-*

servationist. Here another attempt to buy into Arcadia is subverted by the appearance of death. A wealthy white couple buy a farm so as to 'play at' farming in an attempt to bolster up their failing marriage. The story is told from the (distinctly unreliable) point of view of the husband, and its crisis concerns a bungled attempt to arrange the burial of a black man who has died while sheltering with the farm workers. *The Conservationist,* too, like *Antigone* or *Daniel Martin,* is haunted by an unburied body – an anonymous body whose discovery is announced at the beginning and which is finally given a decent burial at the end. This body is balanced out in the symmetries of the novel with another body, that of the white business associate (father of the sixteen-year-old after whom Mehring yearns) who towards the end is found dead in his car, having committed suicide. The figure of the unknown black man represents a kind of centre of gravity for the novel, doubling as the representative of the true owners, those who owned the land before Mehring came and will own it again after he has gone:

> The one whom the farm received had no name. He had no family but their women wept a little for him. There was no child of his present but their children were there to live after him. They had put him away to rest, at last; he had come back. He took possession of this earth, theirs; one of them. (p. 267)

So ends the novel, offering itself as a political and colonial parable.

But the dual valency of this novel proposes a symbiotic relationship between the political parable and its account of creatural existence. For the presence of the man lying by the river is a *memento mori* which at one and the same time links Mehring to his own creatural and somatic existence and affirms the tenuousness of his hold on the land. It is the moment when he himself falls asleep by the river and awakens uneasy, with grit and the taste of earth in his mouth, that forms a turning point in his story, the moment when his queasy relation to his own memory and his own body takes a turn towards dissociation, and the breakdown of conscious mastery:

> For a moment he does not know where he is – or rather who he is; but this situation in which he finds himself, staring into

the eye of the earth with earth at his mouth, is strongly familiar to him . . . (p. 41)

The sense of familiarity, of some kind of unwelcome knowing or knowledge is slow to ebb. As it does, it leaves space in
his mind; or uncovers, like the retreat of a high tide, carrying
away silt. (p. 42)

As suggested earlier, the land in this novel, a locus of vivid and
detailed description, signifies at several different levels. The discourse of place ballasts the tendency of Mehring's story to
weightlessness and flight. At the same time, the hope which
he invests in his farm, and the contrast established throughout
with the city suggest an echo of the tradition of pastoral, as though
the farm promises to be a place of reintegration and abundance.
Specifically, the processes of farming and the primary production
of food not only provide a contrast with Mehring's financial city
world (an unreal city in this binary set), but are of course also
the domain of the black people who actually do the work. Crops,
and the fertility of the land code another aspect of the gender
construction of the novel. The conservationist of the title is
positioned not just within the mythic structure sketched earlier
but within a precisely realised ecology, the terrain of fire and
flood as also of abundant and cyclically replenished life.

Over this domain Mehring (ironically the conservationist of the
title) watches, and his relatedness to the land is homologous with
his relation to women. Both are feminised as the objects of his
erotic gaze, like the 'golden reclining nudes of the desert'
(p. 126) over which he flies.[19] He is constantly, obsessively, exploring
both land and women and his prying gaze is woven into the
rhetoric of the text. After the fire, up 'into some of the older
trees fire has thrust a surgeon's red-gloved hand, cauterizing
through a vaginal gap or knot-hole' (p. 97). But then, as the semi-
neutral narrator explains, as Mehring wanders the burnt land,
'distress is a compulsion to examine minutely', and his compulsion
to examine minutely resonates beyond the particular circumstance
of the fire-damaged land, at least as far back as the scene with
the Portuguese girl on the plane. Gordimer's Mehring, always in
search of something that seems to be missing, is remarkably close
to Freud's and Klein's accounts of the castration horror evoked
in the little boy by his discovery of the female genitals. The terror
of loss necessitates constant reassurance, and recurs in the horror

sequence on the mine dump – 'unmanned when most manly' (p. 262). Mehring's relationship to the land is driven by a compulsion to fill a vacancy.

In the pivotal passage cited above, where he falls asleep in the reeds, there is at least a subliminal suggestion that the reason for his sudden heavy sleep is that Mehring, who is thinking about his nameless lover (entertaining whom was one of his reasons for buying the farm) has masturbated into the earth: 'rolls onto his belly' . . . 'breathing intimately into the earth' . . . a dribble of saliva (p. 41). If so, the scene, with its echo of an older pun on dying, crystallises his infertile relation to the land and to the whole ecology of biological existence. Unlike the dead black man, Mehring is a passenger, not a participant in the cyclical processes of life, and the sterility of his present excludes him from perpetuation (either by genes or by values) into the future. Much as he would like to be remembered, the land will forget him ('No one will even remember where', p. 194).

FLIGHT BETWEEN WORLDS

Mehring's panic rises in stages. There is the disappointment of his son, Terry's, visit (pp. 134–53). Terry, he fears, is homosexual, is easily swayed by political fads, has nothing in common with his father's world. There is the shock of his colleague's suicide, and of the simultaneous realisation that he desires the man's teenage daughter.[20] In his relationship to the next generation he would rather be a lover than a father. It is in this context, late in the novel, that he makes an attempt to put his mark upon the future. I am thinking of the scene where he and Jacobus, the cowhand, plant a pair of expensive European sweet chestnuts, a wistful fantasy of a future where ownership of land and patrilinear succession would inscribe a man's memory upon the face of the land:

– Oh it will be many years before these have any nuts. You and I will be old men, Jacobus . . . These will be big trees . . . when you are very old and walk with a stick. –

– Well, is all right. Is all right when Terry can get them, when he can get marry and bring them nice for his wife, his little children? . . .

It was difficult to decide where to plant the trees. They ought
to be near the farmhouse, really – a farmhouse as one thinks
of one . . .

. . . a sort of dignified approach to where, one day, a farmhouse and its garden would be differentiated from the farm
proper, preside over it. 'Turn right when you come to the big
chestnut trees.' (pp. 224–5)

But in fact the joy of planting is already soured by anticipated
disappointment: these non-indigenous trees, he suspects, will not
survive, and the act of digging the holes arouses the underworld
of the novel's cosmos. It opens up again the imagery of the
earth and burial that runs through Mehring's imagination and
his novel.

Broken in upon, the earth gives the strong musty dampness of
a deserted house or a violated tomb.

There's a vertigo that goes with pits; not that this one could
take him in and conceal him entirely. . . But there are some
for whom it would be large enough; those tribes who bury in
the foetal position. (p. 226)

Immediately afterwards, the earth makes another almost vengeful attempt on the farmer, sucking him into a quagmire from
which he manages to pull himself free. The whole section focuses
a countervailing possibility to the main narrative drift: the possibility of belonging to a land, your place secured in memory, ritual,
and inheritance. It is upon this counter-possibility that Mehring's
rootlessness (the word occurs freshly primed) is mapped.

In wider terms, Gordimer's text (while it insists on following
Mehring where his friends and colleagues cannot) in the end
offers us a version of masculinity characterised by absence,
implosion, vacuum. His disaster occurs in the gap between his
worlds (literally in the sense that the climax occurs just off the
much-travelled road between farm and city), but metaphorically
in a way that takes us back to the cosmos of the novel. Flight,
movement above the surface of the earth, is a motif which,
contrasted in the novel's scheme of meaning with groundedness
in the earth, recurs throughout the novel, reinforcing the narrative
pursuit of a figure in flight. Mehring – at the wheel of his Mercedes,

or on board an airliner – is perpetually between places. Other
people (Jacobus apart) are distanced to memories or the other
end of telephone calls. Increasingly, he uses the farm as a place
of escape, somewhere where people need not know where he
is, or even whether he is abroad or not. His friends' (and his
readers') awareness of his absence is symbolised in the pile up
of ansaphone messages (pp. 200–1). That there is likely to be no
reply seems in a text full of telephones to be embedded in his
very name (May ring?). His story is the story of a disjunction
between public and private worlds, public and private selves.
His work becomes increasingly meaningless to him, reduced to
the absurd in his colleague's death. The places where he might
ground himself – the land, his son, relations with other men –
are glanced at, but remain undeveloped. Instead, and self-
destructively, he throws himself into a trap baited with a woman
whom he does not even find attractive. The ending of his story
raises flight from subject matter to the level of narrative structure: there is no governing voice to impose closure, and the reader
has to grub for clues as to whether he has died, the victim of a
conspiracy of all his accusers, among the yellow mine dumps
(significantly the toxic waste from the pursuit of gold, a dystopic
Eldorado), or fled, his 'death' another self-regarding figment of
his own imagination:

> he's going to make a dash for it, a leap, sell the place to the
> first offer, jump in, the key's there in the ignition, and drive
> off reversing wildly first through the trees . . .
>
> – Come. Come and look, they're all saying. What is it? Who is
> it? It's Mehring. It's Mehring down there. (pp. 264–5)

Yet in the concluding section, Jacobus has 'phoned the farmer in
his office to ask for money for wood to make the coffin for the
man in the reeds. The permission was granted, but 'the farmer
didn't want to hear about it. He was leaving that day for one of
those countries white people go to . . .' (p. 266).

So Jacobus, at 'this' end of the telephone, is in a sense left in
charge. There remains a final suggestion to explore. I suggested
above that one way Mehring might have been located, or
grounded, would have been in his relations with other men. It
appears that for him other men who are equals are competitors

or potential competitors. He does however, have an extended relationship with Jacobus as though the fact that he perceives the black man as an inferior permits him this male closeness, and it is to this that we shall briefly turn. It seems that in this relationship is briefly ghosted another possibility, a glimpse of another way of being.

The passage I am thinking of occurs towards the end of the novel, on New Year's night, when Mehring, who has not gone to any of the parties to which he has been invited, half jokingly invites Jacobus to come and drink whisky with him, then goes out to sit in the darkness among his fields (pp. 202–9). The two men talk, sharing the same glass: the passing of time; cattle; inevitably on to the body in the reeds ('D'you remember at all what he looked like?'). It therefore comes as a shock to the reader to discover that the scene did not, within the realistic norm the text has established, take place at all – 'Jacobus has not come' (p. 209). Instead it has taken place in Mehring's imagination, at once the mental enactment of a wish for male company, and a reminder of the political gulf between black and white.

Mehring's story is one of growing dissociation in several different dimensions. His consciousness, his sexuality, his fantasies come unstitched from his public and social roles. Obviously this dissociation operates at a political level, and I would not want the fact that I have myself colonised this text as an element in a thesis about masculinity to obscure the other level at which this is a parable about South Africa under apartheid. Dissociation along the lines of gender is exacerbated by dissociation along the lines of race and economic power. The patriarchal machinery of white law will make sure that the black hero of Lewis Nkosi's *Mating Birds* (1986) will not get off as lightly as Mehring for his sexual intrusion upon a white woman. But I would want to suggest that the account of masculinity which the novel offers is all of a piece with its account of the political management of land, resources, and people. Both gender structure and political structure, it implies, are sustained by a political economy of energy and psyche which we may with some reservations call patriarchy. Neither, it tells us, are in the end sustainable. That message is not addressed to those countries alone where the interface of first and third worlds is most inescapably obvious.

6

Men in Time

Men or women: complex, mobile, open beings. Admitting the component of the other sex makes them at once much richer, plural, strong, and . . . very fragile. We invent only on this condition . . . This does not mean that in order to create you have to be homosexual. But there is no *invention* possible . . . without the presence in the inventing subject of an abundance of the other . . . persons-detached, persons-thought, peoples born of the unconscious, and in each desert, suddenly animated, a springing forth of self one did not know about – our women, our monsters, our jackals, our Arabs, our fellow-creatures, our fears.

(Hélène Cixous, *Sorties*, in Marks and Courtivron, 1981, p. 97)

I think: 'I wanted to live outside history. I wanted to live outside the history that the Empire imposes on its subjects, even its lost subjects. I never wished it for the barbarians that they should have the history of empire laid upon them.'

(J. M. Coetzee, *Waiting for the Barbarians*, Penguin, 1980, p. 154)

In this chapter I shall consider aspects of the work of four English-speaking male novelists who made their names in the 1980s. Though I have chosen these particular novels to complement and develop the discussions contained in the earlier chapters, my choice of authors and of texts remains in a sense personal. Similar or at least parallel discussions could have been elaborated on the basis of others, but in the end these are texts which I find interesting, and know from teaching them give rise to productive readings. In different but complementary ways they decipher the instability of the male as sign, and in doing so propose different narratives of masculine liminality. In tracing the movement of its subject, and in renegotiating the boundaries between public and private worlds, each text prompts explicit engagement with the narrative performance and variation of masculinity. At the same time each novel potentially refigures the nature of the community of male readers.

The four novels which will form the framework of this chapter will be Graham Swift's *Waterland* (1983), James Kelman's *The Busconductor Hines* (1984), David Leavitt's *The Lost Language of Cranes* (1986), and Ian McEwan's *The Child in Time* (1987). I hope that my account of each of these will throw light upon the others, and, cumulatively, advance understanding of the narrative practice of masculinity and male identities. Inasmuch as the four texts have a common provenance (and there are dangers in compositing unwieldy and disparate histories), it is that of the 1980s in the late capitalist West: an era of the final breakdown on both sides of the Atlantic of the postwar political consensus, the terminal decline of the old heavy industries, the hegemony of neoliberalism, with its fluid labour market, global markets, mass unemployment, and ever expanding service industry. Above all an era of a new and dangerous phase of the Cold War, and a political ferment in which radical energies were principally invested in feminism, environmentalism, and the campaigns against nuclear weapons. It was a period when many received versions of masculinity and male identity were called into question at the level of overt gender debate or simply undermined by rapidly changing patterns of employment, among them the accelerated decline of the unilinear male career. Many male novelists of the period engaged with this turmoil, and their work does not simply *reflect* the crisis of masculinity, but contributes to the debate. Different as their contributions are, it appears to me that Swift, Kelman, Leavitt, and McEwan between them provoke us to think about key issues to do with what it means to be a man at the end of the millennium. Their novels sustain us in the search for new narratives and new ways of thinking and experiencing masculinity. The point will be not that they offer us alternative *images* of masculinity or of relationships (akin, say, to those commercials where a father clasps a clean and cheerful baby to his naked torso), but that their structure and discourses invite us to take part in enacting new patterns, thinking out masculinity and male roles at the level of discourse as much as at the level of referent. What dilemmas are we up against in trying to speak new stories? What are the typical actors and events? Are new stories simply the old ones in updated guise? To what patterns of mastery or exclusion does our knowledge lead? Does the act of telling in itself simply bind the actual more rigidly in place? If we acknowledge that 'man' is no longer the subject of history, what collectivity does the novel of male deeds address? Since the production of the text requires the corresponding activity of readers as they perform their diegetic function, we find ourselves in dialogue with the text and with other readers. And by the same token, the bearers of the anxiety associated with fluidity and change.

THE FATHERLAND OF GRAHAM SWIFT

Graham Swift's novel *Waterland* plainly belongs with that tendency in Western culture for which 'postmodernism' is widely taken as an appropriate, if elastic, label.[1] It is a self-reflexive novel whose narratives and time sequences wind themselves around each other, alternately offering and undermining its own assurances. Its implied epistemology is sceptical, ironic, relativistic. In foregrounding the oral fabrication of memory, with all its deceptions, dubieties and rhetorical self-justifications, the novel belongs with other contemporary successes in a broadly similar genre, like Kazuo Ishiguro's novels *The Artist of the Floating World* and *The Remains of the Day*.[2] To observe this is not to specify a particular literary history: such a genealogical task, if undertaken, would probably have to pursue the antecedents of *Waterland* back to Salman Rushdie's *Midnight's Children* and further still to Günter Grass's *The Tin Drum*. Yet even if we were to dismiss such novels as the products of a passing fashion for untrustworthy and simulated oral narratives, a tad whipped up by publishers, reviewers and film-makers, it would still be necessary to speculate on the reasons why that fashion resonates as it does. *Waterland's* own reflexiveness, and its compulsive dwelling upon stories and story-making, make it germane to our purposes. So, above all, does its investigation in a 1980s context of themes to do with the practice of masculinity and fatherhood, here overtly understood as constructed and propagated through discursive means. A novel, three of whose main characters are named Tom, Dick, and Harry, signals its own generalising intention.

The nature and meaning of paternity has been a recurrent theme in Graham Swift's fiction. Paternity, adoption, childlessness, the 'true heir', are urgent features of stories like 'Hoffmeier's Antelope', 'The Son', and 'Learning to Swim' itself. The obtrusively titled *Shuttlecock* (1981), the novel that precedes *Waterland*, turns upon a son's quest to establish the truth about his father's ostensibly heroic wartime career. Within the novel a triangle is established composed of the narrator (himself an unpredictable and sometimes cruel father), Quinn, his departmental senior, and the now silent father whose reputation may at any moment be destroyed by the revelation of the contents of file C/9E. The son's researches take place in the context of a workplace, the department, which owes a good deal to Kafka.[3] Following his mysterious visit to Quinn and his promotion to Quinn's post, his obsession with his father drops away and he is released to re-engage with his own life, his wife, and his sons. The novel is an allegory not only for obsession but specifically for obsession with the father. The search for the inner truth about the silent elder is too absorbing to allow the younger man any other engagement with life. And yet, the novel refuses to be reduced to a simple contrast between writing and obsession on the one hand, and spontaneous living on the other. For all the narrator's new-found freedom ('And then one day . . . I stopped reading Dad's book' [p. 214]), the cycle of obsession and interpretation will continue. The novel's appeal to the reader 'not to peer too hard beneath the surface of what it says . . . or what it doesn't say' is undermined in its own example. As another of Swift's fathers says of his adopted son, 'Like King Oedipus he's got to ask these fool questions. He's got to find out where he came from' ('The Son', p. 58). The plot of revelation (inch by inch approaching the unspoken truth) lures the reader into a world where originating power is always somewhere else. A pursuit of origins generates endless cycles in Swift's fiction, nowhere more so than in *Waterland*.

In a novel of so many circularities and interlocking cycles, it is hard for a critic to know where to start. The surname of its chief protagonist, Crick, seems to be a signpost to another double helix (and thus perhaps to another occluded woman: Rosalind Franklin)[4] and, as we shall see, the idea of the genetic code of DNA resonates with themes throughout the novel. Perhaps one way of beginning would be by taking one of the novel's cycles – the revolving year. Fifty-two chapters just might be a statistical fluke, but in a novel which places its climactic events in Greenwich, significance is invested in time and the meridian. The choice of Greenwich as

Tom and Mary's later home and thus location of the climactic events of the plot can best be explored through returning to an earlier theme of this book: the dialectic between centrality and margin. Inasmuch as that dialectic is a temporal as well as a spatial process, *Waterland* exemplifies the fecundity of Steven Connor's insight that the novel 'depends upon and is peculiarly defined by [the] mutual adjustment of private time and public time' (1996, p. 129).

In Conrad's *The Secret Agent* (1907), the observatory at Greenwich is the proposed target of a terrorist bomb attack: 'Go for the first meridian,' Mr Vladimir advises Mr Verloc, 'You don't know the middle classes as well as I do. Their sensibilities are jaded. The first meridian' (ch. 2). In the event the attack fails, blowing up Stevie, who has been persuaded to carry the bomb. Swift's bomb is rather more subtle, but nevertheless strikes at the heart of the centrality that the Greenwich Observatory and the Greenwich meridian represent. Greenwich, let us remember, is and has been since 1884 the linchpin on which the world time system has rested, and like Mercator's projection, builds Eurocentrism into global cognitive structures. To be placed on the meridian, to walk your dog along it of a Sunday afternoon, is to assert an implicit claim to be poised at the epicentre of meaning. The text itself brings together astronomy and empire in linking the rise of the Atkinson Brewery to the might of Albion, and in doing so asserts the ambivalent nature of the fixed high point as simultaneously a peak and the place where decline begins: 'Why must the zenith never be fixed . . . why has land reclamation in the eastern Fens become confused with the Empire of Great Britain? Because to fix the zenith is to fix the point at which decline begins . . .' (p. 80).

In a novel preoccupied by time and the telling of history, the meridian represents a husk, a not quite abandoned shell of imperial dominion over representation. Yet for Crick, as husband and historian, Greenwich is not really home, and a park bench 'some fifty yards from the line of zero longitude' is the setting for Mary's revelation about her (imaginary) pregnancy, a revelation which tilts Tom towards a sickening sense of growing unreality: 'The last thing he wants to believe is that he's in fairy land' (*Longitude O°*, p. 129). A text which makes so much of circularity and relativity entertains as its residual counter-supposition the possibility of a fixed point upon which all else would dependably rest.

At different times in the novel the desire for such a centre seems to be invested in the female genitals and in the Greenwich meridian: both places which are subsequently demonstrated to be untrustworthy. What should have been the stable centre, the spot to which all cycles return, is as shifting, as untrustworthy, as any other position. While the narrator has, to take up the metaphor, left the Fens in order to find solid ground under his feet, the aspiration has been cruelly disappointed.

The descent into unreality and the counterposed possibility of security make up between them the novel's underlying dynamic. The fine line between the two is managed by the storytelling propensity. Stories, the novel holds in a characteristically self-reflexive gesture, are told both to 'outwit reality' and to console the frightened. The two motions may indeed come down to the same thing:

For my father . . . had a knack for telling stories (p. 1)

I began, having recognised in my young but by no means carefree class the contagious symptoms of fear: 'Once upon a time . . .' (p. 6)

How did the Cricks outwit reality? By telling stories. (p. 15)

At the centre of what I want to say about this novel is a knot which ties up both an implicit theory about paternity and a theory about narrative and storytelling. In the attempt to pick at this knot I would like to tackle first the subject of storytelling. *Waterland* is a novel which foregrounds oral narration and the situated nature of oral delivery. Much of the novel is presented as Crick's explaining voice, punctuated with the traces of orality, the false starts, repetitions, the characteristic dots trailing into silence. In a printed text this is of course an elaborate tease. The real presence of the narrator is both insisted upon and simultaneously snatched away from us, rather as 'real' paternity is snatched away from Crick ('because you see once I had a child' [p. 224]), and as the claim to reveal historical truth is undermined by the acknowledged relativity of the speaker's position.

For the simulated orality of Crick's delivery – the pretence that 'Crick' and his listeners occupy a mutual time and space – sets before us a contrast between the spoken and the written word.

'Speech is irreversible', Barthes long ago remarked, 'a word cannot be *retracted*, except precisely by saying that one retracts it . . . paradoxically, it is ephemeral speech which is indelible, not monumental writing'. This post-structuralist game with commonsense is relevant here. For Barthes' subject here is the person who is preparing to speak in a teaching situation, some one who has before them the choice of adopting 'in all good faith a role of Authority', or is 'bothered by all this Law that the act of speaking is going to introduce into what he wants to say', in which case

> he uses the irreversibility of speech in order to disturb its legality, correcting, adding, wavering, the speaker moves into the infinitude of language, superimposes on the simple message that everyone expects of him a new message that ruins the very idea of a message and, through the shifting reflection of the blemishes and excesses with which he accompanies the line of the discourse, asks us to believe with him that language is not to be reduced to communication. By all these operations . . . the imperfect orator hopes to render less disagreeable the role that makes every speaker a kind of policeman. ('Writers, Intellectuals, Teachers' [1971], in Barthes, 1977, pp. 190–2)

The speaker's lack of one kind of authority is simultaneously a claim to another.

We the audience are in turn situated as the collective children to whom Crick tells his explanatory stories and then subsequently plunged back into our isolated adulthood. Our reading journey is as unstable and uncharted as the existential journey of the narrative, and raises a recurrent concern in this text and the others in this chapter: the supposed 'speaker' of the novel struggles to retain some kind of hold over the symbolic domain, to find ways of anchoring, organising , and communicating his vision. This is uphill work, since meaning, like the Fens, seems constantly to be threatened by fluidity. Storytelling (like land reclamation) takes place in a perpetual struggle against descent into fluid meaninglessness. It also takes place in a dialectic with the contrary propensity to secrets, the meanings locked in trunks or bottles. The storyteller is he who carries the torch of curiosity, since Mary (the original bearer of curiosity) loses her curiosity with her child, leaving Tom to be the taleteller and the nagging voice of 'why why why'. That the novel offers us this as a male role is something to which we must return shortly. But first it will be necessary to say a little about the topography of the novel, a topography mapped simultaneously upon both time and space.

This is not the place in which to develop at any length an account of Swift's Fenland, or the social history he erects upon it. If, however, we are to understand how the novel's structure instantiates an account of masculinity, we shall have to visit briefly certain principles. I referred just now to another Crick, a textual pointer to a key paradigm of how the shaping past is encoded into the present. The dominant obsession of the novel concerns genesis, explaining the present by working back over the past, detecting the origins of what is in what was, unlocking explanatory secrets. The 'story telling animal' (p. 51) characteristically tells stories about the prehistory of the present, and Crick's chosen profession is directly linked to the narrative function of solace: 'Children, my becoming a history teacher can be directly ascribed to the stories which my mother told me as a child when, like most children, I was afraid of the dark' (p. 52). However, the paradox at the heart of this enterprise is that the pursuit of stability through the compulsive search for origins only ever comes up with yet more instability. As in all flat land, the horizon perpetually recedes. Or, to put it another way, (and the insistent metaphors take us back to the physical topography of the novel and thus to the metaphorical structure on which it rests) firm ground gives way. The only certainty for which the novel seems prepared to vouch is circularity. In a narrative recapitulation of the novel's own underlying theory, the proposition that circular movement characterises both physical and historical domains recurs again and again.[5]

Circularity and return to starting place constitute the underlying paradigm of *Waterland*. They characterise its topography (the drainage, silting up, and renewed liability to flood of the Fens), its biology (the lifecycle of the eel), and its history ('now who says history doesn't go in circles' [p. 180]):

So that while the Ouse flows to the sea, it flows . . . like all rivers, only back to itself, to its own source; and that impression that a river moves only one way is an illusion. And it is also an illusion that what you throw (or push) into a river will be carried away, swallowed for ever, and never return. Because it will return. And that remark first put about . . . by Heraclitus of Ephesus, that we cannot step twice into the same river, is not to be trusted. Because we are always stepping into the same river. (p. 127)

Even successful drainage will result in increased liability to flooding, since the drained peat dries out and shrinks, thus sinking once more below sea and river level. The circling chain of the dredger's buckets, themselves scooping up silt to be deposited at sea, is the dominant image of the later pages of the novel. Yet this passion for circularity and origins is itself deceptive: the same place forever eludes you.[6] As he drives Mary and the stolen baby back to Safeways, the history master whose preoccupation is the French Revolution reflects:

It's called reconstructing the crime. From first to last. It's an analogy of the historical method. It's an analogue of how you discover how you've become what you are. If you're lucky you might find out why. If you're lucky – but it's impossible – you might get back to where you can begin again. Revolution. (p. 270)

What does this recursive paradigm have to do with a masculinity? Let me explain where my argument is heading.

The cycles which form the paradigm of the novel are all in turn associated with biological cycles (hence the lengthy diversion about the breeding habits of eels) to which women are believed to have privileged access. (One of the first things Mary does in the early days of their mutual sexual exploration is to explain to the fifteen-year-old Tom about menstruation.) The attraction of an escape route from the biological cycle lurks in the margins of a narrative in which male protagonists are trying to find some safe ground. This desire for stability, for some guarantee that identity and being might be prolonged into the future is connected with a fantasy about being able to evade biology and natural history altogether. The possibility of symbolically escaping the doomed natural cycle is a notion with which Swift had already toyed when he had his family of clockmakers creating themselves a cultural perpetuity ('The Watch'):

Consider the position of a man who has the prospect before him of extraordinary length of years . . . The limits of his being, his 'place in time' as the phrase goes, the fact of his perishability begin to fade and he begins not to interest himself in those means by which other men seek to prolong their existence. And of these, what is more universal than the begetting of children, the passing on of one's own blood? (*Learning to Swim*, p. 91)

Men's, it seems is the domain of time, women's the domain of childbearing: the mechanical perpetuity to which the race of clockmakers have dedicated themselves is defeated by confrontation with the simple fact of childbirth. Once witness childbirth, and mortality is upon you. Since *Waterland*'s governing preoccupation is with modes of paternity, this drive towards self-perpetuation leads to the fantasy of a mode of paternity that would be superior to the circularity of natural history. 'Which doesn't go anywhere. Which cleaves to itself. Which perpetually travels back to where it came from' (p. 177).

Let us return briefly to the ancestry of Tom's half-brother, Dick. Dick (who ends up diving eel-like into the waters of the Ouse, never to be seen again) is the son of Helen Atkinson and her own father. Despairing of political influence on events, and appalled by the deterioration of the First World War into meaningless slaughter, Ernest Atkinson, looked after by his daughter, has retreated to his country home at Kessling. There his passion for his daughter has grown in inverse proportion to his horror at what is happening in Europe. He 'beats a headlong retreat, backwards, inwards, to Paradise, and starts to believe that only from out of this beauty will come a Saviour of the World' (p. 190). Incest, as the narrator indicates, is one method of trying to stem the forward motion of biology and history. Because 'when fathers love daughters and daughters love fathers it's like tying up into a knot the thread that runs into the future, it's like a stream wanting to flow backwards' (p. 197). Ironically, Ernest's saviour of the world will prove to be Dick, the 'potato head'. But in fact incest is only one of the ways in which male figures in this novel seek to take control symbolically or genetically of their relations with the future.

When, on Martha Clay's orders, young Tom flings the aborted foetus into the river Ouse, he is doing something which haunts him for the rest of the novel. While Mary is physically and emotionally scarred, Tom's wound takes the form of a profound distrust of female inner-space as a suitable container for the future. There is a symbolic absence of sexual reciprocity which he will forever after try to fill. Henceforward, the teacher, like the novelist, will strive to generate his own offspring. Natural history and artificial history are juxtaposed in the very structure of the novel (chs. 27 and 28). One way of summarising the thesis with which this novel is experimenting would be to say that it proposes to substitute cultural for biological paternity.

To influence the young by telling them stories is a form of symbolic fatherhood, more reliable than the other sort. 'I should know', says the teacher, challenged in a pub about the age of the pupil with whom he is drinking, 'he's my son' (p. 209):

> Once upon a time there was a future history teacher and a future history teacher's wife for whom things went wrong, so – since you cannot dispose of the past . . . they had to make do.
> And he made do precisely by making a profession out of the past . . . and thus the history teacher – though his relation with his young charges echoes first the paternal, then the grand-paternal . . . could always say . . . that he looked back in order to look forward.
> Once upon a time there was a history teacher's wife who . . . couldn't have a child. Though her husband had lots: a river of children flowed through his classroom. (pp. 109–10)

Coerced into early retirement, he mentally addresses the children who protest on his behalf, 'I do not expect you to understand that after thirty-two years I have rolled you all into one and now I know the agonies of a mother robbed of her child . . .' (p. 6). If this novel is, as I believe, an enquiry into the status and meaning of patriarchy in late twentieth-century Britain, then one way of encapsulating its theme is to note the metamorphosis of the master of history into the history master.

Tom Crick's chosen method of reproduction is cultural, and operates, as we have already seen, through situated narrative. Yet to make this observation is already to stand on the verge of another. The paradox of a reflexive fiction like *Waterland* is that its allusion to voice generates the fiction of presence that is simultaneously deconstructed by the other spiral of the narrative. Tom Crick the garrulous history teacher is a front man for an enquiry into the novel's own narrative status, its own role in relation to those who may read it, those whom it situates as its own symbolic progeny. The very construction of the novel poses its own claims to symbolic reliability in contrast to the imputed unreliability of women. Thus for example, the chapters about the abortion are interleaved with the chapters in which (nearly forty years later) Mary steals the baby. Mistakenly conflating symbol and referent, she has succumbed in her loneliness to a desire for a literal child, even (perhaps taking the symbolism of her own name literally) to an atavistic desire to bring forth the saviour of the world: 'Your history teacher stands in the doorway, presenting before this bizarre Nativity, the posture of an awestruck shepherd . . .' (p. 229).

The messianic religious discourse into which Mary has been drawn is implicitly set alongside the secular discourse of the novel. Where the male narrator moves in the less disappointing world of the signifier, women, it seems, are identified with real presence, with the signified of biology. But while John Schad (1992, p. 918) argues that 'in the synecdochal guise of the 'menstrual cycle' woman provides the novel . . . with a *bodily* subtext and thus a hint of both the Christian and the Marxist utopian moment', it seems to me that the novel is on the verge of suggesting that motherhood is lent legitimacy only by religious clothing. The womb is an unreliable vehicle for male seed, and its offspring, even where they do grow to term, will not turn out to be the saviours of the world that were prophesied. The novel is thus sanctioned in its continued search for more authentic parenting arrangements. The male storyteller is not only an actor in a circling world, he is the source of a signification which lays claim to a more than momentary persistence, but which in turn sets in motion its own negation.

Swift seems almost to have been carrying out (whether wittingly or unwittingly does not matter) a programme announced by Barthes in the essay quoted above:

Just as psychoanalysis with the work of Lacan, is in the process of extending the Freudian topic into a topology of the subject . . . so likewise we need to substitute for the magisterial space of the past – which was fundamentally a religious space . . . – a less upright, less Euclidean space where no one, neither teacher nor students would ever be in his final place . . . The problem

is not to abolish the distinction in functions ... but to protect
the instability and, as it were, the giddying whirl of the positions of speech. In the teaching space nobody should anywhere
be in his place. (1977, pp. 205–6)

The implications of this radical instability do not simply affect
an undifferentiated 'mankind' as such: they bear differentially
upon a practice of masculinity as validated by patriarchy. To revel
in vertigo has a particular meaning in relation to the warranted
identities of men and fathers. And indeed the drive to paternity
is as suspect in this novel as it is the desired goal:

> Children, beware the paternal instinct ... whenever it appears
> in your officially approved and professionally trained mentors.
> In what direction is it working, whose welfare is it serving?
> This desire to protect and provide, this desire to point the way;
> this desire to hold sway amongst children, where life is always
> beginning, where the world is still to come. (pp. 132–3)

At the level of pragmatic psychology the possibility seems to be
glimpsed here (as in *Shuttlecock* or the short story 'Learning to
Swim') that the lure of fatherhood, a man's obsession with finding or for that matter with acting like a father, might be so
absorbing as not only to block off all other relations and potentials
but to malform those towards whom the fathering impulse was
itself exercised. At the level of narrative, the tale is forever set
against itself.

The outlook for fatherhood as represented in Graham Swift's
novels is bleak. They offer the negative heroism of struggle under
the lifelong burden of inventing a valid presence. Crick's heir
may be 'Price', the pupil with whom he develops a vicarious
father-son relationship, yet there is nothing he can do to allevi-
ate the terror of nuclear war and catastrophe that possesses the
sixteen-year-old founder of the 'Holocaust Club'. He knows as
well as his pupils that the ultimate phallic weapon threatens human
history and even human survival. In the context of patriarchy's
nuclear arms race, history is not in the history master's grip, and
his stories cannot deliver the reassurance that he has believed
all along to be one of the functions of storytelling. While the
novel's underlying mythos enacts distrust of biological process,
the cultural and symbolic process offered in its stead proves itself

unreliable and vertiginous too. All narratives contain within themselves the seeds of their own deconstruction. Dominion over the signifier turns out to be as labile and shifting as dominion over the signified. All that was solid threatens to dissolve: Fatherland transmutes into Waterland.

'THE WEAN AND THAT': PATERNITY AND DOMESTICITY IN *THE BUSCONDUCTOR HINES*

On the face of it, James Kelman's first novel *The Busconductor Hines* could hardly present a greater contrast with *Waterland* in terms of its setting, its language, or its narrative dynamic. However, I hope to be able to show that, despite these dissimilarities, a reading of this novel may be helpfully set alongside the other texts discussed here. Like the others, it is engaged in a renegotiation of the male subject's position on the boundaries of the public and private domains. To start with location – in terms of geography and of class – will prove a way of unpacking some further themes to do with masculinity. To make an obvious but necessary point, the 'world' of James Kelman's novels and stories is – even where, as in *A Disaffection*, the hero has entered the professional middle class – that of working-class Glasgow, its pubs, its betting shops, its closes and estates, its informal gatherings of unemployed men. Kelman has made a speciality of devising a literary notation for Glasgow working-class speech, and any account of his fiction that overlooked Glasgow, that behaved as though this richly coded context could be simply transposed elsewhere, would be a travesty. His linguistic construction of Glasgow is as much part of the fiction as Grassic Gibbon's Kincardineshire is of his.[7] This provenance presents problems to the middle-class English teacher critic, problems better faced now, since they will in any case bear upon the theme of masculinity.

If I try to locate the problem I find it has to do with a sense of embarrassment, of trespass even, a sense of incompatibility of voice: as though I as teacher or writer had no right to speak about Kelman's text, as though the otherness of its subject matter presented an impenetrable barrier to negotiation, the text speaking out of an experience so absolute that those outside that experience have no right to speak of it. If I pause here it is because this is not simply a personal difficulty. I am aware that a reader from another background might equally find – say – Fowles's a class-bound and inaccessible world. But, as I sought to demonstrate in Chapter 1, the universalist stance of 'English' – as to a degree also of metropolitan novel-reading practice – has tended to swallow both class and gender. Part of the endeavour of this book is to find a critical register in which that 'universal' reading subject is opened to question. Yet while the act of humbling oneself before the represented experience is perhaps a useful antidote to the imperialist pretensions of metropolitan criticism, it is a position that will scarcely bear rational examination. Of what represented world *can* we speak if it is a precondition of meaningful speech that we have personally shared the experience from which the discourse originates? Most literature, virtually the whole of history, would be barred to us. Yet my unease is not so easily dissipated, for reasons which have, I think, to do with the topic of this book. That is to say that my own disquiet may itself rest upon a set of myths about masculinity which – while they lie almost below the threshold of conscious thought – are nonetheless potent and widely shared. I mean a deep-seated belief that maleness is more authentic, more straightforwardly instantiated in some sections of society than others. To write this down is to be aware what a preposterous belief it is. But its subliminal ideological attraction is a useful reminder of the importance of social icons to any understanding of what masculinity means.

A set of inverse snobberies and ignorances seems to lead to a semi-articulated and widespread belief that working-class men – a grouping itself forged in the struggle against oppression – somehow express masculinity in a purer form. They thus become the object at once of social horror (in contemporary debates on a range of issues – on literacy and educational exclusion, on the 'underclass', on football hooliganism, on crime) and simultaneously a kind of awed admiration. Such fantasies are organised around icons of uninhibited physicality, strength, drinking, male bonding, and a no-nonsense orientation towards the world, and I enumerate them as a reminder of the projections that working-class men may be carrying on behalf of others. This cast of stereotypical heroes and villains (the two roles are remarkably interchangable) performs nightly in the drama of collective fantasy.[8] I suspect that one element in the runaway success of the film, *The Full Monty*, is its comedic recuperation of the working-class male, so often the villain of contemporary representation. To return to the case of Kelman, demotic language and subject matter can lead either to the reaction of the minority Booker prize judge to *How Late It Was*, or alternatively to a prostration before the experience purportedly behind the words which would lead to the rejection of any criticism as impertinent and contemptible. I do not myself think that either of these positions are tenable, and certainly not in relation to Kelman's novels and stories. We should neither overlook nor patronise Kelman's context, but his novels and stories are themselves highly wrought and complex texts, not primal expressions of some kind of ur-experience.

It follows that Kelman's novels are demonstrably about masculinity and being a man, and that they are at the same time themselves likely to be the focus of fantasies and projections about masculinity on the part of some of their readers, a desire to establish an authenticating connection with the world of the dole queue, the solidarity of hard drinking, chain smoking, gambling, heterosexual males. That his novels are *also* about the vulnerabilities of men could easily vanish beneath the stereotype. Or to put it another way: where so much of the weight of the available narrative stock concerns male success, triumph, or triumph's counterpart, glorious defeat, Kelman (like Dostoyevsky or Beckett before him) is working to find a register for inglorious, day-to-day failure. His narratives tease out the meanings of failure and survival not in relation to some generalised idea of 'man' or humanity, but in relation to the desires of men and the desires invested in manhood. They then proceed further to investigate what could possibly heal the wounds of those who have been discarded by the grand gender narratives. Even to put the case in terms of failure is itself condescending towards the denizens of Kelman's fictive world. So it is necessary to point towards the direction the present argument must take. I shall argue that the domain of Kelman's characters is – to put it in terms of a crude dichotomy – not so much action as language itself. That for the men of his novels language and discourse are the terrain in which to forge identities, and to take steps towards an environment in which their own claims to dignity, humour, or recognition might be realised. In turn, the language in which self-realisation might be attained – while it displays its share of oral aggression – is not so much the language of power, as a language of wit, subversion, and cunning. As Marina Warner has reminded us:

Cunning intelligence has been superseded by force as the well-spring of male authority . . . The very word 'wily', the very idea of subterfuge, carry a stain of dishonour . . . I'm observing a trend towards defining male identity and gender through visible, physical, sexualised signs of potency rather than verbal, mental agility. (1994, p. 26)

However, before we turn to the domain of language as such it is necessary to review other elements of Kelman's novel.

The fictive world of a Kelman novel – here, specifically *The Busconductor Hines* – portrays men both at work among workmates and in the home as actors in the domestic sphere. I want to explore this without falling into an argument about 'images of men', let alone into the implicit or explicit award of points for providing affirmative images. The world of work in Kelman is not a separate domain: work is extended across a spectrum which includes the 'workplace' of paid work (the buses, the factory, the schoolroom) and work at home (cooking, planning meals, budgeting, cleaning, bringing up children). The point of this latter catalogue – which could be considerably extended – is not to conjure up a sort of NVQ in domesticated masculinity, in which representative men could be awarded points for competencies. In talking about Kelman's work we might purloin Clifford Geertz's term and speak of 'thick description' – the project being to devise forms in which to register and to thematise the physical and social detail of living both in and outside the home.

In Chapter 3 I argued that much masculine narrative could be seen as an attempt to define the arena of domesticity as an enclosed and claustrophobic space identified with women, and then having done so, to fantasise escape routes to another domain where being and action could be more authentic. Domesticity was here defined not simply in referential terms, but as the narrative domain of certain sorts of action and certain kinds of identity. As far as Kelman is concerned, male unemployment and the part-time employment of women have created a situation where many choices are occluded, where long-term flight from the family and the domestic sphere (unless into the male enclave of prison) is not an option. To devise ways of thinking about the ecology of male identity is not a matter of simply slotting male figures into different environments. Kelman has set himself the task of developing a narrative technique for registering these shifts.

Let me briefly examine this project in relation to two salient areas of Kelman's fiction, those of male relations and of the home. The domain of male relations (in the pub, on the streets, even, to a lesser extent, at work) is one for which there were in any case plenty of literary antecedents. Developing this theme, Kelman has achieved a highly subtle register for the nuances of certain kinds of dialogue, and for the jostling for footing and status in pairs and groups of men. The technique produces a theatre in which intense attention falls upon verbal and physical gesture. Gordon has suggested to Brian (for whom he has persisted in buying drinks despite his friend's desire to get home to make his small daughter's lunch) that he might consider hiding a load of stolen goods for him for a suitable rake-off:

Then Gordon moved; he rose from the chair and reached for the empties: Just time for another yin eh!
O naw, Christ . . .
Och!
Naw. Naw Gordon honest! Brian was shaking his head and holding his hands aloft. I wish I could, he said.
Ah come on! Gordon grinned.
Naw honest.
A slight pause and Gordon said, You sure?
Wish I could.
Mm. Gordon nodded. He sat back down, then yawned and stretched his arms, flexing his shoulder blades. He looked at Brian. Brian shrugged and made as though to say something but Gordon leaned closer and said: I'm no being cheeky Brian but I think you're fucking daft, no to consider it I mean. That's what I mean, Christ, you don't look as if you're going to even consider it. Brian glanced at the ashtray a moment, then his gaze returned to Gordon who said; Are you?
What . . .
Are you? Consider it – are you going to consider it?
Course.
Gordon continued to look at him.
Course I'm going to consider it.
Gordon nodded.
Brian swallowed the last drops from the lager glass. He paused before saying: I'll need to be hitting the road, the wean and that . . . Heh Gordon, thanks for the drink and that I mean,

Christ . . .
No trouble.
Brian sniffed. He stood to his feet. Course I'm going to consider
it I mean, obviously . . .
Gordon shrugged. No fucking problem Brian dont worry about it.
Brian nodded. Well, see ye eh?
Right.
Seconds later and Brian was pushing his way through the exit.
On the pavement outside he hesitated, then set off, walking
quickly.

('The Wean and That', in *Greyhound for Breakfast*, pp. 179–80)

The theatre of Kelman's encounters is rich in nuance and in
unspoken struggles for dominance and standing. His domestic
theatre is equally densely coded. The common ground is an
insistence upon the social ramifications of biological being: the
planning involved in making and serving food; the problems for
a bus conductor of timing bowel movements or of having a
streaming cold; realising on arrival at work that he smells after
lovemaking. What is sometimes condescendingly known as the
commonplace or the ordinary is reframed by its centrality to the
narrative. Kelman has created a style which registers embodiment.
    The Hines who performs domestic tasks, or on occasion looks
after his child, is not a detached consciousness, but a figure managing non-stop and overlapping demands. When with some
satisfaction he runs over his menus in his head, the resulting
monologue makes an amusing contrast with the non-conditioned
confections of the media chef:

3/4lb beef links, 1lb of potatoes, 2 onions medium sized and 1
tin beans baked. And that's you with the sausage, chips and
beans plus the juicy onions – and they're good for your blood
whether you like it or no . . . And even if your mummy's sick
to death of chips, what should be said is this: she isnt the fucking
cook the day so enough said, let her go to a bastarn cafe . . .
Fine: the items should get dished no more than 4 times per
week but attempt to space it so that 1 day can pass without.
7 days in a week. What is that by christ is there an extra day
floating somewhere? . . . That's the time thing they set you up.
Just think of the days. (pp. 69–70)

The talking heads of Kelman's texts are bombarded by awareness of their surroundings, of their own and others' material existence. They cannot step outside their situatedness for dispassionate reflecion. The medium for registering these multifarious promptings is a complex instrument.

Central to Kelman's whole project is the elaboration of a style for representing consciousness. From early stories like 'Not not while the Giro' onwards, this has been a major drive in his work, and it is to this stylistic project that I next intend to turn. The voice that recurs in his novels is that of a kind of interior monologue, or, more accurately, an interior dialogue, the conversation in the character's head. An attempt to explore the theme of Kelman's masculinities must take account of this evolving style. In examining contrasting representations of the male subject I have drawn attention to a tension which might loosely be expressed as one between the notion of the complete, invulnerable subject, firmly in control of his own boundaries, and the vulnerable subject-in-process, threatened at once by invasions from without and by the unruliness of his own inner world.

So Kelman's representation of men in a whirl of painful excitement is played out against the background of a residual theory which posits the male mind as a site of reflection, dispassionate judgement, disciplined and unemotional attention to what needs to be done. Yet actually many male novels seem to revolve around their hero's *inability* to hold onto a disciplined, dispassionate masculine position, his attempts to blend with his company through frenetic espousal of different discourses – Updike's Rabbit; Bellow's Herzog, Joyce's Bloom. The interior dialogue which Kelman has developed bespeaks the heterogeneity of mind and consciousness. The focal centre of his narratives is a palimpsest of voices, quotations, half-formed thoughts, register shifts, distracting chains of association set going by fortuitous debris from the outer world.

This interior dialogue of Kelman's male characters has to be read against an implicit background: an enduring set of beliefs which credit the normative male mind with self-possession, singularity of vision, a resignedly disappointed judgment on the present in the light of a classical past. In such a paradigm, detached calm and authoritative overview take the place of both playfulness and bodily activity. It is a model for male mind which can be widely illustrated from nineteenth-century debates about the role of mind in society, and after which many figures (of whom Matthew Arnold might stand as a representative) have hankered.[9] Such a model of mind is rationalist in the sense that it is built on a clear-cut mind–body dualism, a hierarchy where mind is envisaged as the superior partner. The corollary of such a model is to project turbulence, unreason, emotion, elsewhere – onto women, working-class men, or colonial subjects. John Barrell has usefully put his finger on the parallels:

> Constructions of gender-difference very often supply or repeat the terms on which class-difference is constructed: women are frequently represented as different from men on the same terms as ignorant men are assumed to differ from educated men, or indeed as children are assumed to differ from mature male adults. (1988, p. 141)

It is crucial to understand that this tradition does not simply provide a recipe for how a man should be, as it were in his own personal experience of himself. It is also simultaneously a theory of social order. The man or group of men who constitute its normative subject rule others by the same token as they rule themselves. Any breakdown of the governance exercised by this hypostatised mind would be followed by social disorder and centrifugal cultural collapse.

This allusion to a model for the masculine mind does not simply redirect us to an abstract intellectual history. A version of it is still evident in Hines' own discourse. Thinking how he is going to build up and educate his son Paul, he thinks first of physical fitness ('it's good too, the swimming, hell of a good for you, the shoulders and that it makes you grow big yins and strong as fuck you'll be able to take care of yourself anywhere anytime'), but then goes on to mentally address the four-year-old Paul:

> you'll be able to do it son, control, take control, of the situation, standing back, clear sighted, the perspective truly precise and into the nub of things, no tangents, just straight in with an understanding already shaped that that which transpires shall do so as an effect of the conditions presented; there will be no other course available; you shall know what to do and go and fucking do it, with none of that backsliding shite. (pp. 90–1)

He projects upon Paul all that he knows is lacking in his own orientation towards things; yet it is at the same time characteristic of the irony of this text that Hines himself at once sees the flaw in this translation of singularity of vision into unambiguous action:

> The backsliding shite. There can be reasons for it. Things arent always as clear as they sometimes appear. You can have a way of moving which you reckon has to be ahead in a definite sense then for some reason what happens is fuck all really, nothing, nothing at all, nothing at all is happening. (p. 91)

In terms of the by now familiar dialectic between centre and margins, Hines (and any number of Kelman's other protagonists) are situated at the margins, where marginality connotes distance from both centre of self and imperial centre. By the same token, they lack control over their own boundaries: their identity is subject to invasion from without as well as lack of governance within.

In a quite physical sense, Hines's attempt to leave his mark on his son has failed. In Chapter 4, making a case about uncluttered heroism, I invoked the ancient symbolism of circumcision. This motif recurs in Hines' contemplation of his son. While he has not succeeded in his ambition, this aspiration represents an attempt to incise the signature of the father in the son's body, laying a surreptitious claim to membership of the chosen people:[10]

> Hines had wanted him circumcised at birth but allowed himself to be dissuaded by a variety of agencies. Why had he wanted it in the first place. He wanted him to be different. He wanted him to think of things. And it could have been a good reminder. Every time he went to the toilet he might have been remembering what was what from his auld man's teachings. Too late now. (pp. 102–3)

Re/membering makes you the embodiment of the father's teachings. But in keeping with the narrative drive of this novel, Hines has not had a free hand in his attempt to sign his son.

How does Kelman's representation of the conditioned and dependent male consciousness work? Perhaps the first note of caution is that his protagonists are not homogeneous, and are not the invariable subjects of the same kind of narrative attention. They differ among themselves, and the triangle composed of 'voice', narrator, and implied reader can be aligned in different ways. Some of his protagonists are case-studies, 'talking heads' the limitations of whose viewpoint – like the speaker of 'Lassies are Trained that Way' (collected in *The Burn*) – constitute a contrast with the implied politics of the narrator and form the subject of the story. More usually, they act as simultaneous self-conscious commentators upon what they themselves are saying. All are garrulous, non-stop commentators on themselves and on the world around them; all are decentred in the sense not only of feeling powerless in relation to the external world, but that their selves are dispersed: they exercise no mastery over internal or external events. They are powerless to avert repetition in the sense that things go round in their heads in cycles which the victim is powerless to break (a propensity which leaks into Kelman's titles – 'Not not while the giro'; *How Late It Was, How Late*). The subject is conscious of himself simultaneously as voice and listener. 'This isnt Hines who's talking. It's a voice. This is a voice doing talking which he listens to. He doesnt think like it at all. What does he think like. Fuck off' (p. 167). At the same time, and in parallel, the text is characterised by a lack of an overall narrative voice which would subordinate and exercise control over other voices. Polyphony here is at once central to the reader's experience and a sign of the lack of masterful narrative interference, a dominating narrator who would correspond to the aspirations of masculine self-discipline.[11]

To discuss an example dispassionately only seems to emphasise what I have just been trying to say, as though detached critical discourse might provide a specious serenity. Believing that Sandra, his wife, has left him, Hines rushes in panic out into the city. On his way back he accosts a crack in the pavement:

There is a crack in the pavement a few yards from the close entrance; it has a brave exterior; it is a cheery wee soul; other cracks can be shifty but not this one. Hines will refer to it as Dan in future. Hello there Dan. How's it going? Cold yin the night eh! This fucking weather wee man. Never mind but, the ice and that, helps you expand. Pity cracks dont wear balaclavas right enough eh! One good thing about these old tenements, however, is the way they refuse to allow snow to hang about. A tough set of bastards so they are. No messing. None of your fucking good king wenceslas rubbish with them. (p. 168)

Hines' world comes alive, is animated as he attaches to his material surroundings his own whirling intellectual and verbal energy. On occasions like this the abundant creativity of this mind-style verges on hysteria. Indeed, the notion of hysteria – associated as it traditionally is with women – is highly relevant.[12] For the idea of hysteria orbits around a loss of control consequent upon the invasion of the 'rational' by the somatic, specifically by the womb and its folklores. Hines, unable to stem the breathtaking whirl of registers, imitations, voices, jokes, becomes the victim of his own verbal creativity. Kelman has developed a syntax of internal flight, a registration for a mind zooming uncontrollably off in all directions, investing its surroundings with frantic energy as it does so.

As internal flight characterises the minds of Kelman's protagonists, so too physical flight is a recurrent theme in their stories. Frequently this is flight into the streets, an abrupt if temporary departure from situations, homes or jobs which for the moment the hero cannot handle. Both Pat (in *A Disaffection*) and the hero of *How Late It Was* set off on attempts at physical flight out of Scotland. But it is internal flight which seems to be the hallmark of men who find their situation intolerable but for whom there is nowhere else to go. Forced by poverty into the private world of flats or lone wandering, the only place to flee is into an interior world, a virtuoso performance to an audience in the head. The isolated man acts out imaginary roles before an interior audience. The theatre of the typical subject of Kelman's fiction has a tendency to move in a solipsistic direction.

On many occasions in this book I have observed how one of the binaries out of which masculinity is constructed is the active/ passive set. The goal for Western men, we have been assured from all quarters, is activity, deeds, achievement, making your mark, as opposed to passivity, dependency, reacting to events. As so often, fictions have transgressed this ideological norm, as countless novels and plays, from Dostoyevsky's underground man through Marcher in James's 'The Beast in the Jungle' to the narrator of Heller's *Something Happened* have adverted to the condition of the man who is not making his mark, or impressing his stamp upon the world around him, the man whose governing theme is the vacuum where his sense of his own purpose ought to be.

James Kelman takes up this problematic from his own angle. Part of the problem for the man who knows that he is not living up to the heroic narratives is the sense of a gap in his own consciousness: the rankling awareness of the disparity between the model and the actuality. Through this gap flows resentment and anger at self and at others. Violence against self or others is one response to the dissonance between ideal and real self: an attempt to act out in however self-destructive a physical form the dominance that you believe you were promised but of which the world has cheated you. A self-pitiful story of superiority unacknowledged underlies the pugnacious distress of the angry white male. Anger and powerlessness are closely related phenomena, and anger as a subject is shot through Kelman's work. To understand why his account of anger is so much more productive than the misogynist spite of something superficially similar, like Osborne's *Look Back in Anger*, we need to turn to his account of the male as victim.

Like Kelman's other protagonists, Rab Hines operates in a small world: the buses and the depot canteen, the pub, the flat he shares with Sandra and Paul. He has ambitions – above all to graduate to driver – and Sandra's parents and his own mother at least once held out hopes that he might go on and educate himself, though all such hopes appear to be doomed to failure. From inside his trap he rages against the world that has so little to offer him, and where he cannot escape the pettiness of those in authority. The folk memory within which he lives is a residue from the proud history of the Red Clyde and concerns a world where men performed manly work in the heavy Clydeside industries. His demonology is one shared by other Kelman males: the bosses, the police, the DSS, the Heads of the Monarchic State. It is difficult framing the questions one wants to put to this narrative, since they could so easily slide over into the possessive individualism of the free-market, and the crass injunction to 'get on your bike'.

Given that *The Busconductor Hines* invites the reader into sympathetic collusion with its hero, what I find myself wanting to articulate is perhaps as simple as the old-fashioned question whether the narrator envisages Hines as having any responsibility for his own fate. Tagged to this question is another one which is gender inflected: 'Hines' is indeed a member of a deprived underclass once ruthlessly exploited and now economically marginalised. But does his masculinity and his consciousness of himself as a man have something to do with the role he himself takes up within that history? His assumption that if he cannot be a 'real man' he will instead act out the child?

One of the striking things about the Hines narrative (which I am here endowing with representative status) is that it reproduces in the reader a sense of being in the presence of another version of the spoiled adult male child. In classes I have found that women readers have felt this particularly strongly – to the point of almost parental fury with Hines for his helplessness. It is as though in telling his story of helplessness and dependency he has usurped a conventionally feminine position (compare Gilligan, 1993). Yet his way of dealing with powerlessness inscribes a male narrative. To try a tentative way of putting it: if Hines cannot have what his culture leads him to expect, then he will sulk, his characteristic pose being to play infantile and self-defeating games with any one who occupies a position of authority. Self-destruction is a mode of revenge upon a world which does not come up with the promised goods, though of course the threat to destroy yourself is only effective if your presence in the world is significant enough for your absence to be felt. It is as though being extraordinarily bad at managing his own life constitutes both an appeal to sympathy, and even a perverse kind of claim to centrality. But if through his own fecklessness Rabbie loses his job on the buses, then it will be left up to Sandra with her despised office job to keep the family afloat.

Hines, like so many of Kelman's men, is a victim, but it is a mark of the complexity of Kelman's work that the spirals of that very victimhood are themselves held up for examination. What could heal the wounded narcissism of the anti-heroic male? Not surprisingly, one plot proffers solace through the woman. Dostoyevsky's underground man seeks solace in his power over Liza the prostitute. Pat in *A Disaffection* believes that his world would fall into shape if only Alison would agree to an affair with him. If such rescues could occur, they would be to the advantage not only of the male protagonist, but of the discourse he represents. I am reminded of the question Alice Jardine poses to male allies of feminism. 'Can you think through the heterogeneity of the subject without relocating the burden of the demised universal subject onto the female?' (Jardine, 1987, p. 61). In terms of relationships, Hines is better off than either the underground man or Pat, and the representation of his relationship with Sandra is a deeply moving aspect of the novel. However, Sandra clearly is not going to be able to meet all his needs, and the strain upon her of attempting to do so is taking its toll. Marriage in this case,

as perhaps in so many others in a world of privatised experience, is being strained to the limit to fulfil all that is coming to
be required of it. We have glimpses of other possibilities of social
fulfilment in Hines' relationship with his workmates, for example
his regular driver, Reilly, a reciprocity of friendly abuse which
seems to be the vehicle of a good deal of warmth and social
pleasure as well as offence and forgiveness (for example, pp. 60–2).
Relationships between fathers and sons are no more straightforward than any other relationships in Kelman's fiction. In
narratives which refuse the climactic beginning, middle, and end;
which are characterised by their episodic structure and low-key
plots, a visit to the parents and a conversation with the father
often seems to form a decisive narrative moment. These are never
stages for the heroics of reconciliation or forgiveness: it is in their
very ordinariness and reticence that these encounters – washing-
up together, oblique arguments over meals, the lurking presence
of the unsaid – figure in the narrative of the sons. Contact with
the father (usually in his house) is both ironised for its emptiness,
its failure to be anything important, and deeply reassuring (for
example, *A Disaffection*, pp. 105–21). The long-anticipated meeting
between Peter and his father constitutes the climax of *How Late
It Was How Late*. There is a very strong sense that when Hines
goes to see his father and in fact ends up talking to his mother
(and coming away with carrier bags of vests and food) he is looking
for some kind of absolution or renewal and that the failure of
that hope is itself constitutive (pp. 128–37). His father, we know,
is typically remembered looking out of the window of the
apartment – gazing at the view almost a form of meditation. As
a child, Hines himself 'got held there by the elbow, a desperate
attempt by the father to instil some peace unto him' (p. 130).
This habit of peaceable, non-appropriative gazing emerges as a
significant motif. It is perhaps the nearest the novel can come to
a kind of redemptive perspective.

Despite the climactic events in the depot canteen, the novel
ends not with any disclosure or climax, but with Hines himself
looking out of the window of his bus. It is as though the narrative in which the father's oblique and almost wordless presence
affirms his son has to do not with action but with passivity, waiting,
looking. If the whole narrative structure of *The Busconductor Hines*
constitutes a reappraisal of masculinity, then the relation between
Hines and his father, and in turn between Hines and his son is

embedded in a deeply unpatriarchal ability to survive what counts as failure, even to survive a man's own judgment on himself for succumbing to the ordinary.

IN SEARCH OF LOST LANGUAGES

In David Leavitt's novel *Equal Affections* (1989), Walter (the lover of the novel's hero Danny) is an Internet man. A lawyer by profession, he spends long hours after work using the computer to converse on gay channels, mixing over the Internet with men with codenames like Sweatpants, Teenage Slavemaster, and NY Jock, shadowy figures who have made a fine art of virtual sex. He eventually has an affair by e-mail and then telephone with a man who (with *Middlemarch* in mind) calls himself Bulstrode. Eventually, sickened by his own flight into a world of virtual reality, Walter returns emotionally as well as physically to Danny. At this point he and his narrator embark on a critique of a postmodernist world in which no pragmatic or epistemological distinction is drawn between simulacrum and creatural reality. The temptation of that world is the way it licences those with access to the technology to leap Faust-like beyond the bounds of physical imperfection:

> Bulstrode, it seemed, had ceased to believe in the barrier between imagination and act. And why not? What are we, after all, Walter wondered, but voices, synapses, electrical impulses? When one person touches another person's body, chemicals under the skin break down and recombine, setting off an electric spark that leaps, neuron to neuron, to the brain. Was that really all that different from what happened when fingers pushed down buttons on a keyboard that sent signals across a telephone wire to another keyboard, another set of fingers? . . . All around him, Walter heard people complaining about how they wished they were different . . . Bulstrode had found a way around all that; he had found out how to become the self he imagined, the self his real life . . . constricted him from fully being. (*Equal Affections*, pp. 139–40)

The counter-statement occurs later on in the novel, and there seems no doubt that it is a statement of the values upon which the novel rests. Walter has been pondering the fate of two Internet regulars who had decided to rendezvous, and for whom he guesses the actual sight of each other has been a disaster, leading them to 'salvage what they could of their fantasies' by fleeing back to the electronic medium:

> The problem with real intimacy . . . is that you cannot just shut it off. Real people have a way of banging against the doors you've closed; they know your name, your phone number. They live with you. And that, he decided, was not altogether bad. What the computer had offered was the safety of isolation, the safety of control . . . And even so, from those heights of safety . . . Walter longed for nothing more than the rich landscape of the dangerous human earth . . . [The] further he went, the more Walter realized that, like it or not, he was inextricably bound with the people who had mattered to him and who mattered to him now, the people whose loves defined him, whose deaths would devastate him. (pp. 240–1)

The route back to 'the rich landscape of the dangerous human earth' is, as the earlier passage made clear, through family:

> Some people invented themselves. And yet there were others – Danny, his mother – who seemed to say, Who I am is who I was, where I come from, who my mother and my father were. The past forms me. The past owns me. The pit of family called endlessly for Walter. (p. 140)

These passages seem to lead us to something of central importance about Leavitt's work, which in the context of this book I might attempt to get hold of like this. The Internet and electronic media represent an exponential further leap in the direction of a Faustian masculine universe where the disembodied wishes of mind can apparently be fulfilled without organic consequences. In such a context, Leavitt's novel seems to be evolving a critique of the postmodernist rhetoric of the self as artefact. In a world of simulacra and virtual reality the gay novel – at least in Leavitt's hands – re-opens commerce both with nature and with history. In doing so, it is returning to the roots of the realist novel. (Butters *et al.*, 1989; Lilly, 1991) Indeed, on reflection this is not surprising, since the gay novel is almost by definition proposing the reinstatement of the male body as an object of desire. It legitimates the male gaze upon himself. An epistemology and a narrative take shape in which the male body – so far from being an imperfect vehicle for male mind – is recovered from the degraded status to which traditional 'high' epistemology had consigned it. By reclaiming the male body as an object, novels like Leavitt's reverse the process identified by Laura Mulvey in her critique of the male cinematic gaze. As argued in Chapter 1, the fixation upon the mediating object of the woman's body has implication for the invisible male body too: 'The male figure cannot bear the burden of sexual objectification. Man is reluctant to gaze at his exhibitionist like' (Mulvey, 1975, pp. 27–8).

Peter Lehman in turn reminds us how if 'we ignore studying images of the male body, we are likely to think of masculinity as an ahistoric, powerfully secure, monolithic position, rather than one riddled with cracks' (1988, p. 108; and see Chapter 1). In representing the penis and the male body as objects of desire, the gay novel proposes a masculinity both fuller but at once more vulnerable. By an analogous process, the bio-social world regains its narrative prominence as a place where all, whether male or female, are subject to similar constraints, but also equal access to joy. There is in fact a utopian current running through the gay novel. The figure of the gay novelist imputed behind his text is another sort of go-between, an intermediary whose task it is to reclaim the male body from being either the subject of denial or the legitimate target of violence and destruction.[13] Consequently one element in the narrative is now explicitly men's vulnerability to other men:

> It seemed to him ironic that he should be doing to Rob exactly what Eliot had done to him. The oppressed, once again, became the oppressor. Men were assholes, Sally had assured him, and now, for the first time, regretfully, Philip felt himself sinking into the ranks of men. (*Lost Language*, p. 205)

And, like all go-betweens, such a novelist is prey to the self-righteousness and dread of subversion entertained by those who are situated at either end of the message system of which he constitutes a key element.

Leavitt's stories and novels have it seems to me a dual address. Inasmuch as they are addressed to a gay community they constitute affirmations of gay narratives and the validity of gay lives and relationships. Inasmuch as they are addressed to a straight audience they constitute a kind of persuasive ethnography, an explanaory discourse addressed to outsiders. The orientation towards either audience results in a form of novel writing which is highly referential in its assumptions: the opposite extreme to an underground anti-representational language of opposition. The act of explaining a society to an audience whom you believe has not shared the experiences to which you refer results in a discourse of realism, a form of novel writing which has curious affinities with didactic narratives, like for example the 'condition of England' novel of the 1840s and 1850s. Both exhibit what I have just called persuasive ethnography, a density of explication and circumstantial detail which is meant not only to set a scene but to initiate the reader into the antechamber of understanding. In Leavitt's work, both narrator and protagonist thus occupy the role of guides and intermediaries familiar from an earlier stage in the novel's history. The gap between the knowledge imputed to the audience and the knowledge of the narrator may in the gay novel as in the industrial novel lead to an explosion of the referential code, a ploddingness of narrative explication. There are moments when Leavitt sounds like no one so much as Judy Blume. And as in Blume, the possibility is entertained that the reader might be more than simply a tourist in the reference world of the novel: he might potentially be an initiate into its systems. In terms of narration, this pedagogical bent means that the novel lacks the spurious purity of intention beloved of mid-twentieth century aesthetics: like the nineteenth-century novel, the story has designs upon its audience, and its heroes and villains are likely to occupy an exemplary status. The novel might even be a vehicle for saving lost languages by inculcating their grammars and idioms.

As the title heralds, the idea of lost languages is a dominant motif in *The Lost Language of Cranes*.[14] It seems to me important therefore to point out that the idea is itself both deeply ambivalent, and also akin to the motif of the lost world of, say, *Le Grand Meaulnes*. Such an idea comes replete with allusions to the dilemmas of primitivism. It is possible to take, that is to say, a tragic, a romantic or a pragmatic view of lost languages, or for that matter to alternate between them. The lost language itself often connotes a form of communication richer, more authentic, more deeply rooted in primal meaning than those we speak now.

(Compare the media image of the wise native American.) On the one hand, it can never be recovered: the speaker of a lost language is forever disinherited, permanently deprived of the ideal communicative resource, perhaps even, like the crane child, of any other means of communication. On the other hand, there is a glimmer of sustaining hope, the possibility of recovering your lost language, of forming a community with other speakers, even of teaching it to others. There is a potential common ground between speakers of different languages, and the novelist as ethnographer and linguist can lead the way. As Leavitt himself has noted, one 'characteristic of pre-eighties gay literature was an assumption that an irrevocable gulf existed between "them" and "us"' (Introduction to *Penguin Book of Gay Short Stories*, p. xxi). By implication, his own work has been devoted to building bridges. As he says elsewhere in the same Introduction, talking of reading novels like Halloran's *Dancer from the Dance*, '[what] I found myself longing for . . . was a gay literature that, rather than fawning over angels made flesh, transformed homosexual experience into human drama; a gay literature that was literature first and gay second' (p. xix). Yet this optimistic activity may be carried on at the expense of all that was represented by the lost language. Jerene's allegory of the crane child may in a way represent the tragic loss of the richly coded, allusive language which has traditionally represented one recourse for the gay writer.[15] But if so it is one on which Leavitt in opting for realism and the referential is in process of turning his back. Inevitably, in bringing his fiction writing project out of the closet, Leavitt has risked disconnection from a rich seam. The advantages and disadvantages of joining the hegemonic culture are finely balanced. With this in mind, let us look more closely at *The Lost Language of Cranes*.

David Leavitt is a novelist of the family as well as of the pair (see, for example, the stories in *Family Dancing*). His couples take the floor in the dance of the generations. In a way, Philip's parents are as central to the narrative of *The Lost Language of Cranes* as he is himself. This family is represented as a cognitive structure which produces ignorance, the family norm one of denial. Owen, Philip's father, is also gay, but he has woven his own life and his marriage around an elaborate series of attempts at flight from his own reality. Rose, Philip's mother, is devoted to the imperative of smoothing things over. This manifests itself in two ways: first, she works as a copy editor who spends her professional life correcting the minute details of text. By implication, her obsessive attention to detail is a bulwark against disaster: editing a book on the care of elderly patients, she finds it 'oddly comforting to read such carefully worded descriptions of collapse and decay' (p. 15). Her form of reading contrasts, as we shall see, with other versions of text and reading which the novel also proposes.

But the other activity with which Rose is associated (through a revival of feminine stereotype) is baking and icing cakes, an activity which the narrator explicitly associates with copy editing:

> In moments of tension she calmed herself by thinking up synonyms: feel, empathize, sympathize; rage, fulminate, fly off the handle; mollify, placate, calm. It was an instinct to put the world in order that powered her, as sitting at her desk she put sentences in order, mending split infinitives and snipping off dangling participles, smoothing away the knots and bumps until the prose before her took on a sheen, like perfect caramel. Cooking was her other pleasure. She gloried in foods that in no way resembled their ingredients . . . Owen sat before the cakes Rose made and gazed, his face filled with a kind of awe. (p. 5)

Books and cakes are juxtaposed in their association with comfort and (stereotypically) mothering. 'At home, he knew, there was cake; there was always cake. There were books, too. It was cold outside, so it would be warm inside' (p. 24). Frosting (that is, icing), smoothing a homogeneous sweet surface over the bumps in things (a metaphor explicitly drawn out later on, p. 249) is the countervailing metaphor to the text's opposed chaotic energy. Rose's desire not to know (especially about her son's and then her husband's sexuality) becomes a key motif in the novel's examination of willed ignorance. At the same time, baking and frosting is a metaphor for the production of text, a narrative smoothing and ordering of the obdurate signified.

The countervailing force to the maintenance of surfaces is one of chaos and decay. Both Owen and Rose (though for different reasons) are appalled at the imminence of losing their apartment, and the likelihood of having to find a new home reinforces their horror at the streets and urban dissolution. Yet it is suggested that there is more underlying this than a perfectly rational horror of 1980s urban decay, that Owen's sense that 'everything had slipped out from under him' (p. 7), is a direct consequence of the denial and flight that characterises his life. His chaos, that is to say, is within him as much as a feature of the world beating on the walls of the apartment. His version of flight, unlike his wife's, is to seek solace wandering the city itself, extending his range year by year into the gay bars and porno theatres. The underlying problematic of the novel turns on the relations between a secret life (with its furtiveness, lies, and role disjunctions) and potential reintegration into society and family.

This drive towards completion and reintegration, this optimism about the emancipatory force of communication, marks this novel as an heir of the enlightenment project. Throughout, shared knowledge and open communication are proposed as the solvents of the deformation of individuals and communities by socially learned prejudices. There can be, observes Sedgwick, 'few gay people, however, courageous and forthright by habit, however fortunate in the support of their immediate communities, in whose lives the closet is not still a shaping presence' (1991, p. 68). In arguing the centrality of the 'epistemology of the closet' she speaks further of the 'risks in making salient the continuity and centrality of the closet, in a historical narrative that does not have as a fulcrum a saving vision . . . of its apocalyptic rupture' (ibid.). Within Leavitt's text, disclosure and the moment of disclosure assume central narrative importance. But, as we shall see, its guarded optimism rests on moments of revelation rather than apocalypse.

If we are to understand how the dialectic of secrets and disclosure takes narrative form in David Leavitt's novel, we need first to return to the motif of reading. As I have already suggested, various kinds of reading enter into *The Lost Language of Cranes*. There is Rose's meticulous copy-editing. Then Philip himself works as an editor for a firm which publishes pulp romances. Centrally, from the age of nine he has been a devoted reader of children's novels by one Derek Moulthorp, who turns out to be the adoptive father of Eliot his lover. With Moulthorp, children's fiction enters the narrative as a distinctive code. It is hard to know what the novel is doing with the figures of Moulthorp and his partner Geoffrey, to whom Eliot eventually introduces the naïvely admiring Philip, unless it is making a programmatic point about a gay couple's capacity for parenting. However, his novels figure prominently, and the trope of meeting the writer seems to underline not only the novel's announced theme of myths of origin, but its implicit attention to the authenticating voice behind a discourse. Framed like this, the book becomes almost a sacred object: returning to his parents' apartment, Philip 'held the book in his hands . . . like one of those rare and ancient Bibles the mere touch of which is said to hold curative powers' (p. 112). Moulthorp's books constituted for the young Philip a richly satisfying alternative world to the strained solicitude of his parents, a world 'the other side of the wall' in which he retrospectively supposes Eliot to have been playing all along (p. 115). His reading of Moulthorp goes back to the summer Philip was nine, when his parents dutifully took him off on holiday: 'In the back seat of the car, while Rose or Owen drove, Philip read Derek Moulthorp's novels' (p. 120).

The novels, for which Philip retains a deep affection, seem to constitute at once a zone of flight and a satisfying alternative world. It is hard to believe that Leavitt or his narrator are simply marking time by articulating a truism about children's fiction. It seems more likely that reading fictions may have a particular significance as a form of social apprenticeship for those whose constituency is still in the process of formation.[16] Further, the metafictional box within box of the children's novel seems to be drawing attention to the status of reading, perhaps even of the praxis of the novel within Leavitt's fictional universe. You can read, the novel seems to imply, both (like Rose) to numb your anxiety, or to seek blueprints for an alternative world, a world where there might be a better fit between being and action. The insistence on children's fiction thus meshes with the utopian and redemptive strand in the novel, and constitutes part of its address to its own reader.

The Lost Language of Cranes, I remarked just now, had a dual address. To the two constituencies suggested there, I must now add a third. To refer to the reader position would only inadequately describe the process by which Leavitt's novel works upon its reader. Position implies singularity, something static where complicity with the discourse of the novel seems to involve process. For one category of readers anyway, the discourse constitutes an invitation not only to self-recognition but to action. One implied reader of *The Lost Language of Cranes* is a potential agent, a figure who, in learning to read himself aright and thus in changing his communicative circumstances, might become able to acknowledge and speak his sexual identity for the first time. To that extent,

Owen is the reader's surrogate within the text. To understand how this might be, we must explore a little further the relations between reading and disclosure.

Rose, as I have indicated, is an ambiguous figure. There is a tendency for her to be scapegoated, to carry much of the blame for the family's mode of repression; even a hint of the folkloric belief about mothers creating homosexual sons (for example, pp. 217, 283)[17]. It is also the case that Leavitt's novels – quite as much as their heterosexual counterparts – are grounded upon the 'dangerous human earth' through female biology. The economy of hope in *Equal Affections*, for example, is structured around first Danny's mother Louise's illness and death, and then his sister April's pregnancy. However, in the later stages of *The Lost Language of Cranes* Rose attains her own dignity, and apparently a share of narrative sympathy. It is her copy editor's capacity to read (so often displaced into furtively purchased puzzle books) that enables her to read clearly the climactic situation in which Owen brings home his young colleague as a gift for his son. Just before this, she has made a vain visit to a bookstore: 'what she needed now was a book telling her how to live in rubble' (p. 271). The point is that while the DIY psychology section holds no such books, Rose's own skills as a reader will stand her in better stead than any book. At first, she scans the nightmare dinner party: 'She was numb, a copy editor, scanning coldly with an eye for detail . . .' (p. 282). But soon she realises the truth: 'It had taken her three minutes to determine what they had been struggling to figure out all night' (p. 286), that Winston their handsome visitor is actually straight. The power politics of the occasion shift, yet it is hard not to receive the impression that – as the focus moves away from Rose again – she is to be punished for her clarity of vision. The last we see of her, she is wearily turning back to a book of acrostics, a reader whose reading has no existential force other than distraction. '"Find fault with" . . . Criticize? Disapprove? Upbraid?' (p. 308). In this text there is passive reading and active reading. Passive reading is close to denial, a way of numbing the subject to anxiety. Active reading substantialises observation with action arising from disclosure. In turn disclosure is the motor of plot.

The related themes of the subject reading himself and his world and of disclosure are not surprisingly often foregrounded in the gay novel. As Ed Cohen has observed, 'more than just a process of emergence and nomination, "coming out" is also a way of telling a life story. Indeed to some extent the "coming out story" becomes the basis for both the production and the reproduction of an identity to which the narrating individual lays claim precisely by pronouncing this story to be his or her own. . . .' (Cohen 1995, p. 87). In *The Lost Language of Cranes* much of the narrative attention is given to the process and ethics of disclosure. To that extent revelation rather than erotic resolution is the goal of Leavitt's plots. Nevertheless, the novel operates in an intertextual relation with the genre of romance: it is significant that Philip's own work lies among heterosexual romantic fiction. It appears, however, that the heterosexual romance is not going to be an adequate model. Like gossip in Lawrence, it figures as a debased form of narrative implicitly compared with the version we are being offered. While at moments the novel appears to instantiate an almost Reichian programme of erotic salvation, the actual pairings it does throw up have an unstable and centrifugal quality. In the end, the novel promotes the understated affection of Philip's relationship with Brad over the glamour and emotional switchback of life with Eliot. The principal narrative investment is in knowledge rather than salvation through courtship and pairing. Such knowledge is grounded in family rather than in the free-floating couple: Eliot's freedom of attachment is an object of longing, but also, the narrative seems to insist, not enough:

> And Philip thought how nice it must be to be able, like Eliot, just to take off from a place you've come to call home, to eject yourself from the complex and dangerous network of friends, lovers, apartments, to sever all ties and leap into the startling newness of the unknown. (p. 257)

In turning its back on the temptations of flight, the passage anticipates the 'dangerous earth' passage from *Equal Affections*.

So disclosure and the personal freedom from which it grows and which it confirms have to be seen not as unqualified goods, but as qualified by and conditional upon the contexts in which they happen. To that extent, Leavitt's novel belongs in the socioethical tradition of the realist novel. Much as his novel has invested in openness between persons, the force of the narrative seems to emphasise that disclosure can take place at the wrong time or for the wrong reasons. Philip's insistence on coming out to his parents as and when he does is examined both from his point of view and from theirs, and it appears that one narrative voice at least has more than a little sympathy with Rose's desire simply not to know: 'I don't believe that just because something's a secret it therefore by definition has to be revealed . . .' (p. 173). But since disclosure and a freeing of communication are essential to the text's system of values, its agents have to confront their dilemmas. Disclosure is a key moment in the proposed life narrative, but those contemplating speaking out or coming out are required to be sensitive to the circumstances in which they disclose.

Perhaps another way of putting this is to say that in David Leavitt's fiction ethics are preferred over aesthetics. Once again, a relevant touchstone may be *Equal Affections*. There, 'Bulstrode's' life history as communicated by e-mail 'was not, it quickly became clear, a thing of the real world' (p. 134). When Walter asks 'How can you love someone you've never seen?', Bulstrode replies: 'In my imagination I've seen you. And isn't that better? That way nothing can spoil you for me. That way you'll always be perfect.' Walter's reply flags the campaign represented by his author's fiction: 'But I'm not perfect . . . and that isn't love' (p. 139). The object of this fiction (however utopian that object may be) is a discourse of the real, its goal a regained language of intimacy and the body social.

As we have seen, moments of disclosure, the drama of coming out, are major plot kernels. They constitute an invitation to the reader to consequential action, an appeal to enact knowledge in the domain of praxis. In *The Lost Language of Cranes* that dynamic is represented through the relationship between Owen and his son. I noted earlier that Owen appears in some sense to act as a surrogate for the reader, an agent on behalf of those possessed by an immense revelation waiting to happen. 'Father and Son' is the title of the last section of the novel, and as in Kelman too, the meeting of father and son carries a specific and potent narrative charge. In existential terms the bonding between the two of them appears at least temporarily to outweigh any other relationship. In narrative terms, their coming together, driven by Owen's desperation and need, provides the cadence of the novel. In physically taking care of his father, being there to take him in, and putting him to bed on his own floor, Philip's story reaches a temporary resolution. It is a resolution which, like the final view of Hines wiping the condensation off the windows of his bus, crystallises in an act of looking, an act dense in suggested meanings: 'He would lie awake for a long time, he knew, looking at Owen's white ankles in the bright moonlight' (p. 319). Affectionate contemplation of the vulnerable paternal body substitutes for dynamic closure.

The Lost Language of Cranes exhibits many of the features of the traditional *Bildungsroman*. But where the novel of (masculine) education through life traditionally worked within a patriarchal structure of authority into which life's apprentice was stage by stage initiated, here the vulnerability of the father and nurturing role undertaken by the son inverts the patriarchal structure. The argument leads to a more permeable, more negotiable fatherhood. Both son and father will have to begin their apprenticeship to their new lives as equals. If Owen is, as I suggested above, in some ways a surrogate for the reader, one condition of his entering a new life phase is giving up such positional status and weight as fatherhood has given him. His new identity, once Philip has rescued him from the street, takes shape as they talk. The metaphor when it comes is in the end not altogether surprising:

[Philip] braced himself against the window, knowing he must keep control, knowing he must not stop his father no matter how much he wanted to. What had started had become inevitable; it was as if Owen were giving birth to something with his words, something that was determined to fight its way out of him. (p. 316)

In this communicative circuit between men, a quasi-biological power of reproduction is attributed to words. The infant that emerges is Owen's new identity. The power of words and thus of the novel to beget and give birth to new realities could hardly be more patently asserted.

In discussing James Kelman, I noted that the reference world of his novels might be the focus of projection on the part of readers who did not themselves belong to it. There may be something analogous going on for straight readers of David Leavitt. The critical story which I am trying to tell cannot evade the gay novel. But I do not feel comfortable with my own appropriation of Leavitt's work for my own purposes, without at least a minimum of self-critical reflection. Gay men and gay communities carry all sorts of meanings for other men who do not so identify themselves. An analysis like that I have just carried out itself risks idealising and homogenising the gay novel. One kind of reading would be to invest in a novel like *The Lost Language of Cranes* utopian hopes, treating it as a place where the contradictions and destructiveness of patriarchy and straight masculinity could be symbolically resolved. But straight men should not make gay men or gay novelists the focus of hope for salvation any more than they ought to invest parallel hopes in women. The hard and frequently unrewarding work of sustaining fragile hope is there for everyone to do. In the final section of this chapter we shall be looking at another narrative of social hope and despair.

THE CHILD IN TIME

Though the narratives are stationed at the contrasting ends of the same event, the disappearance of a child in a supermarket is a trope that links both *Waterland* and Ian McEwan's *The Child in Time*. Similarly, one thread running through David Leavitt's *The Lost Language of Cranes* concerns the horrifying ease with which individuals can vanish into the chaos of an autodestructing urban society:

> The city had always seemed huge to him from this vantage point, and it still seemed huge, but now it was not so much a place where anything might happen as a landscape he might any moment be lost in, disappearing forever the way people seemed to be constantly disappearing in this city. Posters were put up, rewards offered; people posited theories, claimed to have seen their friends wandering, ghosts, on West Street . . . He imagined himself among them now, his own face staring . . . from the makeshift posters on café walls, in the subways. (*The Lost Language of Cranes*, p. 312)

The vanishing of persons moves to centre-stage in *The Child in Time*, with the emphasis shifting from the narrator's own potential disappearance to the loss of his child. Textually, the movement of simulated persons into and out of orderly existence codes the power of narration over its subject matter. We have seen how towards the end of *The Lost Language of Cranes* Philip is present at the metaphorical birth of his father's new, gay, identity. Child-birth of another kind will supply the resolution to *The Child in Time*. Fictional texts propose a stable community of memorialisation, and seek ways of representing the co-existence of different narrative paths. But whereas a countervailing utopian strand runs through David Leavitt's *The Lost Language of Cranes*, the reader of *The Child in Time* is more likely to be struck by its dystopian energies. If the values the narration espouses are to win through it will be against considerable odds, and the outcomes will remain uncertain.

The Child in Time organises narrative energies around an act of social witness, and may be read as a sort of green parable addressed to the late 1980s. The meaning of that parable, and the hope to which it gives a shape has to be read in the context of all the countervailing forces. Those forces are given a temporal habita-tion by a 'futuristic' setting about ten years ahead of the time of writing.[18] The result is to place the narrative within a framework which we might describe as millenarian. *The Child in Time* is a millenarian novel in somewhat the same sense as is Martin Amis' *London Fields* (1989). Which is to say not only that they both organise their prophetic address around the connotations of the coming millennium, but also that the apocalyptic weight resting upon their plots is given precise realisation in terms of the collective fears haunting the moment of writing – nuclear war (accidental or planned), the degradation of the city, the emergence of an alienated and violent underclass, escalating environmental and atmospheric degradation. This is not simply a gratuitous or alarmist setting: as I shall seek to demonstrate, the narrator's pessimistic assessment of the social and environmental moment contours the structure of the novel as a whole.

Let us begin with the futuristic dimension; the argument will then lead to questions about government, power, and public policy, and onward to speculation on the role of the novel and the male novelist within the social and cultural analysis that *The Child in Time* proposes. The prophetic vision of the late 1990s which forms the fabric of the novel, is a result of extrapolating from trends visible enough at the time of writing. As a discourse, the text abjures hyperbole. Whether in science fiction or in the realist tradition, providing readers with the knowledge of another world – even an England a few years in the future – risks protracted pedagogical exposition. McEwan's solution is to insert items of knowledge as they are assumed by his cast. Thus, for example, environmental degradation is all the more chillingly brushed in for being an accepted aspect of the fabric of the world which narrator and speakers take for granted: information that is not foregrounded in some ways resonates all the more. Whereas we can defend ourselves against inauspicious knowledge when it is shouted from the rooftops, the inferences which we draw from textual metonymies penetrate the more deeply for being invested with our own processing energy. We learn casually and almost in passing that broad leaf woods have been almost entirely replaced with conifer plantations, that it is now very difficult to find wild flowers, that there are no longer any newts.

A corresponding degradation is overtaking the social world. The flattening out or marginalisation of diversity is a conspicuous feature of both. The new social world with its gridlocked cities, decayed public services, its armed police and its licensed beggar scheme, is the product of public policy knowingly espoused. Yet the sense of apocalyptic catastrophe which broods over this novel has to do with more than the accelerating destruction of the social and biological environment. This is also a world perched on the brink of nuclear war, a disaster which, again in a chilling flashback, we understand almost happened during the Olympic Games crisis' earlier in the year (p. 34 *et seq.*). Such items are not just part of the stage-set for the plot, a kind of painted backdrop for the story. The vulnerability of human life, and the fragility of the collective arrangements for the maintenance of that life lie at the core of McEwan's novel.[19] The social, ecological, and political environment is at the heart of the story. It is in this sense that I am arguing that *The Child in Time* may be read as a 'green parable'. But if it is a green parable, it is one in which masculinity, fathering, and gender relations figure prominently.

The thread that connects the elements of *The Child in Time* concerns public policy and political power. From the very beginning of the novel it is made clear that the social realm has been given its contemporary shape by acts of public policy, the breakdown of public transport providing a metonymy for some of the results. (The remaining trains have an important narrative function in this novel in bridging separated worlds: journeys towards death and towards new life.) The whole novel is a critique of mainstream masculinity and patriarchal power, and it is fundamental to that critique that the public policy articulated and sustained by such power violates both the natural and the social worlds. The devastation of both environment and nurturing matrix is a masculine accomplishment. Early in the novel Stephen (here the voice of the narrative) reflects that the 'art of bad government was to sever the line between public policy and intimate feeling' (pp. 8–9), and the whole novel appears to be a symbolic attempt to redress that severance by realigning the mutual interaction of the public and the private domains. To that extent, McEwan's novel parallels the argument of the sociologist Anthony Giddens' *The Transformation of Intimacy* (1992), and is shot through with the same contradictions. 'The advancement of self-autonomy in the context of pure relationships is rich with implications for democratic practice in the larger community . . .', Giddens argues (p. 195), and while the utopian lineage of his sociological thesis includes Wilhelm Reich and Herbert Marcuse, it is difficult not to see this as radicalism privatised, intimacy posed as a bulwark against social despair.

The making of policy, and its relation to reproduction and the raising of children is epitomised through a text within the text, the ubiquitous and turgid *Authorised Childcare Handbook* which haunts *The Child in Time* like the persecutory other of its own narrative. Quoted with parodic authority at the head of each section, the *Handbook*, a particular project of the prime minister's, constitutes the agenda of the Whitehall committee on which Stephen, as a noted children's author, has been invited to sit. The sittings of the committee are among the strands polyphonically wound through the novel, and their object is the link between the private and familial and public and political worlds of the novel.

The channel which connects the protagonist Stephen to the making of public policy is his friend Charles Darke, who in one sense presumably represents the dark side of Stephen. Charles is an able and extrovert Tory politician who as a protégé of the prime minister, is clearly going places. Apart from the prime minister, he is the character in the novel who is closest to the seats of power. It is he, not Stephen, however, who is overwhelmed by his proximity to the centre, and his fate is highly pertinent to the argument of this book. Perhaps the clearest summing up, and the one which the narrative apparently endorses, is put in the mouth of Charles's wife, Thelma, after she and Stephen have carried his body home from the wood. Stephen wonders aloud why, if Charles wrote the childcare manual, it was so harsh. Thelma replies:

It's a perfect illustration of Charles's problem. It was his fantasy life which drew him to the work, and it was his desire to please the boss which made him write it the way he did. That's what he could not square and that's why he fell apart. He could never bring his qualities as a child . . . he couldn't bring any of this into his public life. Instead it was all frenetic compensation for what he took to be an excess of vulnerability. (p. 204)

Once again, if in a different form, we are confronted with the figure of the conventionally successful man who implodes into self-destruction. The route traced by that dynamic leads back to a pastoral childhood of boyish adventure. Paradoxically, if we except the baby born at the end, there are no children in the narrative present of *The Child in Time* – Stephen and Julie's daughter Kate has been lost before the novel begins. In a novel which from the title onwards thrusts childhood and its traumatic absence before us, what is incarnated in Charles is yet another version of that now familiar figure, the grown man as child.

The first time Stephen is summoned to Norfolk by Thelma to see his friend it is to find him become disconcertingly a schoolboy out of a 1930s story, the 49-year-old Cabinet Minister as Just William. Charles's breakdown has taken the form of regression to a child self which appears (like the contents of his pockets) to have been reconstructed by 'very thorough research'. The only way he can get in touch with his child self is through this elaborate pretence, his licence to go out and play (and afterwards be put to bed early by Thelma acting mother) in one of the few remaining scraps of broadleaf woodland. At least one of Charles's functions in the novel is to represent a type of masculinity whose public aggrandisement grows out of a lack of inner integration. The result is disastrous at both personal and policy levels. In a programmatic novel, Charles's road represents a dead end. While at one level this can be read as a text about grief and mourning: at another, it concerns the male relationship to childhood and its integration into his adult life.

Relationship to your child is a deeply ambiguous concept. At one level it refers to actual children, at another to the relationship to the child that you yourself were.[20] McEwan's story of grief and mourning alludes to both. It is perhaps not glib to suggest that the little girl Kate has to be sacrificed in order that her father may grow. The psychoanalytic critic Daniel Gunn (1988) may once again help us here.[21] In this passage he is drawing heavily on the work of Serge Leclaire:

> Everyone has a child within. Indeed one has not so much a child as several children: the child one once was, the child one was – and even more the marvellous child one was not – for one's parents, the child one might want to have; and the child one is still every day, when one thinks of what one might have been and done. (p. 45)

He then goes on to quote Leclaire himself:

> For everyone there is always a child to kill, a representation of plenitude and immobile ecstacy . . . to mourn and mourn repeatedly. There is a light to be doused so that it can shine out and fade away against a background of darkness.

The juxtaposition of child and man, of being and unbeing, of paths taken and untaken, provides the fuel-source for the whole novel. And the book, as Gunn and others point out, is another kind of body. The logic of the conditional, of possibility, the wonder and horror of potentiality, leads us to a further set of interlinked ideas: time, books, and reproduction.

Time, like the child, is thematised in the title. It is also the subject of lengthy conversations between Thelma (a physicist by profession in a reversal of the conventional gendering of science) and Stephen:

> whatever time is, the commonsense, everyday version of it as linear, regular, absolute, marching from left to right, from the past, through the present to the future, is either nonsense or a tiny fraction of the truth. We know this from our own experience . . . Time is variable. (p. 117)

The novel thus attempts an accommodation between what is supposed to be a physicist's view of time and experiential time. This accommodation is in turn reflected in the narration. The time structure of the discursive level is no more complicated than that of many twentieth-century novels. Readers of Iris Murdoch, John Fowles, or for that matter Graham Swift, would have little trouble recognising the discourse. Though the locus of concentration moves with the intensity of the protagonist's supposed experience (hence much of the novel is told as reverie or flashback) it is not difficult for the reader to reconstruct the story level in a chronological way. (The person who actually does lose track of the key nine months is Stephen himself.) The novel does, however, introduce elements which clash with its own superficially realistic genre. As in *Le Grand Meaulnes*, the instability within realism set up by this attraction towards the fantastic seems to be at the core of the reader's experience of this novel. I shall examine two such 'uncanny' episodes.[22]

We might borrow a leaf from Freud's theory of the uncanny to suppose that one element of uncanniness is the 'conflict of judgment', the lurking possibility that a phenomenon could be interpreted in more than one way. The first episode at least is open to a 'psychological' or naturalistic interpretation. When, following Thelma's summons, Stephen drives in a hired car to Norfolk to see Charles, the lorry in front of him is involved in an accident. Stephen steers his car to safety and goes back to investigate. The accident is described at a level of detail which slows down both Stephen's and isomorphically the reading experience. Here a direct cue to a naturalistic explanation is offered: 'Julie would have appreciated what had happened to time, how duration shaped itself around the intensity of the event' (p. 95). In the aftermath of the accident, Stephen rescues the driver (who it emerges is not in fact seriously hurt) from his crushed cab in a scene which seems to anticipate – if in hideous parody – his subsequent role in the birth of his child: 'There was a head at Stephen's feet. It protruded from a vertical gash in the steel' (p. 96). The lorry driver's last messages he throws down a drain – their message has been for him rather than for their intended recipients. This event has no bearing on the plot in any direct sense. Its presence therefore seems to be accounted for in terms of a variation on a recurrent theme, a theme repeatedly signalled by an association of key elements: the narrative distortion of time, rescue from death or unbeing, conception and birth.

Prefigured in the road accident is the other occasion which I want to look at, an occasion central to both plot and theme. It seems to represent a junction between the inner and outer dynamic of the novel, and occurs on another outing from London into the country, this time when Stephen goes down to visit Julie, who is by now living on her own in Sussex. It is also the occasion on which Stephen engages in the reflection about time quoted above, a reflection in which he seems to be trying out the thought that women and men have a different relationship to time and to possibility: women comprehending time as more flexible, an arena of change rather than an arena to be dominated by institutions. The outcome of this episode is the conception of their new child. That outcome is heralded by signs of disturbance in the mimetic surface of the novel's discourse. It is as though the genre of realism is inadequate, as though the novel's project requires a shift of genre, or at least of narrative register, in order to accomplish its ends. The whole episode calls for careful examination.

Stephen's visit to Sussex in mid-June follows an exchange of 'neutrally worded postcards' with Julie. In a novel where written messages code the failure or success of the master message of the novel text itself, Stephen finds on arrival at the country station that the rain has smudged and made almost illegible Julie's instructions. His own adventure is itself about to become illegible.[23] On arrival, he sets out on his walk through a rural landscape characterised as the new sterilised domain of the novel's present time: a hypermarket, a motorway, planted lines of conifers 'with their flashing parallax as one row ceded to the next', a 'geometrical forest uncomplicated by undergrowth or birdsong', an 'unbounded prairie of wheat' (p. 51). What appears to happen to him then can be read either in realistic terms as a kind of hallucination or as a transition into a different level of discourse. The disturbance in the narrative is marked by a shift from focalisation through his own consciousness at the present time of narration to an apparently authoritative commentary drawing on Stephen's own later recollection. The narrative distantiation implied by 'afterwards' and a disturbance in the tenses announce a discrete episode about to happen: 'Afterwards, Stephen tried to recall what was on his mind as he walked the three hundred yards between the gate and a well-used minor road. But it was to remain inaccessible, a time of mental white noise.' Stephen's uncertainty is matched by that of the narrator: he 'was aware perhaps of his wet clothes' (p. 55). When he reaches the other side of his time warp his arrival is signalled by the reappearance of broadleaf trees: the 'trees around him were unfolding, broadening, blossoming', chestnuts, as we learn in a moment.

When Stephen arrives outside the Bell Inn with its parked bicycles he has, as he later learns from piecing the scene together with his mother's help, become a silent witness to that moment some forty-five years before when his mother considered having an abortion. The white face she saw at the window matches like the missing piece of the jigsaw puzzle the disembodied Stephen who stares into the pub. Here, as again a few pages later when he and Julie make love again, the text has traced out the alternative narrative, the path which forks from moments of choice. This moment of slippage between time zones, the re-entry of the past into the present, or of the child protagonist as a ghost into the past, is not uncommon in children's fiction – an enactment of an alternative narrative path.[24] Here too it is associated with the figure of the child in time. The figure outside the pub window has been excluded from being and embodiment. His mother 'could not see him. She was listening to his father speak . . . and could not see her son. A cold infant despondency sank through him, a bitter sense of exclusion and longing' (pp. 59–60).

When he and Julie come together again it is this moment which is once more remembered in the flow of a narrative which represents choice as the trace of another potential narrative ('a ghostly, fading Stephen rose, smiled, crossed the room and closed the bathroom door behind him'). He himself feels that this moment picks up and draws out the threads of the earlier moment outside the pub: 'Had he not seen two ghosts already that day and brushed against the mutually enclosing envelopes of events . . . then he would not have been able to choose, as he did now. . . ' (p. 63). The child conceived in this lovemaking will be born, at the end of the next winter, once Charles is dead at the end of the book. We are not told the sex of this child (anymore than that of the prime minister whose structural opposite the child may be), but it is clear that this new child, while it cannot replace Kate, and while Mars still shines outside the cottage window, is a pledge of healing.[25] To understand this ending and reframe the novel's preoccupation with childhood and birth, we need to go back to the subject of books and the role of the male writer as father of his own text.

As an intermediate step I need to pick up the subject of the plasticity of identities, a subject necessarily intertwined with the promotion of narratives in which roles are developed and played out. Jerome Bruner, whose philosophy of education meshes with the theories of the social constructionists I cited in Chapter 1, is talking about the 'transactional self':

For stories define the range of canonical characters, the settings in which they operate, the actions that are permissible and comprehensible. And thereby they provide . . . a map of possible roles and of possible worlds in which action, thought, and self-definition are permissible (or desirable). (1986, p. 66)

At the same time, it is the contention of Stephen and perhaps his novel that culturally, at least, there is a difference between women and men in the shaping of their own lives. On his way to visit Julie, he reflects on the way she has re-made herself since Kate vanished:

Such faith in endless mutability, in re-making yourself as you came to understand more, or changed your version, he came to see as an aspect of her femininity. Where once he had believed . . . that men and women were, beyond all the obvious physical differences, essentially the same, he now suspected that one of their many distinguishing features was precisely their attitude to change. Past a certain age, men froze in place, they tended to believe that, even in adversity, they were somehow at one with their fates. They were who they thought they were. Despite what they said, men believed in what they did and they stuck to it. This was a weakness and a strength. Whether they were scrambling out of trenches to be killed in their thousands, or putting the final touches to a cycle of symphonies, it only rarely occurred to them . . . that they might just as well be doing something else.

To women this thought was a premise . . . Consequently, they were not taken in so easily by jobs and hierarchies, uniforms and medals. Against the faith men had in the institutions they and not women had shaped, women upheld some principle of selfhood in which being surpassed doing. Long ago men had noted something unruly in this. Women simply enclosed the space which men longed to penetrate. (pp. 54–5)

Stephen is here deputising for his narrator, and the project of McEwan's novel may be to reclaim for men – through the agency of the male author – a share of that plasticity and that creative inner space.

In *The Lost Language of Cranes* one strand of the narrative was articulated through children's fiction. Derek Moulthorp, the author and illustrator of many novels for children, figured as an alternative model of parent, a surrogate father whose male parthenogenesis allowed more plasticity of generation than that of the biological parents within the novel. I have already noted the presence of one text-within-a-text in *The Child in Time* in the guise of the portentous extracts from the *Authorised Childcare Handbook*. It is now necessary to link the presence of that text – and all it stands for in terms of back-to-basics parenting – to another text, this time Stephen's own children's novel, *Lemonade*. The point is both that Stephen has been able through his book to address the loss of his own childhood, and that his relatedness to the next generation is conducted in terms of cultural as well as biological reproduction. As Charles (in those days Stephen's publisher) puts it: 'it was your ten year old self you addressed. This book is not for children, it's for a child and that child is you. Lemonade is a message from you to a previous self which will never cease to exist. And the message is bitter' (p. 33).

If Charles is right, then Stephen has made a much better hand of his own departure from childhood than has Charles himself, and it is a sharp reminder of this contrast that when, after a perilous climb, Stephen reaches Charles's tree house, it is professedly lemonade that his uncannily transformed host offers him to drink. Yet the therapeutic effect within the writer's own life is not, we are to understand, the only justification for writing. Writing is performative as well as expressive, and Stephen's writing also gives him influence over the next generation. Specifically he has, according to Charles, taught them about their location in time:

> You've spoken directly to children. Whether you wanted to or not, you've communicated with them across the abyss that separates the child from the adult and you've given them a first ghostly intimation of their mortality. Reading you they get wind of the idea that they are finite as children. (p. 33)

The writer for children is thus perceived not only as the person who successfully bids farewell to his own past, but who by the same act speaks to children as the voice of mortality. The writer is the channel between children and time, the missing link in the implied equation of the title. The writer who can create new beings out of nothingness can also take that life away, or make his symbolic generation messes to gorge his appetite.

I said at the beginning of this section that *The Child in Time* could be read as a green parable. As a parable it is addressed to a social and natural world suffering possibly terminal degradation at the hands of patriarchal policy. While its most powerful and haunting emblem is the disappearance of Kate, that loss in turn symbolises both a more extensive disappearance of viable life forms and the horror of collective amnesia. Yet in describing the novel as a parable I am implying that the novel represents more than a dystopic vision; that it is a kind of prophetic book, a prophecy which points in the direction where solutions to the problems it diagnoses might lie. I shall now attempt to identify the nature of the symbolic resolutions offered by the narrative.

As we have already seen, Stephen has hypothesised a difference between the male and female approach to time and to change. These reflections precede his own entry into a time warp that signifies the co-presence of alternative narratives. The vision of his young parents seen in discussion through the pub window is a grim variant on the primal scene. When he falls away horrified from that scene, he not only revisits a stage before identity solidified, but makes a reverse journey through and out of time, returning to embryo and then eventually to nothingness:

> The air he moved through was dark and wet... He... dropped helplessly through a void, was swept dumbly through invisible curves... saw the horizon below him even as he was hurled through sinuous tunnels of undergrowth, dank, muscular sluices. His eyes grew large and round and lidless with desperate, protesting innocence... he had nowhere to go, no moment which could embody him... And this thought unwrapped a sadness which was not his own. (p. 60)

A similar journey will be made, though this time not in reverse but forwards towards embodiment by the child which brings Julie and Stephen together again. If the novel offers a symbolic resolution, an act of healing which atones for the loss of Kate and by implication all the other absences at which the text hints, that act of healing is connected to – perhaps even identified with – the act of writing. The writer can give birth not only to his own alternative narratives but even to new lives. In the end, *The Child in Time* proposes a reassuringly traditional message.[26]

In this novel, women are in charge of their own lives, and have strength left over not only to tolerate but to support men, as Thelma does Charles. Julie knows better than does Stephen what she needs to do to come to terms with the loss of Kate. Further, unlike Mary in *Waterland*, her maternal role is assured. But while women possess a flexibility in relation to their own insertion into change and history, the metafictional disposition of the novel insists that it is the male novelist who can take charge of change. The strands of narrative and potential narratives are in the hands of someone who can manage the interchange between the actual and the potential. As those potentials are embodied in the text, the male novelist is found reviving the metaphor of writing as a mode of giving birth, a revived mode of paternity. It is through writing that the male subject can atone for the wounds inflicted upon the creatural world. And not just the wounds inflicted by male policy in the abstract. Let us remember that the names Julie and Stephen have occurred before in McEwan's fiction.[27] In chronicling the loss of Kate and the healing narrative that ensues, it appears that the novelist is making amends for the humiliations and bizarre cruelties inflicted upon creatural being within his own novels. It is as though *The Child in Time* is an act of redress to the sadistic infliction of pain and humiliation in novels like *The Cement Garden* or *The Comfort of Strangers*. In the symbolic appropriation of childbirth, there is a close analogy between *The Child in Time* and the childbirth that crowns the ending and rises above the male-inflicted violence and imprisonment of Peter Carey's novel *The Tax Inspector* (1991).[28] Both intimate a perspective of redemption that reframes the narrative of abuse.

The Child in Time addresses itself to a world seen to have gone disastrously wrong. It suggests that the roots of that disaster or near disaster can be traced back to the self-promoting activities of patriarchy.[29] There is a strong sense that it is patriarchy that has got it all abysmally wrong, and that those addressed by the novel are called upon to re-establish the line between 'public policy and intimate feeling'. But can we (and McEwan and Amis are writing in the moment of Greenham, of radical feminism, of Gaia) as men leave it to women to sort the planet out? Is the male novelist a prototype for the man who can dissolve the ossified boundary between the genders? There appears to be a hankering after a harmony that defies Cartesian dualism; an androgynous harmony to which men might gain at least symbolic access. In this there is a strong suggestion of womb envy: as the father of his own text the male writer turns out to be able to give birth as well. *The Child in Time*, suggests Adam Mars-Jones in a witty critique, 'may be the most sustained meditation on paternity in literature'.[30] If so, he argues, McEwan wants to have it both ways – to appropriate the benefits of paternity as an existential condition and to exonerate himself from the charges which must be laid at men's door.

Kate's disappearance figures the aborted plot, or abandoned narrative. Her memory within the text represents the trace of all the 'normal' narratives, all the genres that the narrator cannot deploy but for which he grieves. The implied novelist would like to have been able to tell one kind of story, but it is no longer the time of day to tell the story he had in mind. His story is shaped by other urgencies, driven by other obsessions. What sort of habitations are there in between manipulative power over malleable material and prostration in awe before the sheer complexity of the world? The author's (or narrator's) power over the reader parallels his power over subject matter. How that power is used is therefore a key question. One of the underlying questions in this novel, then, has to do with the way in which the text negotiates its own cultural power to initiate metamorphosis in reader or subject matter. If the narrative voice is surrendering patriarchal domination over material (and reader) what sort of voice does it turn out to be? The trajectory of McEwan's self-referentially fictional career seems to lead from experience back to innocence.

Since writing *The Child in Time*, Ian McEwan has, so to speak, given birth to himself as a children's novelist. *The Daydreamer* (1994) can be seen as emerging from the same problematics as the former novel. A bundle of parallel themes includes the relation of the narrator and the child (as subject and as addressee), the child as focus of alternative narratives, and experiment with alternative paths in time. Anthony Browne's illustrations and McEwan's text mutually reinforce each other, both coding the eerie disturbance of naturalistic surfaces. On another intertextual note, the hero, Peter's, younger sister is called Kate, as though the little girl who went missing in *The Child in Time* has passed through a wormhole in time to resurface alive and well in another universe. To take one of the stories for brief discussion would help to crystallise some themes.

All the stories work upon the narrative trope of the eruption of fantasy or daydream into 'ordinary' situations followed by a return to a transfigured normality. 'The Dolls' strikes me as a story which, like *The Child in Time*, is a self-conscious fiction about male engagement with the symbolic. In this instance, the 'daydream' is that Peter enters his sister's room on his own, and is attacked by her dolls, led by the 'Bad Doll'. The bad doll (humourless though it is to remark on it, obviously a bad object, a key to the splitting that is taking place here) was 'of all the dolls neither boy nor girl. The Bad Doll was simply "it"' (p. 17). Overwhelmed by this onslaught, Peter is dismembered, changing place with the 'Bad Doll'.[31] He is thus by implication castrated as well: the scene seems to represent the apprehension that in playing with dolls (that is to say with fictional people) the imaginative boy will be sadistically feminised.[32] He is rescued by the return of Kate and an ending that is a variant on 'it was all a dream'. Kate reasserts normality by making him put all the dolls tidily back in their places and normality resumes. Yet this conclusion leaves behind it a lurking unease that symbolic action is simultaneously powerful and ineffective, that the author of fantasy might be subject to horrifying punishment for usurping the role of creation.

The dynamic of McEwan's recent fiction is fuelled by an attempt to explore what men could do to heal the world they have made. One way of reading the text would be to see it as an attempt to produce something akin to Shakespeare's *The Winter's Tale*: another green parable of male destructiveness and female reconciliation mediated through the work of the male author. And, like *The Winter's Tale* the symbolic resolution of McEwan's plot both foregrounds and overcomes time through interpellating children into reconciliatory narratives. The figure of the male novelist can father a new child to replace the lost child, and the baby born at the end of *The Child in Time* (unlike the saviour of the world who failed to materialise in *Waterland*) appears as a saviour, a being who may be able to transform the dystopia into which s/he has been born.

In their different approaches to history, to language, to the physical body, and the social body of readership, the four novels discussed in this chapter exemplify some of the paradoxes inherent within any attempt to rewrite masculine narratives. That each of them has at some point bumped up against irresoluble dilemmas in no way invalidates the project on which in very different ways they have been engaged. They all challenge us as readers to take part in that project of making and remaking, unsatisfactory, even dangerous as it may be. For even unsatisfactory speech is preferable to silence and a flickering light better than no light at all.

Afterword

Part of me is inclined to forgo any sort of afterword. Might it not be a way of imposing closure, a last minute attempt to take charge of the reading process? On the other hand, a mysterious silence might connote a superior refusal to do any sort of tidying up, even to see the need to take leave of the reader. I hope that this book might help to challenge the residual equation between the heterosexual male reader and universal experience. More positively, I hope that it may incite critical self-consciousness about 'reading as a man'. To this end, I have implied all along that the practice of reading could not be dissociated from ethical and historical choices. The readings I have carried out may serve as a reminder of the insistence with which patriarchal masculinity seeks to drown out the other, inciting the initiate to concentrate on implanted inner voices, instilling fear of ridicule, humiliation, or loss of status.

Yet to relinquish the reflex claim to superiority and status need not be to collapse into dependent helplessness. The alternative to the ventriloquism of his master's voice need not be peevish and resentful silence. What we need – what I need – is the courage to accept that the self is always in process, that it is what John Shotter (1993) calls a boundary phenomenon. Human communication, as he says elsewhere, is 'ontologically formative . . . a process by which people can . . . literally inform one other's being, that is, help to make each other persons of this or that kind' (1989, p. 145).

To accept and work within cultural mutuality, to seek a reciprocity of voices in or out of fictions requires men to grow out of the horror of dependency. As Stephen Heath has said: 'To respond to feminism is to forgo mastery . . . the impersonal safety of authority can no longer be mine' (1987, p. 6). We need to be clearer about our relatedness to ourselves and to others, and about where our strengths and resources could come from. Anthony Giddens reverses Freud's notorious question:

What do men want? In one sense the answer has been clear

and understood by both sexes from the nineteenth century onwards. Men want status among other men, conferred by material
rewards and conjoined to rituals of male solidarity. But the
male sex here misread a key trend in the trajectory of development of modernity. For men self-identity was sought after
in work, and they failed . . . to understand that the reflexive
project of self involves an emotional reconstruction of the past
in order to project a coherent narrative towards the future.
Their unconscious emotional reliance upon women was the
mystery whose answer they sought in women themselves; and
the quest for self-identity became concealed within this unacknowledged dependence. (1992, pp. 60–1)

It is not that any of our novels provide answers, though they
may suggest other ways of posing the questions – or even suggest other questions. It is rather that in dialogue with them and
their other readers we may move towards the articulation of new
and non-phallic narratives. Such a development would be a small
contribution towards dissolving what Dorothy Dinnerstein calls
the collaboration between men and women 'to keep history mad'
(Dinnerstein, 1976; for example, p. 276).

Two false trails might, I think, be suggested by the readings I
have carried out here. Thus one male reaction to the implied
loss of cultural hegemony might be a paralysing sense of loss
and emptiness. Yet the egalitarian implication of the plural self
need not be implosion, the embarrassed abandonment of authority
roles, or abjection in the face of the supposedly superior emotional experience of the other (Dinnerstein, 1976, p. 72; Rutherford,
1992, ch. 4). Such a reaction – understandable as it is – lays a
spurious claim to harmlessness. More importantly, this 'all or
nothing' syndrome simply transfers the weight of judgment and
the missing universal onto women.

Secondly, there are good reasons to treat with caution the idea
of the unbounded plural self, or any ethic sanctioned in however roundabout a way by deconstruction. A ceaselessly malleable
subject position, like the unending play of signification, can be
endlessly manipulated in the interests of the 'free market'. Writing about American feminism in the 1980s Susan Jeffords points
out: 'a valorisation of plurality as an end in itself . . . may be
misdirected in the context of late American capitalism's own
appropriation of plurality and "excess" as aspects of its own

structures' (1989, p. 167). It would be a bitter historical irony if all we could substitute for a discredited patriarchy were men as perpetual narcissistic consumers.

In accordance with my own subject I had better resist the blandishments of cadence or peroration. So I shall end with a personal note, not a conclusion. It looks as though the only thing for men to do as teachers of reading is quite unheroic: to go on talking, writing, teaching, and learning, in the hope of cultivating the plots in which new narratives may take root.

Notes

INTRODUCTION

1. The interested reader is advised to turn to Chapman and Rutherford (1988); Cohen (1990); Connell (1995); Jackson (1990); Mangan and Walvin (1987); Middleton (1992); Miles (1992); Roper and Tosh (1991); Segal (1990); Seidler (1989); and Sussman (1995); all of which also contain useful bibliographies.
2. Middleton (1992) ch. 6.
3. Compare Mulvey's (1975) puritanical assault on visual pleasure, p. 24. Some of the issues to do with men's pleasure are explored by Frank Mort in Chapman and Rutherford (1988).
4. Compare Gregory Bateson, *Steps to an Ecology of Mind* (St Albans: Paladin, 1973). An anthropological view of the mutuality of knowledge is well-described by Carrithers (1992), for example ch. 4.
5. Claire Pajaczkowska, 'The Heterosexual Presumption' (1981) repr. in *The Sexual Subject: a Screen Reader in Sexuality* (London: Routledge, 1992).
6. I have found Peter Middleton's chapter 'The Lost Language of Emotion' (Middleton, 1992) particularly suggestive here.
7. I am drawing here particularly on Anderson (1991), and more generally on Linda Colley's *Britons: Forging the Nation 1701–1837* (London: Pimlico, 1992) on the rhetorical construction of nationhood. Tölölyan's essay is relevant as he explores revenge as a cultural institution and the 'iconic centrality' in the eyes of a community to be gained by the individual life in becoming the exemplar of a master narrative (Tölölyan, 1989, pp. 105, 108–9, 111). See also Eve Kosovsky Sedgwick's paper 'Nationalisms and Sexualities', in Sedgwick (1994).
8. This process finds poetic representation in many of the poems in Ken Smith's (1987) *Wormwood* (Newcastle: Bloodaxe); and in poems like 'Rough Job' or 'The Inspection' in Fred Voss's (1991) collection *Goodstone* (Newcastle: Bloodaxe).
9. Pajackowska, op. cit.; Middleton (1992) helpfully discusses the senses in which we can say that men are oppressed (p. 145).
10. A paradigmatic example is developed in Lilian Smith's classic study of racial oppression, *Killers of the Dream* (London: Cresset Press, 1950), for example Part 3, ch. 2, 'Two men and a bargain'.
11. For references to historical studies see n. 1 above. Carrithers (1992) ch. 5 is thought-provoking on the idea of social intelligence.

1 MASCULINITY AS FICTION

1. A movement which can be seen to begin with Berger and Luckman (1971), and whose more recent developments can be traced in Billig (1991); Harré (1993); Middleton and Edwards (1990); Shotter (1992); Shotter and Gergen (1989); Bruner (1986). Also relevant here are Middleton's discussion of Raymond Williams' concept of 'structures of feeling' (Middleton, 1992, pp. 205–7), and my own attempt to stitch some of these issues into a discussion of literary text in 'First and Third Persons' and 'Narratives to Live By' (Knights 1992 chs. 4 and 6).

2. See Carrithers (1992) throughout. Beneath their individualism, right-wing arguments are in any case apt to fall back upon the determining influence of the even more intractable structures provided by the more or less spurious sociobiology of sex and race.

3. The imperialism of the linguistic paradigm has been challenged from different directions, for example by Fredric Jameson in *The Prison House of Language: A Critical Account of Structuralism and Russian Formalism* (1972). The appropriation of linguistics by the social sciences has recently been questioned from a linguistic direction by Stephen Pinker, in *The Language Instinct: The New Science and Language of Mind* (Harmondsworth: Penguin, 1994).

4. An example within a contrasting, humanistic, psychological discourse would be John Rowan's *Subpersonalities: The People Inside Us* (London: Routledge, 1990).

5. Another example of thinking through this postmodern idea of the self would be Homi Bhabha (1994).

6. Compare Ross Chambers (1991), *Room for Maneuver: Reading the Oppositional in Narrative:*

> As its title suggests, this book proposes that between the possibility of disturbance in the system and the system's power to recuperate that disturbance there is 'room for maneuver', and that it is in that space of 'play' or 'leeway' in the system that oppositionality arises and change can occur. But not radical, universal, or immediate change; only changes local and scattered that might one day take collective shape and work socially significant transformations. (p. xi)

7. Many references will be found in Knights (1992). To these add McCormick (1994), Bennett (ed.) (1995) and Evans (ed.) (1995).

8. Felman (1977); Brooks (1994).

9. The discussion starts with Barthes' *S/Z*. See also Roger Fowler, 'The Referential Code and Narrative Authority', in *Literature as Social Discourse: The Practice of Linguistic Criticism* (London: Batsford, 1981); and Fairclough (1989).

10. A compelling example of re-reading in the context of the politics of the classroom is recorded in Nina Baym's '"Actually, I felt sorry for the lion', reading Hemingway's 'The Short Happy Life of Francis Macomber"' in Baym (1992).

11. 'The peculiarity of addressivity is that it exists neither fully in the text nor wholly outside it, but in some exchange between the two. The addressivity of a text is what opens or orientates a text to its actual reception in particular acts of reading, as well as the visible impress of this expectation upon its language and form' (Connor, 1996, p. 10).

12. The girl 'who bore a pitcher on her head,/ And seemed with difficult steps to force her way/ Against the blowing wind' figures in the original 'spots of time' passage as well. (Wordsworth, *The Prelude* [1806, version], Book XI. ll. 306 *et seq*).

13. As when Yeats answers Thomas Mann's assertion that 'In our time the destiny of man presents its meanings in political terms.'

> How can I, that girl standing there,
> My attention fix
> On Roman or on Russian
> Or on Spanish politics?

> ('Politics' in *Last Poems*)

14. The poignancy of this novel – significantly the traditional title of the English translation is *The Lost Domain* – is reinforced in its readings by the extrinsic knowledge that its author died in his twenties on the Western Front soon after completing it. The fate of the young tragic male is a re-enactment of the novel's own dynamic as well as a key *topos* of literary modernism. See also Fussell (1975) on the motif of the deaths of young men (chs 7, 'Arcadian Resources' and 8, 'Soldier Boys'). My account of the novel is influenced by Rutherford's chapter on nostalgia (1992, ch. 5).

15. Kosovsky Sedgwick's mapping of homosocial desire underlies my account of the novel as it does so much else in this book (Sedgwick, 1985).

16. Sedgwick (1994), p. 145.

17. Compare Freud's original account of repetition compulsion in *Beyond the Pleasure Principle* (1920). This in turn is illuminatingly discussed by Bronfen (1992, ch. 2, 'The Lady Vanishes').

18. There is an instructive parallel with the disaster attending the attempts of other male watchers to intervene in the lives of those they admire. For example in the case of Ralph Touchett and Isabel Archer in Henry James's *The Portrait of a Lady*. See Habegger (1982) chs. 7 and 8.

19. See Peter Lehman, 'In the Realm of the Senses: Desire, Power and the Representation of the Male Body' (*Genders*, 2, 1988), itself a response to Mulvey: 'Masculinity is not simply a position of power that puts men in comfortable positions of control. If we ignore studying images of the male body, we are likely to think of masculinity as an ahistoric, powerfully secure, monolithic position, rather than one riddled with cracks.'

20. A term which has acquied currency in adult education and staff

development through the work of Donald Schön. See his *The Reflective Practitioner: How Professionals Think in Action* (London: Temple Smith, 1983).

21. The practices and choices of universities feed back into A-level syllabuses and courses. And indeed, through the work of academics like Brian Cox, into the National Curriculum. See for example Cox, *The Great Betrayal: Memoirs of a Life in Education* (London: Chapmans, 1992).

22. Tony Becher, *Academic Tribes and Territories; Intellectual Enquiry and the Cultures of Disciplines,* (Buckingham: Open University Press 1989); Ben Knights, 'Group Processes in Higher Education: The Uses of Theory', *Studies in Higher Education,* vol. 20, no. 2 (1995).

23. This whole section owes a lot to Evans (1993), especially ch. 6, 'Male/Female'.

24. Gilbert and Gubar (1988) speculate that the idea that language is in its nature patriarchal 'may be a reaction formation against the linguistic (as well as the biological) primacy of the mother'. (*No Man's Land,* vol. I, pp. 264, 266). We could perhaps note further that most people, whether female or male, have learned to read under women's auspices. I suspect that this intitiation could be linked to subsequent ambivalence towards the written word – especially in those manifestations where more processing energy is called for.

25. In parallel it seems to me that one of the attractions carried on behalf of English Studies by the alternative philologically-based lobby was precisely its enthusiasm for heroes and the heroic. Beowulf and his thanes, or the bloodthirsty heroes of the sagas could be adopted by even the most gentle and retiring as vicarious guardians of the manly. Indeed, Tolkien's *The Lord of the Rings* might illuminatingly be read in some ways as a gloss upon the the heroic strand in mid-century English Studies.

26. Up to and including the academic year 1993–4 (after which HESA took over) the *University Statistics Register* did not include polytechnics and colleges. This means that my comparative figures – for example for staffing ratios, below, are somewhat rough and ready.

27. Another useful item here is Terence Hawkes' essay on the Shakespearian scholar Dover Wilson (himself a member of the Newbolt Committee). See 'Telmah', reprinted in *That Shakespeherian Rag: Essays on Critical Process* (London: Methuen, 1986).

28. See John Barrell's useful formulation (Barrell, 1988, introduction and p. 6):

> The universal, the fully human position from which properly literary texts and properly literary criticism, can be produced, is also a masculine position. Masculinity cannot of course serve the mediating function between two given opposites that can be served by the position of the middle class ... So in this case one half of the oppostion is elevated into the neutral and therefore, by implication, the balanced position; and the notion that men are generally more 'balanced' than women has no doubt helped to

construct the competent writer as masculine. Thus if women writers
speak with an uncontrolled 'shrillness' of tone . . . this is the sign
of a failure to transcend their femininity – but no male writer
ever lost control of his text through a failure to transcend his
masculinity.

29. A. P. Rossiter's theory of ambivalence – which in many ways set
    the scene for 1950s criticism – seems to me to represent an interest-
    ing extension of this passion for rising above historical struggle. 'That
    is what I mean by "Ambivalence": that two opposed value-judge-
    ments are subsumed, and that both are valid (i.e. for that work of
    art or the mind producing it). The whole is only fully experienced
    when both opposites are held and included in a "two-eyed" view . . . '
    ('Ambivalence: the Dialectic of the Histories', reprinted in *Angel With
    Horns*, London: Longman, 1961).
30. For example: the 'Augustan form, as he adapts it, is perfectly suited
    to his matter and his outlook – matter and outlook that have close
    affinities with Jane Austen's, though he has a range and generous
    masculine strength that bring out by contrast her spinsterly limita-
    tions . . . ' (F. R. Leavis on George Crabbe, *Revaluation*, p. 105).
31. See Evans (1993) ch. 7 for a complementary thesis about the rise of
    theory. Evans quotes one of his respondents: 'Theory represents a
    phallic rigour, it's gender policing' (p. 139).
32. I identify strongly with the position Robert Scholes seemed to be
    working towards in the mid-1980s – e.g.: 'I am struggling to main-
    tain some middle ground between the absolute denial of reference
    and perception, on the one hand, and the absolute refusal to under-
    stand perception and reference as problematic, on the other.' (Scholes,
    1985, p. 111.)
33. This hierarchy reproduces a traditional gesture in the history of beliefs
    about the relation between gender and culture. One of theory's
    favourite patriarchs is discussing the shift from matriarchy to patri-
    archy as represented in Aeschylus' *Oresteia*:

    > this turning from the mother to the father points in addition to a
    > victory of intellectuality over sensuality – that is, an advance in
    > civilisation, since maternity is proved by the evidence of the senses
    > while paternity is a hypothesis, based on an inference and a premiss.
    > Taking sides in this way with a thought-process in preference to
    > sense perception has proved to be a momentous step. (Freud, *Moses
    > and Monotheism* [1938] Part II, C)

    From a different angle, Peter Middleton, whose sympathetic ques-
    tioning of theory has been helpful throughout, argues: 'Emotions
    are assumed . . . by most recent theorists to be personal, humanist,
    sentimental and old-fashioned. Feeling therefore lies outside
    postmodern theories of the subject in language. . . . Desire is the
    only legitimate term' (1992, p. 180).
34. Such an ambition needs to go beyond negative injunction. My own

sympathies are closer to the psychoanalytic tradition. Daniel Gunn, the force of whose work is to demonstrate how fine is the border between psychoanalysis and literature, speaks of analysis as attempting

> to return the world and the body to desiring. It seeks to do this through creation of a space in which patients can voice their story for the first time ... The order of the Symbolic, realm of desire, is founded upon the conditions of language. One enters it (and continually re-enters it) in accepting the primary substitution of the world by words which effect and efface their own conditionality.

He concludes:

> In that very non-identity of language and its referents, in language's non-present presence, a freedom and *a future* are, conditionally, to be found. (Gunn, 1988, p. 131)

2 THE PORTRAIT OF THE ARTIST AS A MAN

1. A scenario re-enacted in those occasions on which Fowles himself has been interviewed, for example, by Carol Bauman in *Modern Fiction Studies* (1985).
2. 'He could read the title of the Freak's book: *The Magus*. He guessed at astrology, she would be into all that nonsense' (p. 65).
3. On this and Alain-Fournier, see Fowles' discussion of sources and influences in the introduction to 'Eliduc' (in *The Ebony Tower*).
4. Relevant here is Marina Warner's feminist rewriting of *The Tempest* in *Indigo* (1992) (London: Vintage 1993).
5. My account of John Fowles has been influenced throughout by Bronfen (1992).
6. The Jungian and archetypal leanings of some of Fowles' critics find themselves anticipated within the text by the implied relationship with the author as a source of wisdom.
7. See for example Ian Gregor's (1980) illuminating account of the process of reading *The Mill on the Floss*, in *Reading the Victorian Novel: Detail Into Form* (London: Vision).
8. 'Feuerbach, not satisfied with abstract thinking, appeals to sensuous contemplation; but he does not conceive sensuousness as practical, human-sensuous activity.' *Theses On Feuerbach* 5 in *Karl Marx and Friedrich Engels: Selected Works* (London: Lawrence & Wishart, 1968) p. 29. See also Seidler, (1989) ch. 2; Lloyd (1993).
9. C. E. Norton, (ed.), *Correspondence between Goethe and Carlyle* (1887).
10. Reference to Carlyle evokes more than abstract ideas. Much of Carlyle's public discourse can be seen as fired by a nostalgia for oral delivery, even where print is his primary medium. It as though the writer enacts the face-to-face situation of rhetoric, asserting as he does so the 'real presence' of the man of letters as hero.
11. Viswanathan notes the problem that the British had with coming to

terms with polytheism with its dispersal of moral authority from a single source (1990, pp. 73, 95).

12. There is a very thought-provoking discussion in Robert Young, *Mental Space* (London: Process Press, 1994).

13. The epigraph which is translated from Cornish (and thus another allusion to the mysterious Celtic source) was also used by Tony Harrison in a much more politically reflexive context ('National Trust'). It is: 'Too long a tongue, too short a hand;/ But tongueless man has lost his land.'

14. Nina Baym makes some very pertinent comments in reply to Eric Sundquist and Harold Bloom on the theory that male writers learn to father themselves (1986, pp. 77–9).

15. The theory (the 'facile translation of the verb 'to author' into the verb "to father"') has led to 'a restriction of literary creation to a sort of therapeutic act that can only be performed by men. If literature is the attempt to *father* oneself by an author, then every act of writing by a woman is both perverse and absurd' (Baym, 1986, p. 78).

3 FICTIONAL FOREFATHERS: CONRAD AND LAWRENCE

1. I am grateful to Bob Burden for saving me from some of my grosser mistakes.

2. Essay on Poe, *Studies in Classic American Literature* (Harmondsworth: Penguin) p. 75.

3. See for example a poem like, 'She Said As Well To Me', *The Complete Poems of D. H. Lawrence*, edited Vivian de Sola Pinto and Warren Roberts (Harmondsworth: Penguin, 1977), p. 254.

4. 'Lorenzo the Closet Queen', in *Nothing Sacred: Selected Writings* (London: Virago, 1982).

5. See for example Peter Buitenhuis, *The Great War of Words: Literature as Propaganda 1914–1918* (London: Batsford, 1989).

6. It is relevant to point out that the other agency of corruption lying in wait for the young hero of 'A Smile of Fortune' is Jacobus, the girl's father, who poses the threat of being brought back within the patriarchal order. To that extent the girl, Alice, is simply a lure and the true threat of enclosure that of the patriarchal dynasty.

7. It seems to me that J. M. Coetzee's *Foe* (1986) represents a reworking of a whole set of cognate issues.

8. F. R. Leavis, *The Great Tradition* (Harmondsworth: Penguin) p. 229.

9. That Lawrence's programme represented a response to feminism and the (limited) advances made by women during the period of the First World War is the argument of Hilary Simpson's *D. H. Lawrence and Feminism* (1982). She sees the 'conviction that female emancipation arises from men's loss of faith in their own masculinity' as the 'primary impulse behind Lawrence's exploration of male bonding and male power' in *Aaron's Rod*, *Kangaroo*, and *The Plumed Serpent* (pp. 108–9).

10. A very different account of Lawrence's fiction from a gender perspective will be found in Kiberd (1985), ch. 6.
11. Here, as throughout, I have been influenced by the argument of Eve Kosovsky Sedgwick's *Between Men* (1983).
12. See for example Tompkins (1992); Baym (1986). The relation of the private domain to femininity may be seen as an unspoken subtext of Richard Sennett's seminal *The Fall of Public Man* (1976).
13. For example in C. F. C. Masterman's , *The Condition of England* (1911), where the condition of the traditional aristocracy is seen as no longer providing the kind of leadership the nation needs.
14. See the discussion in Middleton (1992) pp. 67–77.
15. I am influenced here by the first chapter of Auerbach's *Mimesis* (Auerbach, 1953). Lawrence's style seems in many ways closer to the noumenous, prophetic style Auerbach identifies with the Old Testament.
16. Light and darkness figure as a potent metaphorical set for thinking about both perception and cognition. Lawrence habitually inverts the usual usage. See for example his late poem 'Bavarian Gentians' (*The Complete Poems of D. H. Lawrence*, p. 697).
17. Knights (1978), for example in reference to Coleridge.
18. 'Song of a Man Who Has Come Through' (*The Complete Poems of D. H. Lawrence*, p. 250). See also the creed Lawrence advanced in reply to Benjamin Franklin: 'That gods, strange gods, come forth from the forest into the clearing of my known self, and then go back.' (*Studies in Classic American Literature*).
19. See also Delavenay (1971) pp. 100–2.
20. Compare Gregory Woods on Lawrence: '[h]is most insistent, but necessarily self-contradictory, erotic grail is the passionate, physical union of two heterosexual men' (1987, p. 125).
21. Illuminating throughout on the iconography and meanings of the male body is Joanne Bourke (1996). Here see especially her chapters 1. 'Mutilating', 3 'Bonding', and 5. 'Re-membering'.
22. Letter to Rhys Davies, Christmas Day 1928. Compare Habegger (1982), chs 18 and 23, and Angela Carter's faintly homophobic piece, 'Lorenzo the Closet Queen', in *Nothing Sacred* (Virago).

4   MALE NARRATIVES

1. I have drawn on Edward Said's, *Culture and Imperialism* (London: Vintage, 1994); Said's introduction to the Penguin edition of *Kim*; Bhabha (1994); and Bristow (1991), ch. 5. Michael Ondaatje's *The English Patient* (1992) is in some ways a re-working of *Kim*.
2. See the episode with the woman of Shamleh *Kim*, (ch. 14).
3. I have made particular use of Young (1987), and Shotter and Gergen (1989). The idea of regulative (auto)biography comes from Khachig Tölölyan's luminous essay 'Narrative Culture and the Motivation of the Terrorist', in Shotter and Gergen.
4. Gilligan (1993). See also Shotter (in Shotter and Gergen, 1989) p. 137, on the missing second person. Boys, claim writers like Nancy

Chodorow and Dorothy Dinnerstein, are typically brought up with a stronger sense of ego boundaries than are girls, and thus a greater sense of their own distinctness.

5. Compare this with the account of the life plot of female biography sketched by Jill Ker Conway (*AAAS Bulletin*, May 1995). There is typically 'no adult life stage for a woman'; the 'romantic life plot neglects female adulthood.'

6. See, for example, Nina Baym (1986) pp. 72–3.

7. See Chapter 2 above, for a parallel case about Fowles' *Daniel Martin*.

8. While the analogy with narrative is mine, I am drawing here on Ronald Hyam's hypotheses about the British fashion for circumcision from the 1890s to the mid-twentieth century (1990). In demonstrating that British circumcision was an 'imperial phenomenon', he surveys anthropological evidence that

> it is the establishment of a strong male identity: an assertion of maleness, a conquest of female elements . . . Viewed in [this] light . . . we can see how British circumcision was meant to contribute to the general improvement of the physical and self-confident manliness of the future custodians of empire. (pp. 77–8)

The foreskin 'represents femininity in a boy' (p. 190).

9. See Schwenger (1984) on the association between hunting and rites of passage (for example, p. 97 *et seq.*).

10. I am drawing here also on Robert Scholes' brilliant account of the pragmatics of Hemingway's attempt to eliminate discourse from his writing ('Decoding Papa: "A Very Short Story" as Work and Text', in Scholes, 1982).

11. In his illuminating discussion of the novel, Connor refers to a 'kind of hermeneutic explosion matching the physical explosion of the nuclear bomb' (1996, p. 219).

12. The one exception is old Lorna Elswint, the 'tel woman', whose main role seems to be to function as an element in Riddley's initiation. Sex with Lorna goes along with killing the boar: 'we freshen the Luck up there on top of the gate house. She were the oldes in our crowd but her voyce wernt old. It made the res of her seem yung for a littl . . .' (p. 6).

13. Jeffords examines the theme of the rescue of forgotten heroes in the face of bureaucratic treachery (from p. 116).

14. Bristow speaks of the 'imperialist genealogy of hegemonic masculinity' (1991, p. 166).

15. In the 1970s an interest in the 'absence which constitutes a presence' was one of the first fruits of the liaison between Freudian and Marxian schools which gave rise to literary theory. Compare Toker (1993).

16. Compare Seidler (1989) ch. 2.

17. Kristeva's *Powers of Horror* (1982) is obliquely relevant here, as is Judith Butler's commentary (1990, pp. 133–4).

18. The possibility that self-revulsion is a propellant for some kinds of

artistic creation links the argument here to the themes of Chapter 2. 'Don't talk to me about self-expression!', Thaw the art student shouts at his father at one point in Alasdair Gray's *Lanark*: 'Do you think I'd paint if I'd nothing better to express than this rotten *self*? If my self was made of decent material I could relax with it, but self-*disgust* keeps forcing me out after the truth, the truth!' The context of the conversation suggests that he is implicitly laying the rottenness of his self at his father's door (p. 271).

19. Suttie himself moves away from a gendered account of the taboo on tenderness – for example, pp. 98–9.

20. Freud's account of the totem is, after all, located in an account of the negotiation of father–son relationships. The totem animal is a substitute for the father, and the taboo on killing it arises from the remorse felt by the horde of brothers who have killed and eaten the father. While it might be objected that this programmatic anthropology has little to say to Banks's novel, the point is that it is a classic example of a narrative that privileges father – son relations. Frank's ritual technology of death witnesses to the importance he attaches to the animals who are his targets and his emblems. Rutherford helpfully discusses the privileging of the Oedipal narrative in the context of his discussion of Melanie Klein. He notes that where Klein's 'description of symbolisation places the figure of the mother at the centre of subject formation', both Lacan and Freud 'in their different ways seek to divest the role of the maternal figure in the formation of cultural and gendered subjectivity by privileging the father as the conveyor of cultural meaning and language' (1992, p. 95). Compare Schwenger's discussion of *Totem and Taboo* in Murphy (1994).

21. At the end of *The Face of Battle* John Keegan engages in some interesting reflections on the conditions of modern warfare (ch. 5, pp. 331 *et seq.*) and in a complementary observation Susan Griffin remarks that 'so much of modern warfare is not present to itself' (*New Internationalist*, November 1994).

22. In a characteristically cryptic ending, Barthes in a classic essay alluded to the simultaneous invention by the small human of the sentence, narrative and the Oedipus ('Introduction to the Structural Analysis of Narratives', reprinted in Barthes, 1977 p. 124).

23. Compare the helpful discussion in Rutherford (1992) pp. 111–16, and Schwenger (1994, p. 71):

> I would argue that culture, far from being the passive child of an originary father, may be the means by which we come to a consciousness of the father's stature as something we have conferred on him, and that we can demystify. Rather than again burying the father in our unconscious and that of our culture, we must unearth him from the fictions created by our psyche. When we do so, the gigantic figure of the father dwindles down to the size of us.

5 MALE IMPERSONATORS

1. Jane Miller's book would be a good place to turn for any reader who wanted to follow up the subject of this chapter. The questions she is addressing are, however, very different. As a male reader I am struck by the way in which Miller has reversed the process through which men have written / read women. Her subject is women's experience and expression of dividedness in relation to men. In an important sense, then, 'men' provide the pretext of her book. For a male reader, reading it is a salutary experience.
2. Gilbert and Gubar give a pertinent critique of the formalist tendency to treat the work as autonomous, (for example 1988, p. xiv). For the continuing saga see Sean Burke, *The Death and Return of the Author* (Edinburgh University Press, 1992).
3. 'The narrator's erotic fantasies of penetration and engulfment enact a pursuit:

> violation and persecution of Tess in parallel to those she suffers at the hands of her two lovers . . . The phallic imagery of pricking, piercing and penetration which has been repeatedly noted . . . serves not only to create an image-chain linking Tess's experiences from the death of Prince to her final penetrative act of retaliation, but also to satisfy the narrator's satisfaction with the interiority of her sexuality, and his desire to take possession of her. (Boumelha, 1982, pp. 120–1)

4. Ashcroft, Griffiths and Tiffin (1989); Bhabha (1994); Spivack (1987).
5. My understanding of transference in relation to literary texts owes much to Felman (1977), and Brooks (1994). In some ways I think Felman's account is too literary, or text-orientated, implying as it does that all readings have already been prefigured by the text.
6. In contrast, and in one of those rare fragments of a good press for step-parents, Louie is grateful to Henny that she leaves her alone: 'Like all children she expected intrusion and impertinence: she very early became grateful to her stepmother for the occasions when Henny most markedly neglected her, refused to instruct her, refused to interpret her to visitors' (p. 70).
7. The political context is F. D. Roosevelt's New Deal, of which Sam is an enthusiastic partisan (see p. 327).
8. The biographical trail was laid by Stead herself, and followed by Randell Jarrell in his 1965 introduction to *The Man Who Loved Children*. It has been developed in more detail in Hazel Rowley's absorbing biography (1993). Rowley sees the novel as a way of turning the tables on Christina's own father, and makes the point that her own claim to have written the truth 'word for word' indicates a desire for control reminiscent of her father's. Fiction was a way of turning the tables on David Stead.
9. An inescapable influence in this chapter has been Alice Miller (1987).
10. Foucault (1977). Also of the nineteenth century attempt by men to

control female sexuality. (Mason, 1994a, b; Sedgwick, 1994; Showalter, 1987).

11. In making this point I have been influenced by Bollas (1987), especially his account of 'extractive introjection'.

12. I am thinking for example of the narrator of *The Left Hand of Darkness* (1969). There is an illuminating commentary in Scholes (1985), ch. 7. Relevant to the subject of this book is Le Guin's own introduction to *The Left Hand of Darkness*, and 'Is Gender Necessary?' in *The Language of the Night: Essays on Fantasy and Science Fiction* (London: The Women's Press, 1989). Gordimer's own exploration of male point of view goes back as far as *A World of Strangers* (1958). In view of Walter Ong's observation that there 'is almost no literature by fathers about sons' (1981, p. 103), it is striking that even her polymorphous narrative voice has balked at overcoming this taboo. *My Son's Story* (1990) gravitates inexorably back to the father as the son's object.

13. An example where the genders are reversed would be the narrator's intimate physical knowledge of Gill in Julian Barnes' *Talking it Over* (1991). But the implied male narrator's knowledge of what happens inside a woman's body carries an entirely different weighting. (See Boumelha in n. 3 above).

14. Obliquely relevant is Silverman's question and observations in her afterword:

> What is my own connection to these 'deviant' masculinities? It will perhaps come as no surprise to the reader to learn that while writing this book I have often felt myself to be 'outside' my own corporeal 'envelope', and 'inside' the subjectivities I was exploring. Since the psychic space into which I thereby stepped was one that was familiar to me, I might not seem to have traveled very far away from myself through these exteriorising identifications. However, for a female subject to re-encounter femininity from within a male body is clearly to experience it under different terms – to live it no longer as disenfranchisement and subordination, but rather as phallic divestiture, as a way of saying 'no' to power. (1992, p. 389)

15. A role which in the classroom is often passed on again, this time to the teacher.

16. See Auerbach on the hierarchy of styles, for example on *Henry IV* (1953) ch. 13, especially pp. 312–18.

17. But see Head (1994), pp. 101–2.

18. The unlaid ghost recurs too in the criticism of the novel. Thus Coetzee (1988), seeing it as belonging in an anti-pastoral tradition, questions 'whether it is in the nature of the ghost of the pastoral ever to be finally laid' (p. 81).

19. See Gillian Rose, *Feminism and Geography: the Limits of Geographical Knowledge* (Cambridge: Polity, 1993), especially ch. 5, 'Looking at Landscape: the uneasy pleasures of power'.

20. Namelessness is so ubiquitous as to amount to another of this novel's codes. The paucity of names seems to represent a failure of reciprocity, how little other people register as others to Mehring.

6 MEN IN TIME

1. In relation to *Waterland*, see for example Hutcheon (1989) chs. 2 and 3; Schad (1992); and Cooper (1996). John Schad sets about reading the novel as 'an allegorical exploration of postmodern theories of the end of history' (p. 911).
2. For some dimensions of the literary sociology see Richard Todd (1996). Todd sets *Waterland* in a context that includes Borges, Fuentes, and Morrison. Connor argues that 'where the role of narrative might once have been to call its audiences into the position of the subject of history, narrative in the postwar world has been much more sceptically or modestly concerned to investigate the conditions of possibility under which history may be narratable at all' (1996, p. 133 and ch. 4 in general).
3. This section is influenced by Daniel Gunn's chapter 'Fathers and Sons' (Gunn, 1988).
4. Francis Crick of Watson and Crick. See James Watson, *The Double Helix: A Personal Account of the Discovery of the Structure of DNA* (Harmondsworth: Penguin, 1963). In his analysis of J. G. Ballard's story 'The Voices of Time', Fredric Jameson suggests that the

> universal fascination of contemporary . . . theory with DNA . . . lies not only in its status as a kind of writing (which displaces biology from the physics model to that of information theory) but also in its active and productive power as template and as computer program: a writing that reads you, rather than the other way round. (Jameson, 1991, pp. 155–6)

5. Swift shares with Hayden White the theory widespread since the late 1970s that history is available only through literary and rhetorical procedures. See for example the essays in *Tropics of Discourse: Essays in Cultural Criticism* (Baltimore MD: Johns Hopkins University Press, 1978). The whole bundle of issues concerning the 'linguistic turn' in historical studies is now usefully addressed in Keith Jenkins (ed.), *The Postmodern History Reader* (London: Routledge, 1997).
6. Pamela Cooper (1996) argues that in Swift's novel the landscape of the fens 'externalises the inner spaces of femininity' (p. 387):

> At once spatializing anatomy and anatomizing space, *Waterland* constellates the history/narrative problematic under the sign of gender, rephrasing in this way postmodernism's concern with women's historical agency and with representations of female sexuality within discourse. (p. 372)

7. On the 'dialectics of urbanity' see Drew Milne, 'James Kelman: dialectics of urbanity', *Swansea Review* (1994), especially p. 400.

8. Some of these issues are briefly discussed in an article I wrote about teaching in a men's prison (Knights, 1991).

9. See Mary Ellis Gibson in Harrison and Taylor (eds) (1992); Knights (1978), ch. 4; Roper and Tosh (1991); Seidler (1989).

10. At the end of Bernard Malamud's *The Assistant*, Frank has himself circumcised in an act of identification with his Jewish employer (Penguin edn 1967).

11. In terms of Leech and Short's 'cline of interference' in the narrative report of speech acts, Kelman's text is at the free end of the continuum: 'narrator apparently not in control of report at all' (Geoffrey Leech and Michael Short, *Style in Fiction: a Linguistic Introduction to English Fictional Prose*, London: Longman, 1981). I am grateful to Cris Yelland for reminding me of this formulation.

12. See Showalter (1987), perhaps especially ch. 7.

13. Gazing upon the male body is conventionally permitted when that body is injured. (See for example Bourke on the iconography of the First World War.) It seems appropriate to note further that one of the privileged images of Western culture has been the tormented male body on the cross.

14. For example pp. 51, 53, 92, 131, 153, 181–3. For an oblique commentary, see Middleton (1992) ch. 6.

15. For example, to the oblique and densely allusive poetry of another New Yorker, Hart Crane. See Lilly (1993); and also Woods (1987) ch. 5.

16. The idea of a social constituency taking shape through narrative mediation is helpfully explored, for example, in Elizabeth Ermath's *The English Novel in History 1840–1895* (London: Routledge, 1995).

17. This belief does appear to lurk in the hinterland of the text: for example, the couple with whom Rose, Owen, and their young son live in Italy are significantly called the Mutters, and the wife Rhea puts Philip as a small boy through an ordeal from which he takes refuge in silence. Sedgwick notes that the 'topos of the omnipotent, unknowing mother is profoundly rooted in twentieth-century gay male high culture . . .' (1991, pp. 248–9). Mun-Hou Lo, who has explored the paradox of working with the stereotypical 'etiological mother' in gay fiction, notes that a 'profound ambivalence towards the representation of the mother . . . permeates Leavitt's work' (Lo, 1995).

18. In fact 1996, as Adam Mars-Jones (1997) has pointed out.

19. Not for nothing had McEwan just written the libretto for Michael Berkeley's anti-nuclear cantata *Or Shall We Die*. See also Schwenger on 'writing the unthinkable' (1986).

20. In a culture in which abuse has become one of our central organising categories, 'the child within' has become one of the clichés of contemporary counselling. McEwan's narrative of paternal loss is curiously prefigured in the experience of Marcher in Henry James's late tale of male self-absorption 'The Beast in the Jungle' (1903).

The lost stuff of consciousness became thus for him as a strayed or stolen child to an unappeasable father, he hunted it up and down very much as if he were knocking at doors and inquiring of the police. (Henry James, *Selected Tales* eds Peter Messent and Tom Paulin, London: Dent p. 275).

21. Gunn's book, especially here chs 1 and 2 ('Fathers and Sons' and 'Difficult Births'), is continuously suggestive.
22. Both the 'uncanny' episodes in *The Child in Time* represent the narrative prelude to moments of conception and/or birth. In view of the argument proposed in relation to Swift's *Waterland*, it is perhaps relevant to note that one of Freud's speculative ways of accounting for the phenomenon of the uncanny is in terms of a subliminal memory of 'the former [home] of all human beings ... the place where each of us lived once upon a time and in the beginning', the female genital organs (Freud, 1919, pp. 367–8).
23. On a biographical note, McEwan has himself recorded that this episode which was the starting place for *The Child in Time* originates in a haunting memory 'or perhaps the memory of a dream' (quoted in Ryan, 1994, p. 48).
24. For example, in Philippa Pearce's *Tom's Midnight Garden*, or Robert Westall's *The Windeye*. J. M. Barrie's *Peter Pan* provides the classic example.
25. On literary reactions to the Thatcher years and the prime minister herself see 'The Literary Consequences of Mrs Thatcher', ch. 12 of Taylor (1993).
26. 'Ian McEwan may be one of the few successful literary examples of the New Man ... but in his relationship between the sexes there is much that is atavistic, patriarchal, even patristic' (Mars-Jones, 1997, p. 151). In Freud's in many ways disappointing essay on 'The Uncanny' he argues that the analysis of the uncanny has 'led us back to the old, animistic conception of the universe. This was characterized by the idea that the world was peopled with the spirits of human beings, by the subject's narcissistic overvaluation of his own mental processes ...'
27. Stephen in 'In Between the Sheets', and Julie in *The Cement Garden*.
28. Jeffords discusses a scene in which a group of American soldiers are present as a Vietnamese woman gives birth. She suggests that as reproductive technology extends into a domain traditionally in women's hands, representations respond to the anxiety about the boundaries between life and death by repressing those traditionally assigned cultural and biological power over that realm (1989, p. 109). The metaphor of giving birth has of course recurrently been used by male authors for the act of writing.
29. See Martin Amis on the nuclear debate in the introduction to his story collection *Einstein's Monsters* (Harmondsworth: Penguin 1988): 'In this debate, we are all arguing with our fathers.'
30. Mars-Jones (1997, p. 142). Mars-Jones wittily, if a little unfairly, sees McEwan, like Martin Amis, as having commandeered feminist insight for his own ends.

31. Fascinatingly, Freud's account of the uncanny includes an analysis of Hoffman's story The Sand-Man' in which the protagonist falls in love with a doll.
32. Browne's concluding illustration of the doll's arm looks extraordinarily like a severed penis.

Bibliography

1   CRITICISM AND THEORY

Aaron, Jane (1995), 'Feminism and the DUET Project: Opening Out the Gendered Subject' in Colin Evans (ed.) 1995.

Alderman, Timothy C. (1985), 'The Enigma of *The Ebony Tower*: a Genre Study', *Modern Fiction Studies*, **31** (1).

Anderson, Benedict (revd edn, 1991), *Imagined Communities: Reflections on the Origin and Spread of Nationalism* (London: Verso).

Arlett, Robert (1985), '*Daniel Martin* and the Contemporary Epic Novel', *Modern Fiction Studies*, **31** (1).

Ashcroft, Bill, Gareth Griffiths and Helen Tiffin (eds) (1989), *The Empire Writes Back: Theory and Practice in Post-Colonial Literatures* (London: Routledge).

Auerbach, Erich (trans. Willard Trask) (1953), *Mimesis: the Representation of Reality in Western Literature* (Princeton, NJ: Princeton University Press).

Bakhtin, Mikhail (trans. Caryl Emerson) (1984), *Problems of Dostoyevsky's Poetics* (Manchester University Press).

—— (trans. Vern W. McGee) (1986), *Speech Genres and Other Late Essays* (Austin, TX: University of Texas).

—— (ed. Pam Morris) (1994), *The Bakhtin Reader: Selected Writings of Bakhtin, Medvedev, Voloshinov* (London: Arnold).

Baldick, Chris (1983), *The Social Mission of English Criticism* (Oxford: Oxford University Press).

Barrell, John (1988), *Poetry, Language and Politics* (Manchester: Manchester University Press).

Barthes, Roland (trans. Stephen Heath) (1977), *Image–Music–Text* (Glasgow: Collins).

—— (trans. Richard Howard) (1986), *The Rustle of Language* (Oxford: Blackwell).

Bateson, Gregory (1973), *Steps to an Ecology of Mind* (St Albans: Paladin).

Baym, Nina (1986), 'Melodramas of Beset Manhood: How Theories of American Fiction Exclude Women Authors', in Elaine Showalter (ed.), *The New Feminist Criticism: Essays on Women, Literature and Theory* (London: Virago).

—— (1992), *Feminism and American Literary History: Essays* (New Brunswick: Rutgers).

Bennett, Andrew (ed.) (1995), *Readers and Reading* (Harlow: Longman).

Berger, Peter and Thomas Luckman (1971), *The Social Construction of Reality* (Harmondsworth; Penguin).

Bernstein, Basil (1975), *Class, Codes and Control, vol. 3: Towards a Theory of Educational Transmissions* (London: Routledge).

Bhabha, Homi K. (1994), *The Location of Culture* (London: Routledge).

Billig, Michael (1991), *Ideology and Opinions* (London: Sage).

Bleich, David (1988), *The Double Perspective: Language, Literacy, and Social Relations* (New York: Oxford University Press).

Bloom, Harold (1973), *The Anxiety of Influence* (New York: Oxford University Press).

Bly, Robert [1987] (1991), *Iron John: A Book about Men* (Shaftesbury: Element).

Bollas, Christopher (1987), *The Shadow of the Object: Psychoanalysis of the Unthought Known* (London: Free Association Books).

Boone, Joseph A. and Michael Cadden (eds) (1990), *Engendering Men: The Question of Male Feminist Criticism* (New York: Routledge).

Boumelha, Penny (1982), *Thomas Hardy and Women: Sexual Ideology and Narrative Form* (Brighton: Harvester).

Bourdieu, Pierre, and Jeana-Claude Passeron (trans. Richard Nice) (1977), *Reproduction in Education, Society and Culture* (London: Sage).

Bourke, Joanna (1996), *Dismembering the Male: Men's Bodies, Britain and the Great War* (London: Reaktion).

Bristow, Joseph (1991), *Empire Boys* (London: Harper Collins).

—— (1995), *Effeminate England: Homoerotic England After 1885* (Buckingham: Open University Press).

Bronfen, Elisabeth (1992), *Over Her Dead Body: Death, Femininity, and the Aesthetic* (Manchester: Manchester University Press).

Brooks, Peter (1994), *Psychoanalysis and Storytelling* (Oxford: Blackwell).

Brown, Keith (ed.) (1990), *Rethinking Lawrence* (Buckingham: Open University Press).

Bruner, Jerome (1986), *Actual Minds, Possible Worlds* (Cambridge MA: Harvard University Press).

Burke, Sean (1992), *The Death and Return of the Author: Criticism and Subjectivity in Barthes, Foucault and Derrida* (Edinburgh: Edinburgh University Press).

Butler, Judith (1990), *Gender Trouble: Feminism and the Subversion of Identity* (New York: Routledge).

Butters, Ronald R. *et al.* (eds) (1989), *Displacing Homophobia: Gay Male Perspectives in Literature and Culture* (Durham NC: Duke University Press).

Carpenter, Edward [1896] (1914), *Love's Coming of Age* (London: Methuen).

Carrithers, Michael (1992), *Why Humans Have Cultures: Explaining Anthropology and Social Diversity* (Oxford: Oxford University Press).

Carroll, John (1974), *Break-Out from the Crystal Palace: The Anarcho-Psychological Critique: Stirner, Nietzsche, Dostoyevsky* (London: Routledge).

Chambers, Ross (1991), *Room for Maneuver: Reading the Oppositional in Narrative* (Chicago: University of Chicago Press).

Chapman, Rowena, and Jonathan Rutherford (1988), *Male Order: Unwrapping Masculinity* (London: Lawrence & Wishart).

Clark, S. H. (1994), *Sordid Images: The Poetry of Masculine Desire* (London: Routledge).

Coetzee, J. M. (1988), *White Writing: On the Culture of Letters in South Africa* (New Haven: Yale University Press).

Cohen, David (1990), *Being a Man* (London: Routledge).

Cohen, Ed (1995) 'The Double Lives of Man: Narration and Identification in Late Nineteenth-Century Representations of Eccentric Masculinities' in Sally Ledger and Scott McCracken (eds) 1995, *Cultural Politics at the Fin de Siècle* (Cambridge: Cambridge University Press).

Collecott, Diana (1987), 'A Double Matrix: Re-reading HD', in Sue Roe (ed.), *Women Reading Women's Writing* (Brighton: Harvester).

Connell, R. W. (1987), *Gender and Power* (Cambridge: Polity).

—— (1995), *Masculinities* (Cambridge: Polity).

Connerton, Paul (1988) 'Freud and the Crowd', in Edward Timms and Peter Collier (eds), *Visions and Blueprints: Avant-Garde Culture and Radical Politics in Early Twentieth-Century Europe* (Manchester: Manchester University Press).

Connor, Steven (1996), *The English Novel in History 1950–1995* (London: Routledge).

Cook, Jon (1988), 'Fictional Fathers', in Susannah Radstone (ed.), *Sweet Dreams: Sexuality, Gender, and Popular Fiction* (London: Lawrence & Wishart).

Cooper, Pamela (1996), 'Imperial Topographies: the Spaces of History in *Waterland*', *Modern Fiction Studies* 42(2).

Crews, Frederick (1975), *Out of My System: Psychoanalysis, Ideology, and Critical Method* (New York: Oxford University Press).

Culler, Jonathan (1983), *On Deconstruction: Theory and Criticism after Structuralism* (London: Routledge).

—— (1997), *Literary Theory: A Very Short Introduction* (Oxford University Press)

Davies, Alistair (1984), 'Contexts of Reading: The Reception of D. H. Lawrence's *The Rainbow* and *Women in Love*' in Frank Gloversmith (ed.) 1984.

Dawson, Graham (1994), *Soldier Heroes: British Adventure, Empire and the Imagining of Masculinities* (London: Routledge).

Delavenay, Emile (1971), *D. H. Lawrence and Edward Carpenter: a Study in Edwardian Transition* (London: Heinemann).

Dinnerstein, Dorothy (1976), *The Mermaid and the Minotaur: Sexual Arrangements and Human Malaise* (New York: Harper & Row).

Dollimore, Jonathan (1991), *Sexual Dissidence: Augustine to Wilde, Freud to Foucault* (Oxford: Clarendon).

Doyle, Brian (1989), *English and Englishness* (London: Routledge).

Dyer, Richard (1992), 'Don't Look Now: the Male Pin-Up', in *The Sexual Subject: a Screen Reader in Sexuality* (London: Routledge).

Easthope, Anthony (1990), *What a Man's Gotta Do: The Masculine Myth in Popular Culture* (Boston: Unwin Hyman).

—— (1991), *Literary into Cultural Studies* (London: Routledge).

Ellmann, Maud (1987), *The Poetics of Impersonality* (Brighton: Harvester).

Evans, Colin (1993), *English People: The Experience of Teaching and Learning English in British Universities* (Buckingham: Open University Press).

—— (ed.) (1995), *Developing University English Teaching: An Interdisciplinary Approach to Humanities Teaching at University Level* (Lampeter: Edwin Mellen).

Fairclough, Norman (1989), *Language and Power* (Harlow: Longman).

Felman, Shoshana (1977), 'Turning the Screw of Interpretation', *Yale French Studies*, **55**(6).

Fetterley, Judith (1978), *The Resisting Reader: A Feminist Approach to American Fiction* (Bloomington Ind: Indiana University Press).

Fleishman, Avrom (1990), 'Lawrence and Bakhtin: where Pluralism ends and Dialogism begins', in Keith Brown (ed.), *Rethinking Lawrence* (Buckingham: Open University Press).

Flynn, Elizabeth A. and Patrocinio P. Schweickart (eds) (1986), *Gender and Reading: Essays on Readers, Texts, and Contexts* (Baltimore MD: Johns Hopkins).

Foucault, Michel (1977), *Discipline and Punish* (Harmondsworth: Allen Lane).

Freud, Sigmund, (ed. James Strachey), *The Standard Edition of the Complete Psychological Works* (London: Hogarth, 1954–74): *Totem and Taboo* [1914] (vol. XIII); *Introductory Lectures on Psychoanalysis* [1917] (vols XV and XVI); *Beyond the Pleasure Principle* [1920] (vol. XVIII); *Moses and Monotheism* [1938] (vol. XXIII); 'The "Uncanny"' [1919], repr. in Penguin Freud Library, vol. 14, *Art and Literature*.

Fussell, Paul (1975), *The Great War and Modern Memory* (London: Oxford University Press).

Geertz, C. (1975), *The Interpretation of Cultures* (London: Hutchinson).

Gergen, Kenneth (1989), 'Warranting Voice and the Elaboration' in John Shotter and Kenneth Gergen (eds) (1989).

Gibson, Mary Ellis (1992), 'Dialogue on a Darkling Plain: Genre, Gender, and Audience in Matthew Arnold's Lyrics' in Anthony H. Harrison and Beverley Taylor (eds).

Giddens, Anthony (1992), *The Transformation of Intimacy: Sexuality, Love and Eroticism in Modern Societies* (Cambridge: Polity).

Gilbert, Sandra, M. and Susan Gubar (1979), *The Madwoman in the Attic: the Woman Writer and the Nineteenth-Century Literary Imagination* (New Haven: Yale University Press).

—— and —— (1988, 1989), *No Man's Land: the Place of the Women Writer in the Twentieth-Century*, vols 1 and 2 (New Haven: Yale University Press).

Giles, Howard and Nikolas Coupland (1991), *Language: Contexts and Consequences* (Buckingham: Open University Press).

Gilligan, Carole (revd edn 1993), *In a Different Voice: Psychological Theory and Women's Development* (Cambridge MA: Harvard University Press).

Gilmore, David (1990), *Manhood in the Making: Cultural Concepts of Masculinity* (New Haven, Conn.: Yale University Press).

Girard, René (trans. Yvonne Freccero) (1966), *Deceit, Desire, and the Novel: Self and Others in Literary Structure* (Baltimore: Johns Hopkins).

Gittings, Chris (ed.) (1996), *Imperialism and Gender* (New Lambton NSW: Dangaroo Press).

Gloversmith, Frank (ed.) (1984), *The Theory of Reading* (Hemel Hempstead: Harvester Wheatsheaf).

Gorak, Irene (1991), 'Libertine Pastoral: Nadine Gordimer's *The Conservationist*', *Novel*, **24**(3).

Greenblatt, Stephen (1980), *Renaisance Self-Fashioning: From More to Shakespeare* (Chicago: Chicago University Press).

Gunn, Daniel (1988), *Psychoanalysis and Fiction: An Exploration of Literary and Psychoanalytic Borders* (Cambridge: Cambridge University Press).

Habegger, Alfred (1982), *Gender, Fantasy, and Realism in American Literature* (New York: Columbia University Press).

Hammond, Paul (1996), *Love Between Men in English Literature* (Basingstoke: Macmillan).

Harré, Rom (2nd edn 1993), *Social Being* (Oxford: Blackwell).

—— and Grant Gillett (1994), *The Discursive Mind* (London: Sage).

Harrison, Anthony H. and Beverly Taylor (eds) (1992), *Gender and Discourse in Victorian Literature and Art* (Dekalb Ill.: Northern Illinois University Press).

Head, Dominic (1994), *Nadine Gordimer* (Cambridge: Cambridge University Press).

Hearn, Jeff (1987), *The Gender of Oppression: Men, Masculinity, and the Critique of Marxism* (Brighton: Wheatsheaf).

Heath, Stephen (1982), *The Sexual Fix* (London: Macmillan).

—— (1986), 'Joan Riviere and the Masquerade', in Donald Burgin, James Donald and Cora Kaplan (eds), *Formations of Fantasy* (London: Methuen, 1992).

—— (1987), 'Male Feminism' in Jardine and Smith (eds).

Heilbrun, Carolyn G. (1989), *Writing a Woman's Life* (London: Women's Press).

Henriques, Julian *et al.* (1984), *Changing the Subject: Psychology, Social Regulation and Subjectivity* (London: Methuen).

Heywood, Leslie (1994), 'The Unreadable Text: Conrad and the "Enigma of Woman" in *Victory*', *Conradiana*, **26**(1).

History Workshop Journal, No. 29 (1990).

Hodge, Robert and Gunther Kress (1988), *Social Semiotics* (Cambridge: Polity).

Horrocks, Roger (1994), *Masculinity in Crisis: Myths, Fantasies and Realities* (New York: St Martin's).

Hunter, Ian (1988), *Culture and Government: The Emergence of Literary Education* (London: Macmillan).

Hutcheon, Linda (1989), *The Politics of Postmodernism* (London: Routledge).

Huyssen, Andreas (1986), 'Mass Culture as Woman: Modernism's Other' in Tania Modleski (ed.), *Studies in Entertainment: Critical Approaches to Mass Culture* (Bloomington, Ind.: Indiana University Press).

Hyam, Ronald (1990), *Empire and Sexuality* (Manchester University Press).

Jackson, David (1990), *Unmasking Masculinity: A Critical Autobiography* (London: Unwin Hyman).

Jameson, Fredric (1972), *The Prison-House of Language: A Critical Account of Structuralism and Russian Formalism* (Princeton NJ: Princeton University Press).

—— (1981), *The Political Unconscious: Narrative as a Socially Symbolic Act* (London: Methuen).

—— (1991), *Postmodernism, or, The Cultural Logic of Late Capitalism* (London: Verso).

Jardine A. and P. Smith (eds.) (1987), *Men in Feminism* (New York: Methuen).

Jardine, Alice (1987), 'Men in Feminism: Odor di Huomo or Compagnons de Route' in Jardine and Smith (eds) (New York: Methuen).

Jeffords, Susan (1989), *The Remasculinisation of America: Gender and the Vietnam War* (Bloomington, Ind.: Indiana University Press).

Karl, Frederick R. (1983), '*Victory*: Its Origin and Development', *Conradiana* 15.1.

Keegan, John (1976), *The Face of Battle* (London: Jonathan Cape).

Kiberd, Declan (1985), *Men and Feminism in Modern Literature* (London: Macmillan).

Knights, Ben (1978), *The Idea of the Clerisy in the Nineteenth Century* (Cambridge: Cambridge University Press).

—— (1991), 'Reading Relations in a Men's Prison', *Free Associations*, vol. 2, pt 1, no. 21.

—— (1992), *From Reader to Reader: Theory, Text and Practice in the Study Group* (Hemel Hempstead: Harvester Wheatsheaf).

—— (1995), 'Group Processes in Higher Education: The Uses of Theory', *Studies in Higher Education*, **20**(2).

Koestenbaum, Wayne (1989), *Double Talk: the Erotics of Male Literary Collaboration* (London: Routledge).

Kristeva, Julia (trans. Leon S. Roudiez) (1982), *Powers of Horror: an Essay on Abjection* (New York: Columbia University Press).

—— (ed. Toril Moi) (1986), *The Kristeva Reader* (Oxford: Blackwell).

Lane, Christopher (1995), *Ruling Passions: British Colonial Allegory and the Paradox of Homosexual Desire* (Durham, NC: Duke University Press).

Lave, Jean and Etienne Wenger (1991), *Situated Learning: Legitimate Peripheral Participation* (Cambridge: Cambridge University Press).

Lawrence, D. H. (1923), *Psychoanalysis and the Unconscious* (London: Martin Secker).

Leavis, F. R. (1930), 'Mass Civilisation and Minority Culture' (Cambridge: The Minority Press).

Lehman, Peter (1988), 'In the Realm of the Senses: Desire, Power and the Representation of the Male Body', *Genders*, **2**.

Lentricchia, Frank (1983), *Criticism and Social Change* (University of Chicago Press).

Levenson, Michael (1991), *Modernism and the Fate of Individuality: Character and Novelistic Form from Conrad to Woolf* (Cambridge: Cambridge University Press).

Lilly, Mark (1993), *Gay Men's Literature in the Twentieth Century* (London: Macmillan).

Lloyd, Genevieve (2nd edn 1993), *The Man of Reason: 'Male' and 'Female' in Western Philosophy* (London: Routledge).

Lo, Mun-Hou (1995), 'David Leavitt and the Etiological Maternal Body', *Modern Fiction Studies*, **41**.

Lodge, David (1990), 'Lawrence, Dostoyevsky, Bakhtin: Lawrence and Dialogic Fiction', in Keith Brown (ed.), *Rethinking Lawrence* (Buckingham: Open University Press).

Longhurst, Derek (ed.) (1989), *Gender, Genre and Narrative Pleasure* (London: Unwin Hyman).

Mac an Ghaill, Mairtin (ed.) (1996), *Understanding Masculinities* (Buckingham: Open University Press).

McCormick, Kathleen (1994), *The Culture of Reading and the Teaching of English* (Manchester University Press).

McCracken, Scott (1993), '"A Hard and Absolute Condition of Existence": Reading Masculinity in *Lord Jim*' in Andrew Michael Roberts (ed.) 1993.

Marks, Elaine and Isabelle de Courtivron (eds) (1981), *New French Feminisms: An Anthology* (Brighton: Harvester).

Mars-Jones, Adam (1997), *Blind Bitter Happiness* (London: Chatto & Windus).

Mangan, J. A. and James Walvin (eds) (1987), *Manliness and Morality: Middle-class Masculinity in Britain and America, 1800–1940* (Manchester: Manchester University Press).

Mason, Michael (1994a), *The Making of Victorian Sexuality* (Oxford: Oxford University Press).

—— (1994b), *The Making of Victorian Sexual Attitudes* (Oxford: Oxford University Press).

Meyers, Jeffrey (1980), *D. H. Lawrence: A Biography* (London: Macmillan).

Middleton, David and Derek Edwards (eds) (1990), *Collective Remembering* (London: Sage).

Middleton, Peter (1992), *The Inward Gaze: Masculinity and Subjectivity in Modern Culture* (London: Routledge).

Middleton, Timothy (n.d.), 'Re-reading Conrad's "complete man": Constructions of Masculinity in "Heart of Darkness' and *Lord Jim*''', unpublished paper.

Miles, Rosalind (1992), *The Rites of Man: Love, Sex and Death in the Making of the Male* (London: Paladin).

Miller, Alice (trans. Ruth Ward) (1987), *The Drama of Being a Child* (London: Virago).

Miller, Jane (1986), *Women Writing About Men* (London: Virago).

Miller, J. Hillis (1982), *Fiction and Repetition* (Oxford: Blackwell).

Millett, Kate (1971, repr. 1993), *Sexual Politics* (London: Virago).

Ministry of Reconstruction (1919), *The Final and Interim Reports of the Adult Education Committee of the Ministry of Reconstruction 1918–19*, repr. University of Nottingham, Department of Adult Education (1980).

Modleski, Tania (1991), *Feminism Without Women: Culture and Criticism in a 'Postfeminist' Age* (London: Routledge).

Morgan, Rosemarie (1988), *Women and Sexuality in the Novels of Thomas Hardy* (London: Routledge).

Mulhern, Francis (1979), *The Moment of Scrutiny* (London: New Left Books).

Mulvey, Laura (1975), 'Visual Pleasure and Narrative Cinema', repr. in *The Sexual Subject: a Screen Reader in Sexuality* (London: Routledge, 1992).

Murphy, Peter F. (ed.) (1994), *Fictions of Masculinity: Crossing Cultures, Crossing Sexualities* (New York University Press).

Nash, Cristopher (ed.) (1990), *Narrative in Culture: The Uses of Storytelling in the Sciences, Philosophy, and Literature* (London: Routledge).

Neale, Stephen (1983), 'Masculinity as Spectacle: Reflections on Men and Mainstream Cinema', repr. in *The Sexual Subject: a Screen Reader in Sexuality* (London: Routledge, 1992).

Newbolt Report, The (1921), *The Teaching of English in England* (London: HMSO).

Ong, Walter J. (1981), *Fighting for Life: Context, Sexuality, and Consciousness* (Ithaca: Cornell University Press).

Pajaczkowska, Claire (1981), 'The Heterosexual Presumption: A Contribution to the Debate on Pornography', *Screen*, **22**(1).

Palmer, William J. (1985), 'John Fowles and the Crickets', *Modern Fiction Studies*, **31**(1).

Park, Sue (1985), 'Time and Ruins in John Fowles's Daniel Martin, *Modern Fiction Studies*, **31**(1).

—— , 'John Fowles, Daniel Martin, and Simon Wolfe', *Modern Fiction Studies*, **31**(1).

Pearce, Lynne (1991), 'John Clare's *Child Harold*: the Road not Taken', in Susan Sellers (ed.), *Feminist Criticism: Theory and Practice* (Hemel Hempstead: Harvester Wheatsheaf).

Pittock, Malcolm, '*Sons and Lovers*: the Price of Betrayal' in Keith Brown (ed.) 1990.

Porter, D. (ed.) (1992), *Between Men and Feminism* (London: Routledge).

Potter, Jonathan and Margaret Wetherell (1987), *Discourse and Social Psychology* (London: Sage).

Protherough, Robert (1989), *Students of English* (London: Routledge).

Pykett, Lyn (1995), *Engendering Fictions: The English Novel in the Early Twentieth Century* (London: Edward Arnold).

Radstone, Susannah (ed.) (1988), *Sweet Dreams: Sexuality, Gender, and Popular Fiction* (London: Lawrence & Wishart).

Reid, Su (1989), 'Learning to "Read as a Woman"' in Ann Thompson and Helen Wilcox (eds) 1989.

Rimmon-Kenan, Shlomith (1987), *Discourse in Psychoanalysis and Literature* (London: Methuen).

Riviere, Joan (1929), 'Womanliness as Masquerade', rep. in Victor Burgin, James Donald and Cora Kaplan, (eds) *Formation of Fantasy* (London: Methuen, 1992).

Roberts, Andrew Michael (1996), 'Economics of Empire and Masculinity in Conrad's *Victory*' in Gittings (ed.) 1996.

Roberts, Andrew Michael (ed.) (1993), *Conrad and Gender* (Amsterdam: Rodopi).

—— and Peter Easingwood (1997), 'Beyond the Male Romance: Repetition as Failure and Success in Apocalypse Now', *Critical Survey*, **9**(1).

Roper, Michael, and John Tosh (eds) (1991), *Manful Assertions: Masculinities in Britain since 1800* (London: Routledge).

Rowley, Hazel (1993), *Christina Stead: A Biography* (London: Secker & Warburg).

Rutherford, Jonathan (1992), *Men's Silences: Predicaments in Masculinity* (London: Routledge).

Ryan, Kiernan (1994), *Ian McEwan* (Writers and Their Work) (Plymouth: Northcote House).

Schad, John (1992), 'The End of the End of History: Graham Swift's *Waterland*', *Modern Fiction Studies*, **38**(4).

Scholes, Robert (1982), *Semiotics and Interpretation* (New Haven, Conn.: Yale University Press).

—— (1985), *Textual Power: Literary Theory and the Teaching of English* (New Haven, Conn.: Yale University Press).

―― (1987), 'Reading Like a Man', in Alice Jardine and Paul Smith (eds), *Men in Feminism* (New York: Methuen).

Schweickart, Patrocinio P. (1986), 'Reading Ourselves: Towards a Feminist Theory of Reading' in Elizabeth A. Flynn and Patrocinio P. Schweickart.

Schwenger, Peter (1984), *Phallic Critiques: Masculinity and Twentieth-Century Literature* (London: Routledge).

―― (1986), 'Writing the Unthinkable', *Critical Inquiry*, **13**.

―― (1994), 'Barthelme, Freud and the Killing of Kafka's Father' in Peter Murphy (ed.).

Scott, Bonnie Kyme (ed.) (1990), *The Gender of Modernism* (Bloomington, Ind.: Indiana University Press).

Screen (1992), *The Sexual Subject: a* Screen *Reader in Sexuality* (London: Routledge).

Sedgwick, Eve Kosovsky (1985), *Between Men: English Literature and Male Homosocial Desire* (New York: Columbia University Press).

―― (1991), *Epistemology of the Closet* (Hemel Hempstead: Harvester Wheatsheaf).

―― (1994), *Tendencies* (London: Routledge).

Segal, Lynne (1990), *Slow Motion: Changing Masculinities, Changing Men* (London: Virago).

Seidler, Victor J. (1989), *Rediscovering Masculinity: Reason, Language and Sexuality* (London: Routledge).

―― (ed.) (1991), *The Achilles Heel Reader: Men, Sexual Politics and Socialism* (London: Routledge).

Sennett, Richard (1976), *The Fall of Public Man* (Cambridge: Cambridge University Press).

Shotter, John (1993), *Cultural Politics of Everyday Life: Social Constructionism, Rhetoric and Knowing of the Thrid Kind* (Buckingham: Open University Press).

Shotter, John and Kenneth J. Gergen (eds) (1989), *Texts of Identity* (London: Sage).

Showalter, Elaine (1978), *A Literature of Their Own: British Woman Novelists from Brontë to Lessing* (London: Virago).

―― (ed.) (1986), *The New Feminist Criticism: Essays on Women, Literature and Theory* (London: Virago).

―― (1987), 'Critical Cross Dressing Male Feminists and the Woman of the Year' in Alice Jardine and Paul Smith (eds) 1987).

―― (1987), *The Female Malady: Women, Madness and English Culture, 1830–1980* (London: Virago).

―― (1992), *Sexual Anarchy: Gender and Culture in the Fin de Siècle* (London: Virago).

Silverman, Kaja (1992), *Male Subjectivity at the Margins* (New York: Routledge).

Simons, Herbert W. (ed.) (1989), *Rhetoric in the Human Sciences* (London: Sage).

Simpson, Hilary (1982), *D. H. Lawrence and Feminism* (De Kalb Ill.: Northern Illinois University Press).

Sinfield, Alan (1989), *Literature, Culture and Politics in Postwar Britain* (Oxford: Blackwell).

—— (1992), *Faultlines: Cultural Materialism and the Politics of Dissident Reading* (Oxford: Clarendon).

Spivack, Gayatri Chakravorty (1987), *In Other Worlds: Essays in Cultural Politics* (London: Methuen).

Still, Judith and Michael Worton (1993) *Textuality and Sexuality* (Manchester: Manchester University Press).

Straus, Nina Pelikan (1987), 'The Exclusion of the Intended from Secret Sharing in Conrad's Heart of Darkness', *Novel*, **20**.

Sussman, Herbert (1995), *Victorian Masculinities: Manhood and Masculine Poetics in Early Victorian Literature and Art* (Cambridge: Cambridge: University Press).

Suttie, Ian D. [1935] (1963), *The Origins of Love and Hate* (Harmondsworth: Penguin).

Tannen, Deborah (1994), *Gender and Discourse* (New York: Oxford University Press).

Taylor, D. J. (1993), *After the War: the Novel and England Since 1945* (London: Chatto & Windus).

Thomas, Kim (1990), *Gender and Subject in Higher Education* (Buckingham: Open University Press).

Thompson, Ann and Helen Wilcox (eds) (1989), *Teaching Women: Feminism and English Studies* (Manchester University Press).

Todd, Richard (1996), *Consuming Fictions: the Booker Prize and Fiction in Britain Today* (London: Bloomsbury).

Todorov, Tzvetan (trans. Wlad Godzich) (1984), *Mikhail Bakhtin: the Dialogic Principle* (Manchester University Press).

Toker, Leona (1993), *Eloquent Reticence: Witholding Information in Fictional Narrative* (Lexington. KY: University Press of Lexington).

Tölölyan, Khachig (1989), 'Narrative Culture and the Motivation of the Terrorist' in John Shotter and Kenneth Gergen (eds) 1989.

Tompkins, Jane (1992), *West of Everything: The Inner Life of Westerns* (New York: Oxford University Press).

Trotter, David (1993), *The English Novel in History 1895–1920* (London: Routledge).

Van der Veer, Rene and Jaan Valsiner (eds) (1994), *The Vygotsky Reader* (Oxford: Blackwell).

Viswanathan, Gavri (1990), *Masks of Conquest: Literary Study and British Rule in India* (London: Faber).

Wallace, Anne D. (1993), *Walking, Literature, and English Culture: The Origins and Uses of Peripatetic in the Nineteenth Century* (Oxford: Clarendon).

Warner, Marina (1994), *Managing Monsters: Six Myths of our Time* (London: Vintage).

Waugh, Patricia (1984), *Metafiction: The Theory and Practice of Self-Conscious Fiction* (London: Methuen).

Wetherell, Margaret and Potter, Jonathan (1989), 'Negative Characters and Accounting for Violence' in John Shotter and Kenneth Gergen (eds).

White, Andrea (1993), *Joseph Conrad and the Adventure Tradition: Constructing and Deconstructing the Imperial Subject* (Cambridge University Press).

Widdowson, Peter (ed.) (1992), *D. H. Lawrence* (Longman Critical Readers) (Harlow: Longman).
Williams, Linda Ruth (1993), *Sex in the Head: Visions of Femininity and Fiction in D. H. Lawrence* (Hemel Hempstead: Harvester).
—— (1997), *D. H. Lawrence* (Plymouth: Northcote House).
Woodcock, Bruce (1984), *Male Mythologies: John Fowles and Masculinities* (Brighton: Harvester).
Woods, Gregory (1987), *Articulate Flesh: Male Homo-Eroticism and Modern Poetry* (New Haven, Conn.: Yale University Press).
Woolf, Virginia (1929), *A Room of One's Own* (London: Hogarth Press).
—— (1938), *Three Guineas* (repr. London: Hogarth Press, 1986).
Young, Katherine (1987), *Taleworlds and Storyrealms: The Phenomenology of Narrative* (Dordrecht: Martinus Nijhoff).

2   NOVELS: EDITIONS USED

Where possible I have given references to available paperback editions.

Chapter 1

Alain-Fournier, *Le Grand Meaulnes* (trans. Frank Davison, Penguin Modern Classics)
Bates, H. E., *The Wild Cherry Tree* (Penguin)

Chapter 2

Fowles, John, *Daniel Martin* (Triad Panther)
——, *The Ebony Tower* (Panther Granada)
Gray, Alastair, *Lanark: A Life in 4 Books* (Picador)

Chapter 3

Coetzee, J. M., *Foe* (Penguin)
Conrad, Joseph, *Victory* (Penguin Modern Classics)
Ford Madox Ford, *The Good Soldier: a Tale of Passion* (Penguin Twentieth-Century Classics)
Lawrence, D. H., 'The Primrose Path' in *The Collected Short Stories* (Heinemann) vol. 2
—— *The Rainbow* (Penguin)
—— *Women in Love* (Cambridge text in Penguin Twentieth-Century Classics)

Chapter 4

Banks, Iain, *The Wasp Factory* (Abacus)
Barthelme, Donald, *Sixty Stories* (Minerva)
Dostoyevsky, Fyodor, *Notes from Underground* (trans. Jessie Coulson, Penguin Classics)

Hoban, Russell, *Riddley Walker* (Picador)
Kipling, Rudyard, *Kim* (Penguin Twentieth-Century Classics)
Ondaatje, Michael, *The English Patient* (Picador)

Chapter 5

Barnes, Julian, *Talking it Over* (Picador)
Gordimer, Nadine, *The Conservationist* (Penguin)
—— *Selected Stories* (Penguin)
Stead, Christina, *The Man Who Loved Children* (Penguin)
Nkosi, Lewis, *Mating Birds* (Flamingo)

Chapter 6

Amis, Martin, *Einstein's Monsters* (Penguin)
—— *London Fields* (Penguin)
Bartlett, Neil, *Ready to Catch Him Should He Fall* (Penguin)
Carey, Peter, *The Tax Inspector* (Faber)
Halloran, Andrew, *Dancer from the Dance* (Penguin)
Hollinghurst, Alan, *The Swimming Pool Library* (Penguin)
Kelman, James, *The Burn* (Minerva)
—— *The Busconductor Hines* (Phoenix)
—— *A Disaffection* (Picador)
—— *How Late it Was, How Late* (Secker and Warburg)
—— *Not Not While the Giro* (Minerva)
Leavitt, David, *Equal Affections* (Penguin)
—— *Family Dancing* (Penguin)
—— *The Lost Language of Cranes* (Penguin)
—— (ed. with Mark Mitchell) *The Penguin Book of Gay Short Stories*
McEwan, Ian, *The Child in Time* (Picador)
—— *The Daydreamer* (with illustrations by Anthony Browne) (Jonathan Cape)
Swift, Graham, *Learning to Swim* (Picador)
—— *Shuttlecock* (Penguin)
—— *Waterland* (Picador)

Index